Elements of Mind

Elements of Mind

An Introduction to the Philosophy of Mind

Tim Crane

OXFORD
UNIVERSITY PRESS

OXFORD
UNIVERSITY PRESS

Great Clarendon Street, Oxford OX2 6DP

Oxford University Press is a department of the University of Oxford.
It furthers the University's objective of excellence in research, scholarship,
and education by publishing worldwide in

Oxford New York

Athens Auckland Bangkok Bogotá Buenos Aires Cape Town
Chennai Dar es Salaam Delhi Florence Hong Kong Istanbul Karachi
Kolkata Kuala Lumpur Madrid Melbourne Mexico City Mumbai Nairobi
Paris São Paulo Shanghai Singapore Taipei Tokyo Toronto Warsaw

with associated companies in Berlin Ibadan

Published in the United States
by Oxford University Press Inc., New York

First published 2001

British Library Cataloguing in Publication Data

Data available

Library of Congress Cataloging in Publication Data

Data applied for

ISBN 0–19–289297–5

1 3 5 7 9 10 8 6 4 2

Typeset by RefineCatch Limited, Bungay, Suffolk
Printed in Great Britain
on acid-free paper by
T.J. International, Padstow, Cornwall

For Kati

Preface

In this book I attempt to give an account of what I see to be the main problems of the philosophy of mind: the mind–body problem, the problem of intentionality (or mental representation), the problem of consciousness, and the problem of perception. I also attempt to give solutions to these problems. I do not, of course, pretend that these solutions are without problems of their own, but it seems to me that a book with an opinionated approach to philosophical problems tends to be more interesting than a bland survey. Nor do I pretend, when talking about 'the' main problems of philosophy of mind, that these are the only problems, or that there is only one 'mind–body problem' or 'problem of consciousness'. On the contrary, in my discussion of these problems I will often distinguish a number of things falling under these names, although some of them I do not discuss in any detail. Nonetheless, it seems to me that the traditional names for the problems provide, so to speak, the co-ordinates of a useful map of this field of study, and it is thus that I intend to use them.

The central theme of the book is that *intentionality*, the mind's direction upon its objects, sometimes called the mind's power to represent or be 'about' things, is the essential feature of all mental phenomena. This is *Brentano's thesis*, named in honour of Franz Brentano, the German philosopher and founder of the phenomenological movement. Although I take the name and the inspiration for the thesis from Brentano, the book is not in any sense a book about Brentano or the movement he founded, nor does it defend the thesis in the sense in which he meant it. I explain what I mean by intentionality in Chapter 1, and I give accounts of the intentionality of consciousness, thought, and perception in Chapters 3, 4, and 5. Chapter 2 takes up a subsidiary theme: the mind–body problem, and the extent to which a physicalist reductive account of mental phenomena is possible, or even necessary. One conclusion of Chapter 2 is that much of what is interesting about the mind is left open when the question of physicalism is settled. At its simplest, the point can be put like this: suppose physicalism is true, and mental properties are identical to physical properties. We still need to know which physical properties these are, what are the general characteristics of these properties, how we know about them, and so on. Alternatively, suppose the sort of 'emergentism' I favour is true: mental properties are causally efficacious 'emergent' properties of human beings and other creatures. We still need to know which emergent properties these are, what are the general characteristics of these properties, and how we know about them.

In general, my attitude to physicalism as an overall metaphysical thesis is a sceptical one; and I have a similar attitude towards physicalist explanations of consciousness and intentionality. I do not say that there is anything in principle wrong with the idea of a reductive explanation of mental phenomena; indeed, in Chapter 2, I argue that we should welcome such reduction when we can find it. But the accounts of consciousness and intentionality that have been offered in recent years have failed to command general agreement, and features of the accounts suggest that attention may be better spent looking elsewhere. What we need, I believe, is an understanding of the issues which is neutral on the question of reduction, in the sense that it explores the questions about these aspects of the mind without assuming that a reduction will or will not succeed. This assumes that such an understanding can be achieved, that there is more to the philosophy of mind than sketching reductive projects. I believe this, and I also think that some traditional questions in the philosophy of mind have been neglected through an over-concentration on the question of reduction. Here I have some sympathy with Hilary Putnam's complaint that 'the idea that science leaves no room for an independent philosophical enterprise has reached the point at which leading practitioners sometimes suggest that all that is left for philosophy is to try to anticipate what the presumed scientific solutions to all metaphysical problems will eventually look like' (*Renewing Philosophy*, p. x). The kind of project described here by Putnam is not one discussed in much detail in this book. I do discuss aspects of the reductive projects in my earlier introductory book, *The Mechanical Mind*. (The present book also corrects inadequacies in the description of intentionality given in that book.) Another thing missing from this book is anything by way of detailed discussion of many of the different varieties of physicalist and functionalist theories of mind. I recognize that there is much more to say about these matters than I say here; readers new to the philosophy of mind who are interested in functionalism and the varieties of physicalism may wish to consult Jaegwon Kim's *The Philosophy of Mind*, or *Philosophy of Mind and Cognition* by David Braddon-Mitchell and Frank Jackson, each of which gives an excellent account of these matters.

The idea for this book goes back to 1993, when Frank Jackson invited me to write the entry on intentionality for the new Routledge *Encyclopedia of Philosophy* (under the general editorship of Edward Craig). While writing this piece, I became persuaded that many contemporary discussions of intentionality were incomplete or misguided in certain ways, and that Brentano's thesis was the way to repair the damage. Though he may not agree with what emerged, I am very grateful to Frank for setting me on this track.

I am also grateful to the following institutions: the Arts and Humanities Research Board for a Research Leave award, which enabled me to complete the book; the School of Philosophy of the University of Sydney, for inviting me to be a visiting lecturer in 1999, during which I presented much of the book's material in a seminar; the University of Helsinki, for inviting me to give a course of lectures, based on this book, in 1999; and the Philosophy Department of University College London, for allowing me to take research leave in 1999–2000. Many discussions in Sydney, in and out of the seminar, forced me to change my mind on many things. I would like to express special thanks to David Armstrong, John Bacon, Michael McDermott, Huw Price, Lloyd Reinhardt, and to my students in Sydney, Wylie Breckenridge, Ian Pitt, and Yew-Leong Wong. The late George Molnar contributed vigorously and helpfully to the seminar; his premature death is a sad loss to philosophy in Australia. A seminar in the summer of 2000 gave me a useful opportunity to clarify my ideas under the scrutiny of some London graduate students: I thank especially Matt Soteriou, Guy Longworth, and Jon Webber for their oral and written comments. I would also like to thank the following colleagues and friends for discussions, or for written comments on earlier versions of this work, which have helped me in many different ways: Paul Boghossian, Paul Horwich, Mark Kalderon, Barry Loewer, Hugh Mellor, Greg McCulloch, Lucy O'Brien, David Papineau, Sven Rosenkrantz, Barry C. Smith, Scott Sturgeon, Tuula Tanska, Jerry Valberg, and Alberto Voltolini. For the last decade or so I have been fortunate to have had Mike Martin as a colleague, and have been able to profit from regular discussions of the philosophy of mind, from which I have learned an immeasurable amount. Many of the views expressed here have been influenced by conversations with Mike, although I am certain that he would not agree with many of the conclusions I reach. Katalin Farkas has constantly scrutinized the views expressed here and her insights have made me improve and clarify them. She has been both my sternest and fondest critic; I dedicate this book to her.

London
February 2001

Contents

Chapter 3: **Consciousness**

1

Mind

1. Philosophy of mind and the study of mental phenomena

We have ways of thinking about ourselves which are not scientific in the strict sense of that word. We think of ourselves as conscious, rational creatures, with an outlook or perspective on the world and with needs, commitments, emotions, and values. A part of this view which we have of ourselves is a conception of what these phenomena, the *mental phenomena*, are. This conception is vague in places, and in places perhaps confused; but it is nonetheless pervasive and apparently common, in its broad outlines, to many human cultures at different times.

When I say that this conception is not scientific, all I mean is this: if it is knowledge at all, it is not specialist knowledge. It is not knowledge which requires specific training or a particular degree of intelligence or learning. It is rather something which we inevitably learn as we learn a language, come to understand others, and as we mature within a human society or culture. Some philosophers call this conception 'folk psychology', often intending a contrast with a more scientific psychology. I would like to avoid some of the connotations of the word 'folk' (the connotations the word has in 'folk music' or 'folk dancing'), so I refrain from using this term; nonetheless, what the term refers to certainly exists.

We also have a conception of ourselves and our place in the world which is scientific in any sense of the word. Under this conception, we think of ourselves as organisms, members of a certain species, with an evolutionary history and a biological nature. Our bodies are made up of organs, cells, molecules, and atoms, and various scientific theories describe these things in all their complexity. This scientific knowledge is specialized knowledge; to grasp it requires significant intelligence and extensive (and expensive) education; it is not common to all human cultures or societies, though many of the facts it discovers are true of the members of these societies.

One question which has preoccupied philosophers is this: what is the relationship between these two ways of thinking? Frank Jackson once described his philosophical interests in the following terms: we think we know a lot about ourselves and about the world; science tells us a lot about ourselves and about the world; to what extent is what science tells us compatible with what we think we know?[1] This expresses particularly clearly the framework within which many questions in contemporary philosophy of mind are asked: is the scientific view compatible with our ordinary non-scientific beliefs? Or, does it correct these beliefs? But to what extent can science correct these ordinary beliefs? Could science show, for example, that there is no such thing as thought? If not, why not? If so, how should we conceive of ourselves?

These are important questions, which have been at the centre of philosophical debate for much of the last century. But there is a prior question: what is the content of this non-scientific view of ourselves? What does it mean to have a conception of ourselves as rational, conscious agents with a perspective on the world? To what do we commit ourselves in saying this? Answering these questions is one of the traditional concerns of the philosophy of mind. To have an adequate account of our mental self-conception is surely a precondition for being able to answer fully the questions posed above about the relation between this self-conception and our scientific knowledge.

Some philosophers have claimed that our conception of the mind has no unity or essence; that it is a relatively disorderly collection of ideas which have no unifying thread binding them together.[2] I disagree with these claims. I shall argue that our conception of the mind is unified by the idea of *intentionality*, the mind's directedness on its objects. Intentionality is the distinctive mark of all and only mental phenomena. This is a thesis whose origins may be found, in various forms, in Aristotle, the scholastic philosophers of the Middle Ages, Descartes, and Brentano and his students and followers in the twentieth century. It is sometimes called 'Brentano's thesis', and I shall use this term, though I do not intend this to imply that I am accepting Brentano's philosophy as a whole, or even the precise details of his understanding of intentionality.

In recent analytical philosophy Brentano's thesis is widely rejected, largely for the reason that it cannot accommodate the phenomena of consciousness. I think this objection to Brentano's thesis is mistaken, since I think that the conception of consciousness which it assumes is mistaken. In the rest of this chapter I present a general account of intentionality, and in Chapter 3 I present an intentionalist conception of consciousness. Chapters 4 and 5 draw on these accounts of intentionality and consciousness to provide accounts of thought and perception. Chapter 2 locates these problems relative to the contemporary mind–body problem.

There may be a suspicion at the outset that Brentano's thesis is vacuous without an independent understanding of 'mental'. How are we to tell whether Brentano's thesis is true without being able, in some way, to 'compare' the mental things with the intentional things and 'discover' that every mental thing is an intentional thing and vice versa? Yet without an independent understanding of 'mental' (independent, that is, of the idea of intentionality) this procedure is either vacuous (since 'mental' means the same as 'intentional') or impossible (since we have no idea what the mental is in the first place).

This criticism presupposes that we do not have a rough-and-ready idea of what a *mind* is, which can be sharpened into a more refined philosophical account by employing the idea of intentionality. It is as if any investigation into the essence of our idea of mind, or the mark of the mental, had to start from the assumption that we were in the dark about what we mean when we talk about 'minds' or 'mentality' or 'subjectivity', and that the mark of the mental would be given in the form of an explicit definition of the term 'mind'. But we are not in this position; and if we were, we would not be able to recognize whether any such definition were true. Rather, as with many areas of philosophy, we already have a rough conception of our subject-matter; what we are looking for is not an explicit definition, but a description of the mental phenomena which is sufficiently clear and detailed for us to recognize it as a description of the thing of which we have this conception.

An analogy of Daniel Dennett's may help to make this strategy clearer. Dennett draws the analogy between Brentano's thesis and Church's thesis in the foundations of mathematics. Church's thesis says that every effective procedure or algorithm can be performed by a Turing machine. The idea of an algorithm is just the idea of a step-by-step recipe for solving a mathematical problem; the idea of a Turing machine is the idea of a device which can reduce the application of any such recipe to its simplest mechanical stages. Church's thesis employs the somewhat vague idea of an effective procedure, and sharpens it by means of the more precise idea of a Turing machine. As Dennett says, 'it provides a very useful reduction of a fuzzy-but-useful mathematical notion to a crisply defined notion of apparently equivalent scope and greater power'.[3]

No one could hope that the idea of intentionality could render the idea of the mental as precise as the notion of a Turing machine renders the idea of an effective procedure. As we shall see, the idea of intentionality is in places intractable, and in some places vague. But it is not part of this strategy to claim that all rough ideas can be sharpened to the same degree. We must let the nature of the phenomena be our guide to how far to go, and not impose constraining and distorting assumptions upon them.

2. **Perspectives and points of view**

Among all the living things there are, we distinguish between those which are merely alive and those which have minds—thinking or conscious beings. A daffodil is merely an organic thing; a person has consciousness and the ability to think. What is the basis behind this distinction? What does it consist in? I shall claim that, in its broadest outline, the answer to the question is simple; the hard part is saying precisely what this answer amounts to. What the daffodil lacks and the 'minded' creature has is a *point of view on things* or (as I shall mostly say) a *perspective*. The minded creature is one *for which* things are a certain way: the way they are from that creature's perspective. A lump of rock has no such perspective, the daffodil has no such perspective. We might express this by saying that a minded creature is *one which has a world*: its world. Its having a perspective consists in its having a world. Having a world is something different from there simply being a world. It is true of the rock or the daffodil that it is part of the world; but it is not true that they have a world. A creature with a perspective has a world. But to say that a creature with a perspective *has* a world is not to say that each creature with a perspective has a different world. Perspectives can be perspectives on one and the same world. But at the moment we are interested in the idea of a perspective, and not so much in the idea of a world.

The use I am going to make of the concept of a perspective is to some extent metaphorical, and to some extent vague. One dominant literal use of the word 'perspective' is in connection with pictorial representation. But I extend here the idea to apply to the standpoint or the position of a *person* or *subject*: the 'place' from which they 'see' things. Here 'place', 'standpoint', 'position', and 'see' are strictly speaking metaphorical; but no one will sincerely deny that they understand these metaphorical uses.

The situation is the same with the phrase 'point of view'. Taken literally, a point of view may be thought of as a point (or location in space) from which something is viewed. But although this is part of what I mean by 'point of view' in this context, it is not all I mean. 'Point of view' has also come to mean *opinion* or *belief*; and this dead metaphor is closer to the meaning which my use of 'perspective' is trying to express. However, having a perspective is not having a belief. When I talk of perspectives, I do not mean that a perspective *is* a state of mind; it is meant to be a *condition* for being in a state of mind.

As well as being metaphorical, I said that the idea of a perspective is vague. By 'vague' I don't mean *woolly* or *unclear*, but vague in the philosophical sense: an expression is vague when its application does not have sharp boundaries. Which creatures in the world have perspectives and which do not? Is there a sharp division between these two classes of things? It is hard to say. The reason it is hard may be because reality is vague and there is no fact of the matter about where perspectives begin and end; or it may be because there is a fact of the matter, there is a sharp boundary, but we cannot know where it is.[4] Do fish have a perspective on their world? Some would say so. Does a bacterium? Surely not. So where is the line to be drawn? Does a shrimp have a perspective? Some might say yes, some say no. What settles it? Here we confront the vagueness of the idea of a perspective. I do not need to solve this problem here, so long as any vagueness in the idea of a perspective is matched by a vagueness in the idea of mind: the extent to which we wonder whether a shrimp has a perspective is the extent to which we wonder whether the shrimp has a mind.

A sceptic may wonder at this point how we can *ever* know that a shrimp has or hasn't got a mind or a perspective. The question—how do we know whether something has got a mind?—is a good question. But it is not relevant here. It may be relevant in other contexts: for instance, a debate about whether it is wrong to eat oysters alive may turn on whether they can feel anything, and therefore whether there is anything like the oyster's perspective. Someone who denied this might deny it because they couldn't make sense of the idea of the oyster's perspective. The sceptic's worry is that this debate is irresolvable because we can never know enough (in the right kind of way) about oysters to know whether they have a perspective. Therefore, we will never be able to know the answer to our question, as far as oysters are concerned.

But although this question about knowledge may (or may not) be relevant to the question of what we should eat, our question is more fundamental: *what is it* that we are wondering about when we wonder whether something has a mind? The sceptical question—how do we know whether anything has a mind?—is not one which we must answer before we answer this question. I could raise the question, how do I know (*really* know) that you have a mind? After all, the only things I ever see are the movements of your body, all I ever hear are sounds. I never (it could be said) see or hear your *thoughts* or your *perspective*. If a perspective is something hidden behind your behaviour, then what assurance do I have that even the rock does not have a perspective?[5]

These questions have their place; but their place is not in the answer to the question about the nature of mind. For the sceptical question takes for granted that we have some idea what a perspective is; and then asks whether we really know that others have *this*. Perhaps this question rests upon deep misunderstandings—about knowledge, or about perspectives—but we will not know this until we know something about what a perspective is. How should we start?

The starting point should be that we do as a matter of fact draw a distinction—sceptical questions aside—between those living things which clearly do have a perspective, and those which clearly don't. There are unclear cases in the middle, but as I observed above, the extent to which we are unclear about whether these cases are cases of *minds* parallels exactly our unclarity about whether they are cases of something having a *perspective*. Does this mean that 'mind' and 'perspective' are practically synonyms, and so no real illumination can be cast on the concept of mind by talking about perspectives? No. Starting with the idea of a perspective, I claim, we can begin to introduce the idea which unifies all the phenomena of mind, and forms the basic subject-matter of the philosophy of mind. This is the idea of *intentionality*, the traditional technical term for the mind's 'directedness upon its objects'. Intentionality, I claim, is what is common to all phenomena we call mental.

3. **Perspectives and their objects**

As I just noted, when I say that having a mind is having a perspective, I am using the word *perspective* in an extended, metaphorical sense. To get a better grip on this metaphorical sense of perspective, consider first its literal use. The techniques of perspective drawing provide a way of representing (say) a three-dimensional scene on a two-dimensional surface. For our interests, two features of this kind of pictorial representation are notable.

First, the picture is a picture *of* things; the perspective in the picture is thus a perspective *on things* other than the perspective itself. To say that there is a certain perspective in the picture is to say that *things* are presented in a certain way: the picture's being a perspective drawing is a matter of the things represented standing in a certain represented relation to the point at which they are viewed. There is a distinction, then, between the perspective itself and the things presented within, or in, or from that perspective.

Second, the things in the picture are presented in a *certain way*. Some surfaces are visible, some are not; things are seen as having certain patterns of shadows and illumination. This is a consequence of the fact that a drawing contains, implicitly, the point of view itself from which things are seen. The perspective drawing is not a 'view from nowhere' (to use Thomas Nagel's phrase); rather, it is a view from a certain place and certain time. Rather than being a view from nowhere, our drawing might be a view from *now, here*.[6] So this means that certain things are included in the picture, and certain things are excluded. (A. W. Moore uses the term 'perspectival' in a similar way when he says that an outlook is perspectival iff (if and only if) there is some other possible outlook that it excludes.[7]) I will express this exclusion by saying that the picture essentially presents things under a certain *aspect*. 'Aspect' is used here in a general way, to mark out any property or feature of the things presented which is evident in the presentation.

These two features of perspectives—that a perspective is a perspective on things, and that from a perspective, things are presented under a certain aspect—are part of what gives the point to talking about the mind in terms of a perspective. The first feature brings out the simple but important truth that in a state of mind, such as a thought, experience, or desire, something is presented, there is something which the state of mind is directed at. As Brentano put it, 'in the idea, something is conceived, in judgement something is accepted or rejected, in love, loved, in hate, hated, in desire, desired; and so on'.[8] We can express this by saying that states of mind have *objects*. This is the heart of the idea of intentionality: for a state of mind to have intentionality, it must have, or be 'directed' on, an object.

The idea of intentionality also contains the second feature of a perspective, its necessary partiality or 'aspectual' character. Mental states such as thoughts and desires present things in the world in certain ways: an experience of a boat in the harbour presents the boat by presenting one side of the boat, with certain colours, certain shadows. The boat might seem to be a seaworthy vessel, but in fact be full of holes—this fact need not be presented in the experience. The kind man who taught you Latin may not present himself to you as the spy he really is; the spy whom you meet on the secret mission may not present himself as the kindly Latin teacher he really is.

I introduced the idea of perspective through its literal (and therefore visual) use. But this is not because I am only concerned here with how things are presented visually, or visual presentations. In the sense which shall concern us here, presentations may be (for example) presentations of sounds, which are experienced as independent of the experiencing of them. Or, a presentation can be merely the phenomenon of thinking about something. Thinking about something may involve imagining it, visualizing it in memory, or having words running through one's mind. (We shall also need the idea of unconscious presentations, but I shall postpone discussion of this until §21.) Presentation from a perspective in my sense is not supposed to be essentially visual.

The two features we have uncovered in this reflection on the idea of a perspective are: first, the fact that presentations must be presentations of something; and second, the fact that they present these things under a certain aspect. I shall call the first feature *directedness* and the second feature (following John Searle[9]) *aspectual shape*. Then I can express Brentano's thesis as follows: all and only mental phenomena exhibit directedness and aspectual shape.

This is a somewhat abstract and general definition of mind or mental phenomena. By talking in terms of 'phenomena' I mean to express two things. First, the category of phenomena is a broad category which encompasses anything which goes on mentally in a person's life (or the life of any minded creature who is not a person). So I am not restricting myself only to mental *events* or only to mental *states*. I am attempting to cover all mental goings-on and conditions (for more on states, events, etc., see §10). Second, I mean 'phenomenon' in the sense of an *appearance*. We are talking here about the appearance of mind, how minds seem to those who have them. Hence, most of the rest of this book will in a sense be an exercise in *phenomenology*, the theory (the '-ology') of the phenomena or the appearances. Sometimes the word 'phenomenology' is reserved for a particular kind of theory of phenomena, deriving from Edmund Husserl.[10] Husserl thought that the way to study the phenomena of mind was to 'bracket' the reality outside the mind, and investigate things only as they appear, where this involved no commitment to there being any such things. This technique of bracketing is a specific approach to the theory of appearances, and is not required by the mere idea of such a theory. When I say that this book is an exercise in phenomenology, I mean the word in the general sense, and not in Husserl's more specific sense.

I shall use the term *intentionalism* for the view that all mental phenomena exhibit intentionality. Intentionalism is controversial. Many philosophers reject it on the grounds that there obviously are states which are indisputably states of mind, but involve no perspective in the sense just explained. Some philosophers think that certain kinds of bodily sensations, like pains, involve no directedness nor aspectual shape. Others think that there are certain emotional states or moods which have no directedness (being unhappy, say, but not about anything in particular). These philosophers would deny that the answer to the question—what is the essence of our idea of mind?—is exhausted by talking about the perspective or point of view of the creature in question. Even once we have granted the facts about the perspective of a creature, we still have not said everything about the conscious life of the creature. Naturally, I reject this view, but the reasons for the rejection must wait until Chapter 3. Here I merely state what the thesis of intentionalism is; its defence will emerge. The first thing to do in explaining the thesis is to give a brief sketch of the origins of the idea of intentionality.

4. The origins of the concepts of intentionality and intension

The term 'intentionality' has a long and complex history, not all of which is relevant to our concerns in this book. But a glance at the origins of this somewhat unusual term will help illuminate its utility.

The Scholastic philosophers of the Middle Ages were interested in the logical structure of concepts. The term 'intentio' was employed as a technical term for a concept or notion. Like much Scholastic terminology, the term originates from Aristotle's philosophy. Aristotle had used the word *noema* (concept) for what is before the mind in thought. Through the Arabic commentators on Aristotle, this word was translated into the Arabic terms which the Scholastics themselves translated as *intentio, intentiones* (plural), and *intentionale* (adjective). 'Intentio' literally means a tension or stretching (from the verb *intendere*, to stretch). G. E. M. Anscombe once claimed that the word 'intentio' was chosen because of an analogy between stretching or aiming one's bow at something (*intendere arcum in*), and 'stretching' or aiming one's mind at something (*intendere anima in*).[11] Hence *intentio* as the noun derived from intending in this sense: the *intentio* is the concept which is the 'object' of a state of mind, in the sense that it is what is aimed at by the mind, or 'before the mind' in thought. This word has survived into contemporary English in the phrase, 'to all intents and purposes'. Here the idea of an intent is the idea of what was meant.

We will not go far wrong if we think of an *intentio* as a concept. But it is useful to distinguish two senses of the word 'concept'. In the logical sense a concept is thought of as an abstraction, an abstract entity. Concepts in the logical sense are what logical relations hold between. In the psychological sense, a concept is a component of a state of mind. (I don't mean to imply that this was a distinction which was clearly drawn in the Middle Ages; it is one which we can draw now, looking back.) Many Scholastic philosophers were very interested in concepts in the logical sense; as they conceived it, in the abstract relations between *intentiones* or intentions. First intentions were concepts which applied to particular objects, whereas second intentions were concepts which applied to first intentions. Some Scholastic philosophers thought that second intentions were the subject-matter of logic.

Others, notably St Thomas Aquinas, were interested in concepts in (what we can now call) the psychological sense. Aquinas developed Aristotle's theory of sense-perception, according to which the mind takes on the 'form' of the perceived object, into an account of thinking in general. Aquinas's view was that what makes your thought of a goat a thought of a goat was the very same thing that makes a goat a goat: namely, the occurrence of the form of a goat. But the form of goat is instantiated in your mind in a different way from the way it is instantiated in an actual goat: in an actual goat, the form has *esse naturale* (natural existence), while in the thought of a goat, the form has *esse intentionale* (intentional existence).[12]

Related to the idea of an *intentio* is the idea of an object. Readers of Descartes's *Meditations* are sometimes puzzled by the distinction he makes in the Third Meditation between 'formal' and 'objective' reality. When Descartes argued that a cause must have as much reality as its effects, he applied this principle to ideas by distinguishing the *formal reality* of the cause of an idea from the idea's *objective reality*. Formal reality is just what we would call today *reality*; but objective reality is (perhaps rather confusingly) the content of the idea, considered as an idea. The objective reality of the idea of a dog consists in the fact that it is about dogs; thus the objective reality of an idea is its intentionality: the characteristics it has as a representation of something.

After the Scholastic period the term 'intentionality' fell into a certain disrepute, as did many terms arising from Aristotelian philosophy. In *Leviathan*, Hobbes scathingly dismissed the idea that the concept of intentionality is needed to give an account of the beginnings of language:

and so by succession of time, so much language might be gotten, as [Adam] had found use for, though not so copious, as an orator or philosopher had need of. For I do not find anything in the Scripture, out of which, directly or by consequence can be gathered, that *Adam* was taught the names of all figures, numbers, measures, colours, sounds, fancies, relations; much less the names of words and speech, such as *general, special, affirmative, negative, interrogative, optative, infinitive*, all of which are useful; and least of all, of *entity, intentionality, quiddity*, and other insignificant words of the school.[13]

Logic, however, survived the demise of the terminology of intentionality; but logicians also introduced some terminology which is strikingly similar to that terminology, so similar that it might be confused with it. In the seventeenth-century *Logic: or The Art of Thinking* (the 'Port Royal Logic') a distinction was made between the *extension* and the *comprehension* of a term. The extension of a term is the set or class of things to which the term applies—we can think of it as the set of things over which the term 'extends'. So the extension of the term 'marsupial' is the set of all marsupials: kangaroos, wallabies, wombats, and so on. The comprehension of a term is, as the label suggests, what is understood by someone who grasps it. Thus the comprehension of the term 'marsupial' may be something like *creature that suckles its young and keeps newborns in a pouch.*

Leibniz made use of this distinction, but introduced the term 'intension' as a variant of 'comprehension', thus providing an elegant counterpart for the term 'extension':

When I say *Every man is an animal* I mean that all the men are included amongst all the animals; but at the same time I mean that the idea of animal is included in the idea of man. 'Animal' comprises more individuals than 'man' does, but 'man' comprises more ideas or more attributes: one has more instances, the other more degrees of reality; one has the greater extension, the other the greater intension.[14]

Leibniz puts the point vividly: the more is in the extension, the less is in the intension, and vice versa. In other words, the more general a term is—the larger its extension, or the set of things to which it applies—the less specific the intension has to be; and the more specific the intension, the smaller the extension.

The contrast made here between intension and extension survived into twentieth-century logic, although it is not formulated in the way Leibniz did. These days the terms 'intensional' and 'extensional' are normally applied to languages (or contexts within a language), or to the logics which study these languages or contexts. (The following brief exposition will not be news to those familiar with philosophy of language, and may be skipped.) A context is extensional when it is one in which the following principles of inference apply (where 'a' and 'b' are singular terms):

Substitution of co-referring terms

From '. . . a . . .' and 'a = b' infer '. . . b . . .'

(For example: from 'Vladimir is taller than George Orwell' and 'George Orwell = Eric Blair' infer 'Vladimir is taller than Eric Blair'.)

Existential generalization

From '. . . a . . .', infer '∃x . . . x . . .'

(For example: from 'George Orwell is shorter than Vladimir' infer 'There is someone who is shorter than Vladimir'.)

An intensional context is one where one or both of these principles is not generally valid or truth-preserving. For example: the sentence 'Dorothy believes that Vladimir is taller than George Orwell' is an intensional context, since together with 'George Orwell = Eric Blair' it does not entail 'Dorothy believes that Vladimir is taller than Eric Blair'. The first two sentences could be true while the third is false (if Dorothy does not believe that George Orwell = Eric Blair). Intuitively, the way to understand the distinction is to see extensional contexts as those where truth or falsehood depends solely on the extensions of the expressions involved (hence the above principles), and intensional contexts as those where truth or falsehood depends on the way the extensions are conceived.

Frege's famous theory of sense and reference is an attempt to account for the logical and semantic properties of certain intensional contexts. Frege distinguished the *reference* of an expression, what it refers to, from its *sense*, the 'mode of presentation' of the reference. In our example, the same reference (the man, Orwell) is presented in two ways, by the sense associated with the expression 'George Orwell', and by the sense associated with the expression 'Eric Blair'. Now, since Frege's discussion in 'On sense and reference', such psychological contexts have been at the focus of many discussions of

intensionality. But it is important to emphasize that contexts other than psychological contexts are intensional. (For example, the inference from 'the
number of coins in my pocket is five' and 'five is necessarily odd' to 'the
number of coins in my pocket is necessarily odd' is invalid, because '...
necessarily ...' creates an intensional context.) The general feature of intensional contexts is that their logical properties (e.g. whether they allow the
validity of inferences) are sensitive to the ways in which things are described
(e.g., picked out as 'George Orwell' or as 'five'). Insofar as the truth of sentences, and their logical properties, are determined only by the extensions of
the expressions in question, then logic does not need to take account of
the way in which the extensions are picked out, the intensions of these expressions. Logics which attempt to display the logical properties of intensional
contexts are called intensional logics.

When the terminology of intentionality was reintroduced by Brentano in
his 1879 book *Psychology from an Empirical Standpoint*, there was no mention
of intension and extension. Brentano's concern in this book was to distinguish
the newly emerging science of psychology from physiology on the one hand,
and philosophy on the other. He made this distinction not in terms of the
different methods of these disciplines, but in terms of their different subject-
matters. The subject-matter of physiology was the body, while the subject-
matter of philosophy included questions such as the immortality of the soul,
and so on. Psychology's subject-matter, by contrast, was mental phenomena,
and the difference between mental phenomena and physical phenomena was
that mental phenomena exhibited 'what the Scholastics of the Middle Ages'
called 'the intentional inexistence' of an object.[15] Mental phenomena are
intentional, they have objects. So the link with the Scholastic idea of *esse
intentionale* is made explicitly.

But Brentano did not characterize intentionality in terms of the intensionality of psychological contexts. It is somewhat mysterious, then, that when
R. M. Chisholm introduced Brentano's ideas to English-speaking philosophy
in the 1950s, he defined intentionality in terms of criteria of intensionality.[16]
And when Quine, in his *Word and Object* (1960), talked about Brentano's thesis
of the 'irreducibility of the intentional', he was talking about the irreducibility
of intensional language to extensional language, not Brentano's claim that mental phenomena are irreducibly intentional.[17] And as we saw above, the ideas of
intentionality and intensionality are distinct, and have distinct origins.

This conflation of the distinct ideas of intentionality and intensionality is
perhaps more understandable given Quine's method of 'semantic ascent',
which asks us to investigate phenomena by investigating the language we use
to speak about phenomena. But nonetheless, the conflation has given rise to
nothing but confusion, and we need to be absolutely clear about this at the
beginning of our enquiry. For it is plain, despite what Chisholm says, that

intensionality cannot be a criterion or sufficient condition of the presence of intentionality. Regardless of whether intentionality is the mark of the mental, there are intensional contexts which are nothing to do with intentionality.[18]

When I said above that I was defending Brentano's thesis, I did not mean that I was defending the idea that intentional phenomena are irreducible to physical phenomena (this is what some mean by the 'irreducibility of the intentional'[19]). I am defending the thesis that all mental phenomena are intentional. This thesis is distinct from the thesis that intentional phenomena are irreducible to physical phenomena, since one could hold the former without holding the latter. This would be so, for example, if one held that all mental phenomena were physical, but what made them mental was their intentionality. (For more on reduction, see §15.)

5. Directedness and intentional objects

So it is very important to distinguish clearly between intentionality and intensionality. It would be wrong, however, to think that the ideas of intension and intensionality have nothing to do with the mind.[20] After all, part of the point of these ideas is to explain aspects of reasoning: to explain how concepts (in the logical sense) should relate to one another. But it would be hard to see the point of an investigation into how concepts (in this sense) relate to one another unless it had something to do with the relations between concepts in the psychological sense. Reasoning is something which is done by thinkers, by reasoners; so it would surely be strange if the ingredients of reason had nothing to do with the ingredients of thought.

The link between intensions and intentionality will be appreciated as we develop further the ideas of directedness and aspectual shape. I shall claim that, in broad outline, the intensionality of the ingredients of reason is the logical expression or reflection of these two ideas. To argue for this, I will first say something about directedness, and in the next section I will discuss aspectual shape.

Directedness is the idea that intentional states have objects. The object of an intentional state is often called an 'intentional object'. But what is an intentional object? It is sometimes asked: is an intentional object something in the mind, something in the world outside the mind, or something 'in between', an intermediary between the mind and the world? In response to this sort of question, John Searle says:

an Intentional object is just an object like any other; it has no peculiar ontological status at all. To call something an Intentional object is just to say that it is what some intentional state is about. Thus, for example, if Bill admires President Carter, then the Intentional object of his admiration is President Carter, the actual man and not some shadowy intermediate entity between Bill and the man.[21]

Searle is surely right that there is no intuitive case for there being 'shadowy intermediaries' between thinkers and the things they are thinking about. When I remember President Carter, my thought goes—as it were—straight to Carter himself. I do not first think about some non-physical 'stand-in' for Carter, and then move on to the man. (Things are more complex in the case of perception: see §41.) But nonetheless, there are two problems with Searle's claim that intentional objects are just 'ordinary objects'. Concentration on these problems will bring out what should be meant by the phrase 'intentional object'.

First, there is a tension between the claim that an intentional object is just 'what some intentional state is about' and the claim that intentional objects are objects in the ordinary sense—if objects in this sense are things like houses, people, tables, and chairs. For there seem to be many kinds of entity which can be the things I am thinking about, none of which are objects in the ordinary sense. I can think about the First World War—but this is an event, not an object. If I am thinking about Newton's second law of motion, I am thinking about the relation between force, mass, and acceleration—but these are physical quantities or properties, not objects. In these and many other cases, the natural answer to the question 'what are you thinking about?' does not pick out an object in the ordinary sense.[22]

However, perhaps Searle does not mean *object* in the ordinary sense—the sense in which events and properties are not objects. Perhaps he just means 'existing entity'; if so, properties and events are objects in this sense. But this gives rise to the second problem with his claim that intentional objects are ordinary objects. It is an undeniable fact that some intentional states can be about things which do not exist. That is, one can think about, desire, wish for, or anticipate things which do not exist. And if someone is thinking about something which does not exist, then obviously the *intentional object* of their thought—thus defined as *what they are thinking about*—does not exist. But non-existent entities are not shadowy, intermediate entities: they are not entities at all! (This claim has been denied by some philosophers; their denial will be discussed further in §7.) So, on the face of it, the following claims are in tension:

- Intentional objects are the objects of intentional states (e.g. the object of a thought is what a thought is about);
- Intentional objects are ordinary objects (e.g. people, chairs, tables, etc.);
- Some intentional objects do not exist (e.g. one can think about Pegasus, or Santa Claus, etc.).

These claims jointly imply that some ordinary objects do not exist. But clearly this is not what Searle intended.

What is the solution to this puzzle? I think it is correct to say that some intentional objects do not exist. So, for reasons to be given below, I think we should keep Searle's equation of 'intentional object' with 'object of intentional state' but deny that intentional objects are ordinary objects in any sense.

This claim seems paradoxical. If Carter is the object of my thought, then Carter is an intentional object. But Carter is an ordinary kind of object—a person—so how can *this* intentional object, at least, not be an object in any sense? To remove the (understandable) sense of paradox from the claim, we must first say something about the idea of an object. In §7 we will apply this way of thinking to the question of thought about the non-existent.

A very common use of the word 'object' is in phrases like 'physical object' or 'material object'. But there are many contexts in philosophy and elsewhere where we use the idea of an object in a different way. For instance, a question in the philosophy of mathematics is whether numbers are objects. This debate would be impossible to understand if the only sense we could make of the word 'object' is the sense it has in the phrase 'physical object'—since of course numbers are not physical objects. Sometimes numbers are called 'abstract objects', intended to suggest that they are not 'concrete', where concreteness is sometimes explained in terms of existence in space-time.[23] This conception of an abstract object, like our conception of a physical object, is what we might call a *substantial* conception of an object. It is a metaphysical theory that there are these kinds of objects, with this kind of nature. This use of the term 'object' is not a pun or a homonym of its use in the phrase 'physical object': on many views, what makes abstract objects *objects* is (e.g.) that they are particulars, the referents of singular terms, or the values of variables bound by first-order quantifiers—things they have in common with physical objects. (Then something more has to be said about what makes them abstract—but we need not worry about this here.)

This substantial conception of an object—the conception of a kind of object having a certain nature—can be contrasted with another kind of conception, which we could call the *schematic* idea of an object. This is the kind of idea we find expressed in phrases like 'object of attention'. An object of attention is something to which someone is or can be attending. But clearly there is nothing which all objects of attention need have in common: objects of attention have no 'nature'. Another example of a schematic idea of an object is the grammatical idea. Transitive verbs are verbs which take objects. This is a claim which we find easy enough to understand when learning grammar; but to understand it we do not need to have a substantial conception of what an object, in this sense, is. All we need to know is that the object is something which plays a certain role in the sentence. The object of the sentence 'Vladimir ate the banana' is the banana, the object of the sentence 'the directors threw a party' is a party, and the object of the sentence 'Anna and Bert made a verbal agreement' is a verbal agreement; but there should be no puzzlement about the idea that the grammatical category *object* contains such things as bananas, parties, and verbal agreements. A grammatical object is whatever stands in the relevant relation to a transitive verb. The object of a sentence is an object in the schematic, rather than the substantial, sense.

Now it is possible to hold that intentional objects are a substantial kind of object—this is presumably the kind of view that Searle is alluding to when he talks of shadowy intermediaries. One could say, for instance, that the objects of our thoughts—what we are thinking about—are *ideas in our minds*, or *representations in our heads*, and then go on to give a substantial account of what ideas or representations are. But Searle is right to dismiss these views at the outset. When we think *about* ideas, then ideas are the objects of our thought, but when we think about people (say), there is no reason to suppose that we think about them by *thinking about* ideas (though having ideas may be part of the story of what enables us to think about them: see §8). This much of what Searle says is quite correct.

But my main point here is that to deny that intentional objects are shadowy intermediaries does not imply that intentional objects are objects in the ordinary sense. The first point I made against Searle was that, unlike the category of 'objects in the ordinary sense', the category of 'things thought about' has no chance of being a metaphysically unified category: objects of thought are not just particulars, not just properties, and not just events. And the second point I made was that 'object' cannot just mean 'existing entity', since some intentional objects do not exist. To these two considerations we can add the familiar point that intentional objects can be indeterminate. As G. E. M. Anscombe puts it: 'I can think of a man without thinking of a man of any particular height; I cannot hit a man without hitting a man of any particular height, because there is no such thing as a man of no particular height.'[24] So 'the man' thought about is, in a sense, 'indeterminate': he is 'no particular man', or in Russell's (unintentionally comic) phrase, an 'ambiguous man'.[25] Some intentional objects, then, are indeterminate in this sense; but no ordinary objects are indeterminate. So rather than introduce a class of objects which includes real events and properties, indeterminate entities, and things which do not exist, we should conclude that intentional objects, unlike abstract objects, *have no nature of their own*. The idea of an intentional object is a schematic idea of an object, not a substantial idea. Further clarification of this view comes from J. J. Valberg's observation that we can sensibly replace the word 'object' with the word 'thing' in the phrase 'physical object'; but we cannot do likewise with the word when it occurs in the phrases 'object of experience', 'object of attention', or 'intentional object'.[26]

We can say the same about the grammatical idea of the *direct object* of a transitive verb. 'Object' here does not mean *thing*: 'direct thing' makes no sense. What I mean when I say that an intentional object is not a kind of object is the same kind of thing as what is meant by saying that a *grammatical* object is not a kind of object. This comparison, between the direct object of a transitive verb and the intentional object of a state of mind, was originally made in a classic paper by Anscombe.[27] Unlike Anscombe, however, I do not say that an intentional object *is* a kind of grammatical object, or that the idea of an intentional object is a purely grammatical idea. I think that intentional objects and grammatical objects are both objects in the schematic sense, but the first is not explained in terms of the second. The idea of an intentional object is a phenomenological idea, not a grammatical one. It is an idea which emerges in the process of reflecting on what mental life is like. The connection between the ideas is this: there is a perfectly legitimate use of the word 'object' according to which to be an object of this kind is not *ipso facto* to be an entity of any kind, where an entity is something which has a nature.

What is it, then, for something to be an intentional object? The answer I shall give is simple, and at first sight uninformative: it is to be that upon which the mind is directed when in an intentional state. In the case of thought, for instance, the intentional object of your thought is what is given in a (correct) answer to the question, 'what are you thinking about?' Likewise, the intentional object of a desire is the thing desired, the intentional object of a wish is the thing wished for—and so on. This formulation is not intended to imply that there can only ever be *one* answer to the question. One could be thinking about the Iran–Iraq war, and the answer to the question, 'what are you thinking about?' could be 'the war' or 'Iran' or 'Iraq'. If one gave all three answers, it would be pointless to keep pushing the question, 'yes, but which one are you *really* thinking about?' There is no reason to suppose that there is only ever one intentional object of a state of mind.

One of my reasons for denying that intentional objects form a kind of object is that I take seriously the proposition that some intentional objects do not exist. This proposition entails that there is no category of intentional objects: for all members of a given category of things exist. This conclusion assumes Quine's conception of existence, according to which the idea of a thing (something) and the idea of existence are two sides of the same coin. To be a thing (to be something) is to exist: so strictly speaking the phrase *things which do not exist* is an oxymoron.[28] For there are no things which do not exist: 'there are' is a form of words which we use to express existence. (Here I merely state the Quinean view, rather than argue for it. We will return to the matter in §7 below.) This point provides a link with the concept of intensionality. One of the marks of intensionality is failure of existential generalization: from 'Vladimir believes that Pegasus flies' we cannot infer 'There is something x such that Vladimir believes x flies'. I see this logical feature as a product of the fact that intentional states can be about things which do not exist.

However, this feature—failure of existential generalization—is not an uncontroversial feature of all reports of intentional states, if intentionality is just directedness on something. For it appears that some reports of intentional states do license existential generalizations. Perhaps the simplest case is the case of knowledge: if I know Vladimir, then he must exist. If Vladimir is a mere figment of my imagination, then I cannot know him. But this case is controversial, since it is controversial whether knowledge itself is a state of mind, or a composite state involving a thought about something, plus its existence. Similar claims (on both sides) have been made, though, for reports of seeing: some claim that 'A sees B' does entail 'There is an x such that A sees x'. Other cases are reports of certain object-directed emotions: 'A loves B' (arguably) entails 'There is an x such that A loves x'; and certain kinds of belief-reports: 'A believes, of B, that he is a spy' entails 'There is an x such that x is believed by A to be a spy'.[29]

One could conclude from this that there are two kinds of intentional state, those whose ascriptions license existential generalization, and those whose ascriptions don't. In other words, there are two kinds of directedness, the intensional and the extensional. Or one could conclude that there are not two kinds of directedness, but that there are two ways of *reporting* directedness, the intensional way and the extensional way. The phenomenon of directedness can be described in various ways, but this does not necessarily require a distinction between kinds of directedness. As will become apparent, I favour this latter view. But we will return to the details of this difficult question in §35.

6. Aspectual shape and intentional content

The second feature of intentionality is the idea of aspectual shape. This is a term which I take from Searle to express an idea which should be familiar from other areas of philosophy. The term is useful because it is free from some of the acquired connotations of some other terms used for the same or a similar phenomenon.

The basic idea of aspectual shape is very simple: in any intentional state, the objects on which the mind is directed are presented in a certain way. Suppose that you are thinking of St Petersburg—with its elegant baroque buildings and its harsh climate. You are thinking about it in a particular way: maybe you are visualizing it in the imagination, on the basis of pictures you have seen or on the basis of experience. Or maybe you are just thinking about it as *St Petersburg*—that is, a thought which you would express by using the name 'St

Petersburg'. You may just think to yourself, 'Vladimir is in St Petersburg; I wonder what the weather is like there?' When you think about St Petersburg as St Petersburg, the aspectual shape of your thought is different from when you think about St Petersburg as Leningrad, or when you think of it while listening to Shostakovich's *Leningrad Symphony*. Similarly, when you visually perceive St Petersburg, you see it from some particular place, in certain particular conditions of illumination, and so on. You see it under a certain aspect. Your experience, like your thought, has a certain aspectual shape.

These truisms are just ways of expressing the simple idea that one cannot think of something without thinking of it in some way. This is related to Frege's idea of *sense*. As we saw above (§4) Frege distinguished between the reference of an expression and its sense. The sense he called the *mode of presentation* of the reference, the way the reference is presented. St Petersburg is presented in a different way when referred to by the name 'St Petersburg' than it is when referred to by the name 'Leningrad'. Some commentators on Frege have spelled out the idea of a mode of presentation in terms of the idea of a 'way of thinking' of the reference of a word. Thus Gareth Evans:

Frege's idea was that it is a property of a singular term in a public language that, in order to understand utterances containing it, one must not only think of a particular object, its reference, but one must think of that object *in a particular way*: that is, every competent user of the language who understands the utterance will think of the object in the same way.[30]

Sense, on this view, is a way of thinking of reference. The reference is thought about under some aspect. To say that something is presented under an aspect is not to say that the aspect itself is what is presented. The aspect is the *mode* of presentation (to use Frege's term) of the reference. So it is not as if one is presented with a reference (a real existing thing) by *first* being presented with an aspect. This would make one's access to the references of one's words 'mediated' by access to the aspects; but we have already rejected (§5) the obscure idea that there are such intermediaries in thought. As Evans says,

The fact that one is thinking about an object in a particular way can no more warrant the conclusion that one is not thinking of the object in the most direct possible fashion, than the fact that one is giving something *in a particular way* warrants the view that one's giving is somehow indirect.[31]

One can of course turn one's attention to the aspects under which things are given. Suppose you see a familiar person watching you in a strange way. You can perhaps turn your attention to the way in which they are watching you. The *way* then becomes the object of your attention, and it too has an aspectual shape.

So, at its most general, the idea of aspectual shape is just the idea that there is no such thing as a thought about, or an awareness of, an object *as such*—that there is no such thing as what we might call 'bare' presentation of an object. Indeed, the idea scarcely makes sense. I can illustrate this with a comment on a famous analogy of Frege's. In his essay 'On sense and reference', Frege uses an analogy to distinguish between the sense of a term, its reference, and the idea associated with the term:

Somebody observes the moon through a telescope. I compare the Moon itself to the reference; it is the object of the observation, mediated by the real image projected by the object glass in the interior of the telescope, and by the retinal image of the observer. The former I compare to the sense, the latter is like the idea or experience. The optical image in the telescope is indeed one-sided and dependent upon the standpoint of observation; but it is still objective, inasmuch as it can be used by several observers. At any rate it could be arranged for several to use it simultaneously. But each one would have his own retinal image.[32]

Frege's main point here is to distinguish the sense of a word from ideas in the minds of speakers. For him, ideas are subjective and private, while senses, though partial and perspectival, are objective and public: this is his 'anti-psychologism' about sense. The analogy makes this point nicely. But when it comes to the relation between sense and reference, the analogy could mislead. For one might be tempted to think that there is a more 'direct' way of getting at *the Moon itself*, a 'pure reference' unmediated by the telescope—after all, one can step aside from the telescope and look at the moon with the naked eye! The thesis of aspectual shape is that, where states of mind are concerned, there is no such thing as a pure reference. All mental access to objects is 'one-sided and dependent on a standpoint': in the terms of the analogy, the naked eye is just another standpoint. (Here I aim only to draw attention to a possible confusion in understanding the analogy; of course Frege himself did not think in this way.)

Frege's theory of sense is an attempt to give an account of the aspectual shape involved in grasping the meanings of words. But although I am following Frege in some respects, I do not want to restrict myself to his terminology in describing the phenomenon of aspectual shape. For Frege's theory involves taking stands on certain issues which it would be well to leave open for the time being: for instance, his anti-psychologism noted above, his view that sense 'is not something subjective . . . it does not therefore belong to psychology'.[33] Also, Frege has no place for the idea of an intentional object in the sense in which I am using this term. At this stage, we are trying to characterize the phenomena to be explained and understood; it would be wrong to describe the phenomenon of aspectual shape in a way that makes certain accounts of it impossible.

However, this connection with Frege's theory of sense shows a clear link between the idea of aspectual shape and the idea of intensionality. A state of mind's having aspectual shape is a matter of its partial presentation of a thing. Therefore, if in reporting an intentional state we want to report how things are from the subject's perspective, we need to convey this partiality. If I believe Napoleon died on St Helena, then a report which attempts to capture my view of things can report it in this way. A report that says I believe that Josephine's sometime husband died on St Helena, or that Napoleon died on an island in the Atlantic Ocean, might not capture my way of seeing things, since I might believe that Napoleon died in this place without believing that he was married to Josephine, or while having the false belief that St Helena was in the Mediterranean. Hence belief-reports are often intensional: when the aim is to capture the subject's perspective, whether the belief-report is a good one depends on the way it describes the objects of the belief. Hence not all descriptions of the objects involved are equally good for this purpose: substitution of co-referring expressions in a belief report do not always preserve the truth-value of the report. And likewise for reports of other intentional states.

What counts as capturing the subject's perspective in any particular case can be a difficult matter. And it is clear that there are reports of intentional states which do not aim to capture the subject's perspective and yet still can be true: it is true that Oedipus wanted to marry his mother, although he would not have put it that way himself. The conclusion I would draw from this is not that there are two kinds of intentional state, the intensional and the extensional, but (as with the discussion of directedness in §5) that there are two ways of *reporting* or *ascribing* intentional states, the intensional and the extensional. The intensional ascriptions of intentional states are those which are sensitive to the subject's own perspective. (We will return to this question in §35.)

So the link between intentionality, our subject, and intensionality, the logical concept, is complex. The heart of this link may be expressed as follows: when ascriptions of mental states are intensional, this is a reflection of, or an expression of, their intentionality. The failure of existential generalization is a expression of the fact that the objects of some intentional states do not exist; the failure of substitutivity is a expression of the aspectual shape of intentional states. But not all ascriptions of intentional states are intensional. This is because: (a) some ascriptions of intentional states are not made unless the objects of those states exist; and (b) some ascriptions of intentional states serve purposes other than to capture how things are from the subject's perspective. Intensionality is not, then, a necessary condition for the ascription of an intentional state. (Nor is it sufficient, for the reasons given in §4.) But it does not follow from this that there are intentional states which lack aspectual shape.[34]

7. **The problem of intentionality**

So far, I have outlined the origins of the ideas of intentionality and intension-ality, and described what I take to be the connection between them. I have also expounded the thesis that all intentional states have objects and aspectual shape but that intentional objects are not objects in the ordinary sense. I gave three reasons for saying that intentional objects are not objects in this sense: intentional objects can be entities of many metaphysical kinds, they can be indeterminate, and some of them do not exist. But saying this does not mean that intentional objects are objects in a *non-ordinary* sense (as abstract objects like numbers might be). Instead, I said that 'object' in 'intentional object' should be understood in what I called a *schematic,* rather than a *substantial* way, following Anscombe's analogy with the grammatical use of 'object'. The object of a sentence is not, as such, a certain kind of entity, and the object of a thought is not, as such, a certain kind of entity. If we were dividing the things in the world up into metaphysical kinds we might list the properties, relations, physical objects, abstract objects, events, processes . . . but we would not need to mention, in addition, the intentional objects.

But what should we say about the case where someone is thinking about something, say President Carter, that does exist? Shouldn't we then say that Carter is the intentional object of my thought, and that he is something real, so there is at least such a thing as the class of intentional objects which are real. So aren't *some* intentional objects things (e.g. Carter)? What can I mean, then, by saying that intentional objects are not things? The short answer to this is that what makes Carter an intentional object is the fact that he is the object of my thought; and this is not something distinctive of *Carter,* but only of *Carter-as-thought-about,* and *Carter-as-thought-about* cannot be an entity in the same way as Carter is. Carter would be what he is regardless of whether he is thought about by me.[35]

So: I express the idea that intentional states can concern things which do not exist by saying that some intentional objects do not exist. Perhaps I could have talked in another way: I could have said, with Searle, that all intentional objects exist, but that some intentional states have no intentional objects. But then I would have been at a loss to say what makes this latter class of states *intentional.* Intentionality, it is often said, is 'aboutness': but what is the thought that *Pegasus flies* about, if the thought has no intentional object? If we say 'well, it is about something, but that thing does not exist', we do not avoid the problem, we restate it. (Likewise with the answer: 'the thought contains a Pegasus-representation', to which the obvious response is: we knew *that!*) My alternative strategy, outlined in §5 above, is to keep the slogan 'some inten-tional objects do not exist', but interpret the phrase 'intentional object' in the way suggested. The reason behind this is that we need the idea of an intentional object as much as we need the idea of *a thing thought about* or the idea of an *object of thought.* Since I don't see how we should do without these ideas, I don't see how we should do without the idea of an intentional object.

If some intentional objects do not exist, then as I said in §5, there is no such thing as the class of all intentional objects, since all members of a given class exist. It follows from this that not all intentional states are relations to intentional objects, since the existence of a relation entails the existence of what it relates (its *relata*). If Vladimir is taller than Ivan, then the relation *x is taller than y* holds between Vladimir and Ivan; therefore they must both exist. This seems obvious. We might hesitate when thinking about examples from fiction—it is true that Desdemona loves Othello, even though neither Desdemona nor Othello really exist. But this puzzle is best solved by treating statements about fictional characters as disguised statements about the fiction itself. Thus 'Desdemona loves Othello' must surely be understood as something like 'In Shakespeare's *Othello*, Desdemona loves Othello'.[36] Putting this kind of thing to one side, it seems an undeniable fact that if a relation relates any two things A and B, then A and B must exist.

This indicates the general way to formulate a persistent and traditional problem, which I shall call the problem of intentionality.[37] (Other things have been called the problem of intentionality; I will have something to say about them later.) Concentrating here on the case of thinking about an object—analogous things can be said about desire, hope, and other intentional states—this problem of intentionality can be expressed as the conflict between three propositions:

(1) All thoughts are relations between thinkers and the things which they are about.
(2) Relations entail the existence of their relata.
(3) Some thoughts are about things which do not exist.

It is clear that (1)–(3) cannot be true together. So one of these propositions must be denied. I claimed above that (1) must be denied. To defend this claim, I must show why (2) and (3) are undeniable.

It seems to me that (3) is a proposition which is not really up for dispute. We can think about unicorns, phlogiston, Pegasus, Vulcan, the Golden Mountain, the fountain of youth (which are merely contingent non-existents), as well as necessary non-existents like the round square and the greatest prime number. Perhaps these thoughts are not very frequent, surely they are exceptions to the rule. But the thoughts certainly exist, and so a solution to the problem which denies (3) would have little to be said for it; it would not be solving the problem but avoiding it by denying a manifest fact.

(We should not, of course, say that our thoughts are really about the *idea* of

Pegasus or the *idea* of phlogiston. This is a confusion. Debates about whether phlogiston exists are not debates about whether the idea of phlogiston exists. The idea of phlogiston certainly exists! Therefore, thoughts about phlogiston are not *ipso facto* thoughts about the idea of phlogiston.[38] A more striking example: a debate about the existence of God is not normally a debate about whether the idea of God exists.)

But what should be said about (2)? It seems on the face of it obvious that if two things are related, then they exist. But this has been disputed. For it has been argued that since we are prepared to say things like 'there are lots of things which do not exist: for example, Pegasus', then we are actually committed to there being non-existent objects. On this view, some objects exist while others do not, just as some objects are red and others are not. This view, therefore, rejects Quine's account of existence, according to which there are no things which do not exist. As I said above, for Quine, 'There are Fs' and 'Fs exist' say the same thing. Those who believe in non-existent objects deny this, since they are prepared to quantify (say 'There are . . .') over things which do not exist. Among all the things that there are, some exist and some do not. So although a relation might entail that its relata *are*, or are *real*, it does not thereby entail that they *exist*: (2) is therefore false.

What should we make of this view? It certainly solves our problem of intentionality in a very elegant and simple way. By appealing to an ontology of non-existent objects, we can preserve the idea that every intentional state is a relation to a real object while still maintaining that we can think about things which do not exist (since real ≠ existent). And it is certainly true that 'there are many things which do not exist' is an intelligible thing to say (haven't I just said that some intentional objects do not exist?). Moreover, as noted above (§5), we should not restrict the use of the term 'object' simply to talk about physical objects, at least not if we can make sense of the ideas of (say) mental or abstract objects. So perhaps we can allow non-existent objects too?

Yet despite its agreeably quick way with our problem, I find the view impossible to believe. Russell once said: 'Logic, I should maintain, must no more admit a unicorn than zoology can; for logic is concerned with the real world just as truly as zoology, though with its more abstract and general features.'[39] The same is true of other parts of philosophy. But how should we respond to the view that certain objects exist and others do not, if not by simply denying it? It does not help here to appeal to the Russell–Quine view that 'exists' is not a first-level predicate but a quantifier; for one thing, this is another way of expressing what is at issue; and for another, the view that 'exists' is never a predicate is not plausible.[40] So somehow we have to get our minds around the idea that not all objects exist; some do not. Presumably all these objects are real, so the real divides into the existent and the non-existent. It sounds then as if we ought to be able to distinguish these two kinds of object from each other. But what distinguishes them? A unicorn has a horn and four legs, and a tail. A rhinoceros has a horn, four legs and a tail. The rhino exists and the unicorn does not. What does this further difference amount to? There seem to be two possibilities. Either existence is a primitive property, inexplicable in other terms, which some things have and others lack. Or there is some analysis of existence, and the idea of existence can be spelt out in other terms. Neither possibility is very promising. If existence is a primitive property, then how can it be explained to us what it is to deny existence to something real, if we do not already understand the distinction? But if existence is explained in terms of some property F—say, for example, location in space-time—then the view that some real things do not exist seems only a terminological variation of the view that some existing things do not have property F (e.g. do not exist in space-time).

These points merely shift the burden of argument; they do not refute the view that there are non-existent objects. As far as I know, there is no knock-down plausible refutation of this view.[41] But the view is hard to understand and seems to stipulate an answer to our problem of intentionality where more detailed investigation is what is needed. I admit that I cannot refute the view to my satisfaction; but nonetheless I reject it.

But haven't I said that some intentional objects do not exist? So am I not in the same boat as those who deny (2)? No. As should be clear by now, the question misunderstands what I mean by 'intentional object'. For when I say 'some intentional objects do not exist', I do not mean that there are some real, but non-existent, intentional objects. Rather, I mean that there are intentional states which can be truly described as being 'about Pegasus', 'about unicorns', etc.—and it is not the case that there is anything corresponding to these quoted words. The words have no reference: there are no unicorns, and no Pegasus. Nothing: not a non-existent but real thing, just nothing. This is what I mean when I talk about 'intentional objects which do not exist' and 'thoughts about the non-existent'.

Yet the question may be pressed: why talk about intentional objects in these cases at all, if there is no real thing which one is thinking about? My reason is this. There are many thoughts about non-existent objects, and not all of them are of exactly the same type. A thought about Pegasus is a different kind of thought from a thought about Zeus. Yet neither Zeus nor Pegasus exists; both Zeus and Pegasus are nothing. So the fact that there is no real thing (nothing) to which these thoughts refer does not mean that the thoughts are the same: one is about Pegasus, the other is about Zeus. (It is all very well to say that the thoughts involve different *ideas* or different *representations*; this just raises the question, what makes the ideas or representations different?) I use the idea of an intentional object to express this difference. The intentional object of a subject S's thought is given by an answer to the question 'what is S thinking about?'. The answer 'Zeus' is (in this case) a better answer than the answer 'nothing'. This is what makes Zeus the intentional object of S's thought. So long as we do not think of intentional objects as a kind of object, there should be no confusion introduced by this way of talking.

We can put the matter in another way. The problem of intentionality presents a dilemma about the idea of an *object of thought* or an *intentional object*. Given that there can be objects of thought which do not exist, are these objects real? If they are, then we can say that all thoughts are relations to their objects, but at the price of accepting the reality of non-existent objects. But if they are not, then 'they' are nothing, so thoughts cannot consist in relations to them; so how do we distinguish apparently different thoughts about nothing? My attempt to steer between the horns of this dilemma involves appealing to the understanding of 'intentional object' given in §5. An intentional object is not a kind of object, but rather the intentional object of a thought T is what is given in answer to the question 'what is T about?' If this question has an answer, then the thought has an intentional object. If the answer refers to some existent thing, then the intentional object is something real: perhaps an object in the more normal sense—a material or physical object—or perhaps a place, or a property or an event. To say that an intentional object is real is to say that the phrase which gives the intentional object has a reference. It is not to say, for example, that one set of things (the set of intentional objects) shares a member with another set of things (the set of real things).

If this is right, then it will already be obvious why (1) is false: for relations must relate real things, yet the intentional object of a thought is not a real thing. After all, intentional objects are not, as such, things (§5). So of course any adequate solution to the problem of intentionality should begin by denying (1): all intentional states are relations to things they are about. This must be agreed by everyone who holds (2) and (3). For the case of thought:

NOT-(1): Not all thoughts are relations between thinkers and the things they are about.

But to say this is not to say that *no* thoughts involve relations to real existing things; it is just to say that not all of them do. So the next question is: even if there are thoughts which do not involve relations to real things, are there any thoughts which *do* involve relations to real things? To answer *yes* is to say that thoughts fall into two categories: those which are relations to existing objects on which they are directed, and those which are not. To answer *no* is to hold that no thoughts involve relations to the real things they are about. To introduce some terminology which will be helpful later: the first view is the view that some thoughts are *broad*; the second view is the view that all thoughts are *narrow*. Then, generally speaking, we can say that the doctrine of *externalism* in the philosophy of mind is the doctrine that intentional states are broad; the doctrine of *internalism* is the doctrine that intentional states are narrow.

There are many different varieties of externalism, depending on how many (and which) kinds of thoughts the doctrine holds to be broad. If a mental state S is broad, then the existence of S entails the existence of its object. To take an extreme example: if knowledge is a mental state, then knowledge is a broad mental state: if I know that Caesar crossed the Rubicon, then Caesar and the Rubicon exist. Knowledge is a *factive* state: being in this state entails that the content of the state expresses a truth.[42] As we saw above (§5), seeing is a somewhat more debated example of a broad mental state: but if seeing is, as some claim, factive, then if I saw Caesar cross the Rubicon, Caesar and the Rubicon exist. Another kind of putative example of a broad mental state is thought about a perceived object, which one might express by using a sentence of the form 'that F is G', containing the demonstrative pronoun 'that'. Some have argued that one cannot be in such a state of mind unless the thing referred to by 'that F' exists. Still another view is the view that certain kinds of thought metaphysically depend on causal relations between thinker and object; since causation is a relation, these thoughts must be broad.

The internalist view of thought does not, of course, deny thoughts are often about real things. But it does deny that being in an intentional state always entails the existence of the thing it is about. A thought is narrow when its existence does not entail the existence of its objects. So thoughts about non-existent objects are on the face of it narrow, but according to an internalist, so are thoughts like *that apple looks tasty*, thought while looking at an apple in front of one. According to an internalist, this thought does not entail the existence of that apple; the thought could exist even if the apple didn't. This is what is meant by saying that the thought is not a relation to the apple.

As this example shows, to make sense of narrow thoughts, we have to make sense of at least two ideas: (a) that there could be a thought even if there is no real thing thought about; and (b) that the existence of the thinker and the apple does not entail the existence of a relation, *thinking*, between them. The internalist will say that we have already begun to make sense of (a) when we denied (1) above. And (b) is unproblematic so long as we accept that it cannot suffice in general for an arbitrary relation to exist between A and B that A and B exist. Consider the causal relation: no one should think that a causal relation exists between A and B simply when A and B exist. So a thinker can exist, the thing thought about can exist, and yet thinking may not be a relation to that thing. For if thinking about something were a relation to it, then the thought could not exist in the absence of the object: the object is essential to the thought. This means that internalism must distinguish between whether a real thing *is* the object of a thought, and whether the existence of that thing is *essential* to the thought. If one could have had the thought S in the possible absence of its object, then S is not a broad thought. But this does not imply, as I have explained things, that the actual thought has no object.

The dispute between the externalist and internalist views of thought will be discussed further in §§36–7. The aim of this section has simply been to explain what solution to the problem of intentionality we must recommend. As I mentioned above, sometimes something else is called the problem of intentionality: the problem of giving an account of intentionality in physicalist or naturalist terms.[43] This is a problem that assumes the truth of physicalism, whereas my problem is more general: it is a problem whether or not physicalism is true. (For physicalism, see §§12–15.)

My problem of intentionality is the problem of thought about the non-existent. I have to admit that no solution to this difficult problem is entirely satisfactory. I have been considering three. The first denies that such thought is possible; the second holds that it is only possible if there is a realm of 'non-existent objects'. And the third denies that all intentional states are relations to real things. I argued that this solution arises naturally out of the idea that all intentional states have intentional objects, plus the particular way I am understanding the term 'intentional object'. I said that one gives the intentional object of a state of mind by giving an answer to the question 'what is the state of mind directed on?' But what does it mean to 'give' the intentional object? This requires that we return to the idea of intentional content.

8. The structure of intentionality

I have introduced a number of pieces of terminology—presentation, directedness, intentional object, aspectual shape, intentional content, and intentionalism. Here is a summary of how I intend these ideas to be related. In an intentional state, something is presented to the mind. So any intentional state is a presentation. What is presented is called an intentional object; for a state of mind to have an intentional object is for it to be directed on that object. So, insofar as a state of mind is directed, it has an intentional object. The intentional object of a thought is given in the answer to the question 'what is your thought about?/what is your thought directed on?' For a state of mind to have aspectual shape is for it to present its object in a certain way. And so, insofar as the state of mind has aspectual shape, then it has intentional content. The intentional content of a thought is given in an answer to the questions 'what are you thinking?/what is in your mind?' Since, according to intentionalism, all mental states have directedness and aspectual shape, then all mental states have an intentional object and intentional content.

It will help if I compare what I have just said to the famous and often-quoted passage from Brentano's *Psychology from an Empirical Standpoint*:

Every mental phenomenon is characterized by what the scholastics of the Middle Ages referred to as the intentional . . . inexistence of the mental, and what we, although with not quite unambiguous expressions, would call relation to a content, direction upon an object . . . or immanent objectivity.[44]

On the face of it, this passage suggests that 'intentional inexistence', 'relation to a content', 'direction upon an object', and 'immanent objectivity' are all ways of saying the same thing; and I think this is the right interpretation. By 'intentional inexistence' Brentano means the existence of the intentional object *in* the state of mind itself. This does not mean that everything we think about is in our minds in the sense of being a mental entity, but rather that the object individuates the state of mind: different intentional object, different state of mind. (In itself, this does not mean that the intentional object need not exist; but that is another question.[45]) The terminology of 'immanent objectivity' derives from the Cartesian idea of 'objective reality' (see above §4): the state's having an object is immanent (i.e. not transcendent) in the state itself. And Brentano did not distinguish between the relation to a content and the direction upon an object. All of these phrases are just ways of expressing the fact that mental states have intentional objects. The main point of this passage is to insist that all mental phenomena have this feature: this is Brentano's thesis, the characteristic thesis of intentionalism, the thesis to be defended in this book. (There are of course differences between Brentano's metaphysical assumptions and the assumptions I am making. But we can ignore these for the purposes of stating this thesis.)

Brentano's student Twardowski, however, did distinguish between direction on an object and relation to a content, and I shall follow him in this.[46] I expressed my version of this distinction above by saying that an intentional state has an intentional object (or objects), and the way (or ways) that the object is presented is the intentional content of the state. 'Intentional object' is defined in terms of directedness, and 'intentional content' is defined in terms of aspectual shape. I need this distinction because neither directedness nor aspectual shape on their own is enough to characterize what I mean by the subject's perspective on the world. Directedness on an object alone is not enough because there are many ways a mind can be directed on the same intentional object. And aspectual shape alone cannot define intentionality, since an aspect is by definition the aspect under which an intentional object (the object of thought) is presented.

The following question arises. When an intentional state is ascribed to a thinker, does the ascription specify the intentional object, or the intentional content? As we shall see, this is ultimately a confused question. If one tries to put into words what the intentional object of one's state of mind is, one cannot do this without doing it in some particular way. An analogy with Frege's theory of sense and reference might help make this clear. Discussing Frege's theory, Dummett says that 'in saying what the reference [of an expression] is, we have to choose a particular way of saying this'.[47] This means that one cannot use some words to give the intentional object of one's state of mind without also *ipso facto* giving the content of one's state of mind. If, in response to the question of what I am thinking about, I reply 'that charming restaurant in Capri', then the object of my thought is the restaurant in question, and the phrase 'that charming restaurant in Capri' gives the content of my state of mind. One consequence of this is that when describing an intentional state, one does not have to go on to mention the intentional object if one has already given the content of the state: since doing the second is a way of doing the first. When I am thinking about the charming restaurant in Capri, I can give the intentional object of my thought by stating its content: 'that charming restaurant in Capri.'[48]

This does not mean that the idea of an intentional object is redundant; for there are many ways in which one may be thinking about the same thing, and hence many contents associated with the same object. But how do we answer the question of when two thoughts have the same intentional object? As noted, it is not necessary that the object be presented in the same way. 'Bratislava' and 'Pozsony' are two names for the same city. Someone could be thinking of Bratislava as Bratislava, and someone else thinking of it as Pozsony. The fact that they are thinking of the same thing is fairly easy to establish in this case, since we know how to establish the truth of the identity statement 'Bratislava = Pozsony'. But what about when the intentional object does not exist? P. T. Geach famously discussed a story in which a number of villagers attributed various evil deeds to a (non-existent) witch. What determines whether the villagers are thinking of 'the same' witch? Geach calls this the problem of 'intentional identity':

we have intentional identity when a number of people, or one person on different occasions, have attitudes with a common focus, whether or not there actually is something at that focus.[49]

Plausible as this view is, the question now turns into a question about what constitutes a 'common focus'. It seems to me that there is no reason to think that there will always be a fact of the matter about whether two thinkers are focusing on the same intentional object when that object does not exist. For without a real object to give us an independent criterion, all we have to go on is sameness of words used. But this need not be worrying, since there is nothing in our ordinary way of understanding thoughts which requires definite answers in these kinds of case. Indeed, one of the distinguishing marks of the case when the object of thought exists is that we are entitled to think there is an answer to questions of this kind; when an intentional object does not exist, then we should not necessarily expect an answer.

I claim, then, that we need both the idea of an intentional object and the idea of intentional content. My use of the word 'content' here is somewhat more general than the standard use in contemporary philosophy. For I have said that something like *that charming restaurant in Capri* or *St Petersburg* can be the content of my thought. Orthodox usage tends to insist that content must be *propositional*, where a proposition is something that is capable of being true or false. St Petersburg is not true or false, and neither is a restaurant. What is true or false is something that is expressed by a whole sentence and is reported as the content of intentional states such as beliefs. A belief is generally the *belief that p*, where *p* is replaced by a sentence; I shall say that the sentence expresses a proposition. States of mind which have propositional contents are called *propositional attitudes*. An orthodox view is that all intentional states are propositional attitudes (see §§33–4); thus, this view must reconstrue my examples of thinking about an object in propositional terms. To be thinking about St Petersburg must be reconstrued as a thought of something like the form, *St Petersburg is F.*

I agree that the contents of many intentional states are propositional, where this just means that they are assessable as true or false. But I reject the view that *all* content is propositional. I will defend this rejection in §§24 and 34; but for the time being let me just record my opinion that there are many everyday examples of psychological states whose content we do describe in non-propositional terms—loving or hating someone, or contemplating/thinking about an object are paradigm examples. I intend to take this view at face value for the time being.

This being said, let me return to the main theme. Although giving the content of an intentional state is a way of giving its object, giving the content of an intentional state does not wholly *individuate* that state—that is, distinguish it from all others. For I may imagine that little restaurant in Capri, and I may remember it. These states of mind are different, but their contents are the same. To distinguish these states, we need to mention the different ways in which I relate to this content: by memory and by imagination. From what I said at the beginning of this section, the following abstract structure of intentionality suggests itself:

Subject—Directedness/Presentation—Object/Content

There are three terms in this structure. The nature of the subject is not something which is within the scope of this book (strange as that may sound). Object and content I have already explained. Directedness is the converse of presentation: if X is directed on Y, Y is presented to X. What the point about memory and imagination shows is that we need to distinguish between different kinds of presentation or directedness. I will borrow another term from Searle and call these different *intentional modes*. (They should not be confused with Frege's 'modes of presentation', which fall on the 'content' side of the above structure. To avoid confusion, and because this book is not about Frege's semantics, I will not mention Frege's term 'mode of presentation' again in this book.)

Now since, as I argued above, we do not need to mention the intentional object *in addition* if we mention the intentional content, then we can re-describe the general structure of an intentional state as follows:

Subject—Intentional Mode—Content

This is the general structure of intentionality which I shall be assuming in this book. Intentional modes are the relations one stands in to the contents of one's intentional states. Obvious examples are belief, hope, and the other propositional attitudes (I could have used the word 'attitude' rather than 'mode', but this might have the confusing connotation that all intentional states are propositional attitudes: a doctrine I reject). Desire, thought, intention, perception, love, fear, regret, pity—these are all intentional modes. My aim here is just to characterize the general structure of an intentional state. The simple idea is that a person's intentional state is individuated by two things: the intentional mode and the intentional content. And, as I have said, the intentional content fixes the intentional object, what the intentional state is about. So, to fix a subject's intentional state, one needs to fix the mode and the content.

This general structure has the form of a relation: subjects are related to contents by means of intentional modes. It turns out, then, that intentionality does have a relational structure after all: but we should think of it, not in terms of relations to 'objects of thought', but in terms of relations to contents. There is nothing puzzling in the idea that a state might seem to be a relation to one kind of thing, but turn out to be a relation to another kind of thing. For example, one might initially take the dispositional property of solubility in water to be a relation to its manifestations (dissolvings), but then reject this idea on the grounds that something could be soluble even if nothing had ever dissolved. But one could also say that water-solubility is nonetheless a relation to the thing in which something dissolves; viz., water. (I do not believe this view of dispositions, but the example is for illustration only.)

What does it mean to say that intentional states are relations to intentional contents but not to intentional objects? The relevant point is this: the content of the state must always exist, but the object of the state need not exist. My argument for this claim is as follows. The intentional object of a thought is the thing the thought is about. Some intentional objects do not exist. So although there is always an answer to the question, 'what is your thought about?', *sometimes* it makes sense to say that what you are thinking about is, strictly speaking, nothing: one's thought is like a fired arrow with no target. It makes some sense for the subject to say something like 'I was thinking about Pegasus, but Pegasus does not exist, so in a sense my thought was about nothing!' But it makes no sense to say this about the *content* of a thought. Whether or not the object of a thought exists, it cannot be the case that a thought has no *content*, that its content is nothing. There is a sense in which a thought can be about nothing: one's mind can be directed, as it were, to a certain location where there is nothing there (as Geach says, there is nothing 'at the focus of one's attitudes'). But there is *no* sense in which the content of a thought can be nothing. We can put the point in terms of a distinction between what someone is *thinking about* and what someone is *thinking*. And let us say that while the object of a thought is what one is thinking about, the content of a thought is what one is thinking. Then my point is that while there is a sense in which one may be thinking, and yet thinking *about* nothing, there is no sense in which one may be thinking, and yet *thinking* nothing. This is a consequence of the fact that thoughts (and other intentional states) are relations to their contents.

This claim about intentional content captures the truth behind the confused response to the problem of intentionality mentioned above (§7): 'in a sense Pegasus exists, because the idea of Pegasus exists!' The obvious response to this is that the idea of Napoleon is not what your Napoleon-thoughts are about; so why should the idea of Pegasus be what your Pegasus-thoughts are about? But this does not mean that 'ideas' have no role to play; it's just that they cannot be intentional objects. If there are ideas, then it makes sense to say that they can be (*contra* Frege) the contents of one's thoughts, even if they are not the objects. In discussing the intentional attitude of worshipping, where the object of worship Y does not exist, Anscombe says:

It will not be right to say that X worshipped an idea. It is rather than the subject's having an idea is what is needed to give the proposition [that X worshipped Y] a chance of being true.[50]

What ideas in this sense are, and what intentional content is, and how they are related to intentional modes, shall occupy us in the rest of this book.

2

Body

9. Interaction between mind and body

When we reflect on our experience of the world, little is more obvious than the fact that our perspective is the perspective of an embodied being. As Descartes says, 'there is nothing nature teaches me more expressly, or more sensibly than that I have a body, which is ill disposed when I feel pain, which needs to eat and drink when I have feelings of hunger and thirst, etc.'.[1] Descartes's view was that this awareness of our bodies gave our sensations and other experiences a special character, which he memorably described as follows:

Nature also teaches me by these feelings of pain, hunger, thirst, etc., that I am not lodged in my body, like a pilot in his ship, but, besides, that I am joined to it very closely and indeed so compounded and intermingled with my body, that I form, as it were, a single whole with it. For, if this were not so, when my body is hurt, I would not on that account feel pain, I who am only a thinking thing, but I should perceive the wound by understanding alone, just as a pilot sees with his eyes if any damage occurs to his ship; and when my body needs to drink or eat, I would know this simply without being warned of it by the confused feelings of hunger or thirst. For in truth all these feelings of hunger, thirst, pain etc., are nothing other than certain confused ways of thinking, which arise from and depend on the union and, as it were, the mingling of the mind and the body.[2]

These remarks of Descartes describe well the way in which our relationship with our body is immediate and intimate. We are aware of things happening within our bodies, but not in the way we are aware of things distinct from our bodies. We do not observe our bodies as we observe other things. I do not have to look and check now what the position of my limbs is, whether I am hanging upside down, or whether my arms are above my head. Normally, I know this immediately, without having to look. Our position contrasts with that of those patients who have suffered a certain kind of brain damage and as a result have lost all sense of the position, location, and movement of their bodies. They have lost their proprioception (the sense of the body's position) and kinesthesia (the sense of the body's motion). They have to observe their bodies moving in order to gain any awareness of them. The simplest movement is an exhausting trial; they are, in a sense, lodged in their bodies like a pilot in a ship.[3]

It is an insight of Descartes that our normal relationship with our bodies is not like this. But Descartes is perhaps more famous for another view: that minds and bodies are separate entities, which causally interact. This is his *dualism*, a doctrine he never satisfactorily reconciled with the view of our awareness of our bodies quoted above. The quotation itself is permeated with this tension in his views: I am *joined* to my body, my mind and body are *mingled* (suggesting two distinct entities), but nonetheless my mind and body form a *union* and a *single whole*. There is a tension in these two ideas. The phenomenological insight about bodily awareness suggests a unity, while the dualism denies this. How, then, should we conceive of the relationship between mind and body?

A natural first answer to this question is that the relation is a causal one. Mind and body interact causally, in the sense that mental states and events cause physical states and events in the brain, body, and external world. The question, raised repeatedly since Descartes's day, is whether this is compatible with a dualism of mind and body. To understand this problem properly, we need an understanding of what dualism is, and why causal interaction poses a problem for it.

Descartes's dualism is a dualism of *substances*, where 'substance' here is meant in the traditional, technical philosophical sense. There are two ideas contained in the traditional concept of substance. The first is that there is a distinction between a substance and its properties (or attributes) and that a substance is the bearer of properties. The second idea is the idea that a substance is something capable of independent existence.[4] In the next section we shall outline the idea of substance and related metaphysical ideas; then in §11 we shall return to causal interaction.

10. Substance, property, event

Metaphysics has traditionally contrasted a substance—such as a unified object, like a person or an animal—with its properties or attributes or characteristics (I will use the word 'property', and I will not distinguish between properties, attributes, qualities, or characteristics). A substance is what *has* properties, what is the *bearer* of properties. Properties are *possessed* by a substance, they *belong* to a substance or they *inhere* in a substance. In seventeenth-century philosophy a further contrast is made between an attribute and its modes. So, for example, in Descartes's philosophy extension is the characteristic attribute of matter or material substance, and the particular way in which a piece of matter is extended is a mode of extension, and thus a modification of material substance. But this further distinction is not one we need for present purposes.

We can talk about substances, and we can also talk about kinds of substance. When Descartes says that there are two substances, he means that there are two kinds of substance: mental and material. Each person's mind or soul is a distinct substance, but these substances are all of the same kind: they are all mental. For reasons which need not detain us here, Descartes (unlike Aristotle) thought that there was only one (that is, *one*: not just one *kind* of) material substance. But the term 'dualism', as it is usually meant, plainly connotes the number of kinds of substance that there are, not the number of substances.

We can also distinguish between a particular and a substance. A particular is an unrepeatable, singular entity: that is, it is only ever at one place at a given time. A specific flood or a specific hurricane is a particular, just as a particular horse or tiger is. But a flood, for example, is not a substance: it is an event. It is something which happens, not something to which things happen. In standard terminology, the flood itself does not *persist* through change in its properties; rather, we should say, the flood itself simply consists of changes in other things. An example of a particular which is a substance might be an animal, like a tiger, for instance: a tiger persists through changes in its properties. (Some philosophers will say that substances form a sub-class of particular objects: some objects or 'continuants' are not substances because they do not have a sufficient unity. We need not consider this distinction here.)

To say that something persists through changes in its properties is to say that it is *wholly present* throughout each moment of its existence. The flood is not wholly present throughout each moment of its existence—at each moment only a *part* of the flood is present, not the whole flood—whereas the whole tiger is.[5] If a person is a substance, then a person is wholly present throughout each moment of its existence: it is not merely part of me which is present during 1999, and another part which is present during 2000. I exist throughout all these periods of my life. If a person is not a substance, then this is not true, and we should think of people as having temporal parts like floods and hurricanes; but we need not address this question here. All I am doing here is describing the idea of substance; I am not attempting to defend the idea that people are substances in this sense.[6]

The second aspect of the traditional idea of substance is the idea that a substance is capable of independent existence: that is, existence independent of other things. On the Aristotelian view, the existence of something's properties is dependent on substances which instantiate them. The notion of *substance* therefore has a certain kind of priority over *property*. But this, of course, depends on the Aristotelian idea that there cannot be uninstantiated properties—properties with no bearers—so for us it is not a good general way of expressing the idea of substance in terms of independent existence. In the modern period independent existence came to be understood in terms of *independence from all other things*: thus (according to Descartes) my mind is a substance if its existence is independent of all bodies and all other minds. As it happened, since the existence of everything is dependent on God, but God's existence is dependent on nothing else, it turns out that God is the only substance properly so-called. While Descartes was prepared to be somewhat relaxed about this conclusion—in a strict sense, God is the only substance, but in a looser sense matter and minds are substances too—Spinoza pursued the matter to its strict conclusion and held that there is only one (numerically one, and one kind of) substance, which is God, or Nature.[7]

This illustrates one way in which the idea of independent existence is somewhat tricky to spell out precisely. But things get worse when we try and understand what 'independent' actually means. Ignore God, and let us ask: what does it mean for minds and matter to be independent substances? As we have seen, Descartes held that minds and bodies form an intimate unity: what he called the 'substantial union of mind and body'. So as things actually are, mind and body are joined together. But he also thought that they *could* exist independently: my mind *could* exist without this body, and it *could* even exist without any body at all. In other words, the soul could be disembodied. (Remember that one of Descartes's aims was to explain how the immortality of the soul was possible.[8]) So it seems like Descartes's view is this: mind and body are joined as a matter of fact, but it is possible that they could exist separately.

This sounds initially like a good way of understanding the idea of 'capable of independent existence'. But it raises a problem. For some of those who deny dualism and uphold *monism* claim that their monism is a contingent truth: that it is true, but it might not have been. One way of expressing this is as follows: there is a possible world in which there are disembodied minds or souls. But if this is their view, then it seems to be dangerously close to Descartes's dualism in the following sense: minds are embodied in the actual world, but there is a world in which they are not embodied at all. And now it seems hard to express the difference between monism and dualism at all! Yet surely this difference ought to be easy to express: dualism says that there are two kinds of thing, monism says that there is one. (The problem we have unearthed here is not with 'two' or 'one' but with 'thing'.)

We can offer two possible responses on behalf of the monist. The first response is to deny that monism is a contingent truth after all: a consistent monism must deny that disembodied minds are possible. The second response is to hold that, although disembodied minds are possible in some sense, it is not possible that any *actual* mind in the actual world could be disembodied. There might be a mind in a possible world which is exactly like me, but it would not *be* me, since I am essentially embodied. On this response, then, I (or any other actual embodied mind) am a fully material, embodied being, and I cannot be disembodied—even though the idea of *some disembodied being or other* is a coherent metaphysical possibility.

Despite these difficulties with the idea of independent existence, we have arrived at enough of an idea of substance to understand substance dualism. It should be plain that it would be wrong to represent Descartes's own view as the view that bodies are made of one kind of stuff, and minds of another. For the truth is that on this view minds are not made of stuff (or anything else) at all.[9] If minds were made of something, then they would be divisible; but on Descartes's view, a mind is not divisible. Unlike the body, which can be broken down into smaller parts, and therefore can be said to be made of those parts, the mind cannot be broken down into any parts at all. Perceptions and emotions, beliefs and desires, are not parts of the mind, but properties of it. (More precisely, on Descartes's view, they are *modes* of its characteristic *attribute*: thought. More precisely still, on Descartes's view, sensory perception and emotion are only properly attributable to the substantial union of mind and body.)

Sometimes dualism is presented as the view that there is a special kind of 'mind-stuff' out of which our minds are made, like some sort of ghostly 'ectoplasm'. The criticism is then sometimes made that we are not told anything about the nature of this stuff, and that dualism is therefore characterized entirely negatively: we are only told what mental substance (in the sense of 'stuff') is *not*, rather than what it *is*.[10] But since the view that minds are made of mental stuff has been invented by its critics in order to be refuted, and has not been proposed by any philosopher worth taking seriously, it is hardly surprising that we have not been given a characterization of mental stuff in this sense. We can safely put this view to one side.

Now Cartesian dualism of substances is often contrasted with a dualism of properties, or property dualism. According to property dualism, mental properties are distinct from physical properties, even though they are properties of one substance. For example, property dualism may say that the human body or the human person is the substance, but that it has two kinds of property, mental and physical. (More on physical properties in §12.) Or it may say that all substances—all persisting subjects of predication—are physical, in the sense that they all have physical properties, but that some of these physical substances have mental properties. For example, a property dualist may say that the mind is the brain, but what makes the brain the mind is the fact that it has mental properties.[11]

This would perhaps be a good place to clarify further the rest of the ontological terminology I will employ in this book. It is common for philosophers of mind to talk in terms of a general category of mental *events* as if these were the only mental phenomena. I suppose it would be possible to stipulate that 'event' simply picks out the most general kind of entity, but this stipulation is misleading. For whichever way we decide to talk, there is an important distinction which we need to make between those particular happenings which take time, are unrepeatable, dated, and have temporal parts—and other kinds of entities. This first kind of entity—particular parties, wars, conversations, meetings, and so on—is what I call an *event*. The other kind of entity includes those which are constituted by some particular having a property at a time, or over a period of time: I call these entities *states*, though they could also be called *states of affairs* or *facts*.[12] So, for example, me swimming the English Channel yesterday is an event—it took a certain amount of time, it is unrepeatable, dated, and has temporal parts. But me being six feet tall now is a state of me, or a fact about me: it consists in my having a property at a certain time. It is not something that happens.

Not all mental phenomena are events. Mental events are mental happenings, like noticing something, watching something, feeling a pain, or thinking aloud. I shall sometimes use an older terminology and call mental events 'mental acts'—this is a variant on 'event', so 'act' should not have the connotation of something which is freely or intentionally done (and nor should it have the opposite connotation). The important thing about these acts or events is that they are particulars, which can have properties and stand in relations, and they take time: for example, Geach describes acts of judgement as 'plainly episodic', by which he means that they 'have a position in a time-series'.[13] But mental *states* like beliefs are not events at all. Beliefs are not episodes, they do not take time, they do not have temporal parts ('the first part of my believing this was more interesting than the second' makes no sense). To have a belief is to have a property. Events, on the other hand, can *have* properties, but they do not consist in the instantiation of properties alone. They are, like objects, basic particulars: their nature cannot be further analysed.

If objects and events are both basic particulars, then the question arises as to what distinguishes them from one another. This is an important question, but here I only have space to answer it dogmatically by repeating the claim made above: while events have temporal parts, objects do not. While there is such a thing as the first day of this week—a temporal part of this week—there is no such thing as me on the first day of this week.[14] Many objects (like people, for instance) are substances, and are therefore wholly present throughout each moment of their existence. It is not as if part of me is present in the early part of my life, and another part is present in the later part of my life. I am *all there* at each moment. Many will dispute this; but nothing significant turns on it in this book, so I will not debate this issue here.

I am also dogmatic in assuming the existence of properties, conceived of as universals. But once again, little turns on this (except a point about physicalism: see §14), so nominalists, those who deny universals, can reconstrue my talk as they like. On other ontological issues I remain neutral: on whether processes are something other than the events which make them up; or on whether there are 'tropes' or particularized properties, in addition to properties conceived of as universals.

Having clarified these ontological questions, we can return to the question of the causal interaction between mind and body. What is the problem with causal interaction for dualism, for any kind of dualism? Many problems have been suggested; some are proposed as problems for substance dualism alone, while others are problems for all kinds of dualism. Let us start with substance dualism, and examine the problems as they are supposed to arise there. It will turn out that, in the only sense in which there is a real problem for substance dualism, there is also a problem for property dualism too. Therefore the question of whether the mind is a substance is not the most important question here. The important question is whether any kind of dualism can explain causal interaction.

11. The 'intelligibility' of mental causation

At its most general, the charge against Cartesian dualism is that it makes mental causation unintelligible. This was a charge brought by Princess Elizabeth of Bohemia, in her correspondence with Descartes.[15] In claiming that mental causation is problematic, or unintelligible, we could be locating the problem in one or more of three places: first, we could be saying that there is something about *the physical world* which makes mental causation problematic; or second, that there is something about *mental phenomena* (on a dualist conception of them) which makes such causation problematic; or third, that the kind of *causal link itself* required for such an interaction is unintelligible or unclear. Let us take these points in reverse order.

The last point may be dismissed fairly briefly. When we talk about causation in this context, we are using a very abstract and general idea: the idea of something making something else happen. To say that there is mental causation, or psychophysical causation, is just to say that mental things—thoughts, experiences, sensations—make things happen in the physical world. What is 'making something happen'? At this level of generality, that question is answered by a theory of causation. Of course, a theory of causation does not explain particular ways in which various kinds of thing make other things happen: a theory of causation does not explain electromagnetism, or transfer of heat, or the collapse of the stock market. But if all of these phenomena are causal, then a theory of causation tells us what makes them so. It might say, for instance, that A is a cause of B just in case the following is true: if A had not existed, then B would not have had existed (counterfactual theories). Or it might say that A is a cause of B just in case the chance of B occurring is higher if A had occurred than it would have been otherwise (probabilistic theories). We have no difficulty understanding that such claims can be true where A is mental and B is physical—or at least, if we find them hard to understand, that is because of something to do with A and B themselves, or with some philosophical theory of A and B, *not* because of anything to do with causation.

(An exception to this claim is the kind of theory which identifies the 'real essence' of causation with the transfer or flow of physical energy.[16] If mental entities are not physical, and this is what causation is, then it follows straight-forwardly that mental causation is impossible, not just problematic. The only ways for such a view to defend mental causation is to hold that mental entities are really physical—see below for this kind of view—or that there is mental energy. The latter view, it seems to me, has little to recommend it.)

So the problem of mental causation does not derive from something to do with causation. This leaves us with two possibilities: either mental causation is problematic for dualism because of something to do with the mental, or because of something to do with the physical. Both points are made in this remark of Jerry Fodor's:

> The chief drawback of dualism is its failure to account adequately for mental causation. If the mind is non-physical, it has no position in physical space. How then, can a mental cause give rise to a behavioural effect that has a position in space? To put it another way, how can the nonphysical give rise to the physical without violating the laws of conservation of mass, of energy and of momentum?[17]

Fodor's first point is that non-physical things have no position in space, and therefore they cannot interact with something which has a position in space: the problem of mental causation arises for dualism because of something to do with the mind. The second is that the interaction between non-physical mind and physical body breaks some law of physics: it is because of something to do with the physical, with physical law, that the problem arises.

Why say that non-physical things have no position in space? In Descartes's metaphysics, of course, mental substances have no *extension* in space, but strictly speaking lack of extension does not imply lack of position—a point has position, but no extension.[18] However, it is not Descartes's view, and nor is it very plausible for the dualist, to hold that the mind has location at an extensionless point. So let's agree with Fodor for the moment that the substance dualist must hold that mind has no location in space at all. Why does this mean that mind and body cannot causally interact?

It might seem obvious. Causation requires that causes precede (or at least are simultaneous with) their effects. For A to precede B, or for A to be simultaneous with B, A and B have to be located in time. But how can something have a location in time unless it has a location in space? The world we experience is a spatio-temporal world: to have a location in that world, an object or event must occupy a point of space and time (or: space-time). We can't make much sense of the idea of something having an existence in space but no existence in time; or even if we could, we couldn't make sense of such a thing being a cause. How, then, can we make sense of something which is in time but not in space as being a cause? One difficulty is that we would have no understanding of why these unlocated entities cause things *where* they do. Why should my unlocated mind move this body rather than that one? In the case of located entities, the answer to this question is so straightforward that it needs little consideration: this ball breaks this window because it's this one it *hits*, and so on. Even when we allow the possibility of action at a distance, we think in general of this action as mediated by a force (e.g. gravity) or by a field: we picture lines of force acting between the objects, say. The supposed unlocated minds give us no way of answering the question, because it gives us no way of starting to understand why *this* rather than *that*. Note here that I am not saying that the very idea of something *mental* causing something is problematic. I'm saying that it is problematic only because one combines some uncontroversial claim about causation with a controversial *thesis* about the mind: that it has no location.

But although it might be a part of some dualist views that the mind has no location in space, is it required by the very idea of substance dualism? No. A substance here is defined as the bearer of properties which is capable of independent existence. A mental, non-physical, substance is one which is a bearer of mental properties, capable of independent existence—no clash here with the idea of existence in space. So we should grant that there can be a non-physical substance which has a location in space. What makes it not physical is that it has non-physical (in this case, mental) properties and no physical properties. Imagine, in this vein, that you are a blend, a mixture of your body, which is a physical thing, and a non-physical thing which occupies the same space as your body. You and your body coincide in space, so there are two things in the same space at the same time. But that is allowed by the fact that one of them is a non-physical object. Two physical objects of the same kind cannot occupy the same place at the same time; but perhaps non-physical substances are not subject to the same sorts of constraints.[19]

I introduced this example of a dualist view, not because I find it plausible, but rather to bring out the separability of the ideas of dualism and non-spatiality. For if these ideas are genuinely separable, then Fodor's first objection is not to dualism as such, but only to a dualism which holds that the mind is non-spatial. It would be an interesting historical task to determine which kinds of dualism advocated by the philosophers of the past fall into which category, but there is no room for this task here. My point is that if we can make sense of the idea of a substance dualist view which does allow for the existence of the mind in space, then Fodor's first point is not relevant to a general attack on substance dualism.

However, it turns out that we would not need this first point against dualism if Fodor's second point is sound: that causation by non-physical substances would violate the laws of physics. For if this second point is true, then *whatever* non-physical substances turn out to be, they cannot have effects in the physical world unless the laws of physics are false. And in fact, it turns out that this criticism is even more powerful than this: for, as we shall see, it is an objection not just to substance dualism, but to any form of dualism whatsoever. So if the second point is sound, we do not need the first. It is important to emphasize this, since it is sometimes assumed that the arguments against dualist causation are essentially of the first kind. If I am right, this is a mistake.

But what exactly is Fodor's second point? The objection is not that the dualist's conception of interaction between the mental and the physical is unintelligible, that no sense whatsoever can be made of it. The claim is rather that the apparent fact of mental causation is inconsistent with other things we know. So let us start with the idea that the mind affects the body, and ask: with what known fact about the physical world is this incompatible? This requires a brief digression into physics, the physical, and the influential doctrine known as *physicalism*.

12. Physics and physicalism

Dualism, as its name suggests, classifies things in the world by number: it says there are two things, or two kinds of thing. Therefore it is naturally contrasted with monism, which says there is one thing, or one kind of thing. Monisms have been traditionally divided into two kinds: idealism, which says that all is mental, and materialism, which says that all is material.

But contemporary philosophers talk about a contrast and opposition between dualism and *physicalism*. Is there a difference? Sometimes the word 'physicalism' is used as a synonym for 'materialism', and 'physical' used as a synonym for 'material'. This is perfectly natural insofar as physics is the science of matter, but it is nonetheless possible to make some useful distinctions between monism, materialism, and physicalism. Making these distinctions will help us to understand the objection to a dualist account of mental causation.

Monism is a commitment to what we might call one-ness: the world is one, of one nature. A truly monistic view is Spinoza's monism, which holds that there is only one substance, which can be called *God* or *Nature*. As we saw above, Spinoza adopted the traditional conception of substance as that which can exist in and of itself, and is not dependent on anything else. So it is not hard to see how he came to the conclusion that there can be only one substance, since God is the only thing which is genuinely independent of everything else. Contemporary versions of monism tend to say not that the world itself is one substance, but that everything in the world is made of the same *sort of thing*: materialism says that the world is made of matter, idealism says that it made of ideas, and Russell's 'neutral monism' of the 1920s says that the world is of one nature, while remaining neutral on whether it is mental or material.

Here I am interested in making a distinction between materialist monism and physicalism. A materialist monist holds that everything is material, that is, made of matter. But it is obvious that physics (the science of matter, among other things) says that there are many things in the world which are not made of matter: there are forces, waves, fields, and so on. A physicalist, traditionally, is someone who gives a certain kind of authoritative role to physics. This role is partly epistemological—physics has an authority in telling us what to believe—and partly ontological—physics has an authority in telling us what there is. This conception of the special role of physics has complex origins.[20] But at its heart is the idea that physics is the science which aims at what W. V. Quine calls 'full coverage'. Physics aims, by using exact quantitative methods, and its categories of mass, energy, force, and so on, to give an account of the properties and behaviour of everything which has a spatial and temporal position. The laws of physics are laws which are intended to be true of all objects in space and time. There are no objects which are exempt from these laws. Let's call this claim, 'the generality of physics':

The generality of physics: All objects and events in space-time have physical properties, and the laws of physics govern or describe the behaviour of all objects and events in space-time.

The generality of physics is a monist principle. But it is not yet physicalism. For physicalism is the view that the physical story told by these laws is, in a sense, the whole story.

And full coverage is one thing, the whole story is another. Physicalism is the view that physics is the whole story, but this does not follow from the fact that physics has full coverage. (Thus it could be misleading to call a theory which unifies the fundamental physical forces a 'theory of everything' just because everything is *subject* to these forces.) In what sense, though, is physics supposed to tell the whole story, if 'whole story' does not just mean 'full coverage'? Physicalism says that physics tells the whole story about the causation of *physical events*: that is, events which have physical properties or features. According to physicalism, everything physical which happens, everything which is an effect, must be a result of purely physical causes in accordance with physical law. This doctrine is a doctrine about causation. Following David Papineau, I shall call it 'the completeness of physics':

The completeness of physics: Every physical event has a physical cause which is enough to bring it about, given the laws of physics.

The label 'completeness' should not lead us to think that physics is a complete science in the sense that it has been completed—that physics is 'finished'. (In any case, it is not clear what it would be for a science to be 'finished'; the idea reminds me of a cartoon I once saw, with a picture of a road leading to a city, and a sign on the road saying something like: 'No more building; this city is finished.') Rather, the idea behind the phrase is that physical causes are complete in the sense of being *enough* to bring about all physical effects.

The completeness of physics should also be distinguished from the claim that physics can explain everything. Consider the view that David Lewis calls 'the explanatory adequacy of physics':

there is some unified body of scientific theories of the sort we now accept, which together provide a true and exhaustive account of all physical phenomena. They are unified in that they are cumulative: the theory governing any physical phenomenon is explained by theories governing phenomena out of which that phenomenon is composed and by the way it is composed out of them. The same is true of the latter phenomena, and so on down to fundamental particles or fields governed by a few simple laws, more or less as conceived in present-day theoretical physics.[21]

This is a stronger claim than the completeness of physics, because one could hold the completeness of physics and deny the explanatory adequacy of physics, but not vice versa. We may reject the idea of the explanatory adequacy of physics because we may believe (as seems plausible) that the different sciences have their own different explanatory domains, which they treat in their own way, in terms of their own concepts and principles. Explanations in biology, for instance, appeal to biological concepts and categories, and no one believes that they can really be expressed in the language of fundamental physics. Or that they need to be. Yet this explanatory autonomy for biology is compatible with both the generality of physics—biological interactions are among things with physical properties, and no biological interaction is in conflict with the laws of physics—and the completeness of physics, since the completeness of physics says that whatever physical events occur have a physical causal history which fixes their occurrence.

The completeness of physics may be illustrated with a theological image.[22] Imagine God creating the universe. God has to decide how to set things up, to arrange the matter at the beginning of the universe and to choose the laws according to which the matter will behave and so on—in such a way that he gets the universe he wants. The completeness of physics says that in order to get every *physical* effect in the universe, God does not have to do anything else except set up the physical laws and initial conditions. All God has to do to make anything physical happen is to set the physical part of the world in motion.

The image seems to imply determinism: the doctrine that the present is completely fixed by the nature of the past and its exceptionless laws, in such a way that if the universe were to be started all over again, with the same initial conditions and the same set of (deterministic) laws, it would have the same particular history. But in fact, the completeness of physics does not imply determinism, and it is consistent with an indeterministic view of the physical universe, according to which physical events happen only with a certain probability. According to indeterminism, it does not follow that if the universe were started all over again with the same laws of nature, it would have the same particular history. There is only a certain *chance* that it has the same particular history, where chance is understood as objective physical probability. Whether the universe is deterministic, or (as contemporary physics seems to suggest) indeterministic is a question which is independent of the truth or falsehood of the completeness of physics. Strictly speaking, then, when discussing the completeness of physics, we should express it in the way Papineau does, when he says:

The completeness of physics 2: Every physical event is determined, or has its chance determined, by purely physical causes in accordance with physical law.[23]

But no harm will be done if we simplify and talk as if determinism were true in this chapter.

Physicalism has been defined in many ways. What it (or the completeness of physics) really amounts to depends almost entirely on what 'physical' means. I have been taking the meaning of 'physical' to be given by the content of physical science, where physical science is the science which aims at full coverage. The nature of this science is not something which can be established by purely *a priori* reflection; it is an empirical question what the content and scope of physics actually is. This marks one difference between physicalism and older forms of materialism, which fixed the content of its doctrine in a relatively *a priori* way: for instance, by saying that everything is material, and matter is solid, impenetrable, conserved, interacting deterministically and only on contact. Since modern physics has shown this conception of matter to be wrong in perhaps every respect, it is reasonable for a materialist to become a physicalist, and take the approach: 'rather than say *a priori* what the world of matter must be like, I will rather let physics, the science of matter, tell us what matter, and the rest of the world, is like.' The point of calling yourself a physicalist rather than a materialist is chiefly to express this attitude to physical science.

This does mean that there is an open-ended character to the doctrine of physicalism itself.[24] Should we say that the content of physicalism is fixed by present-day physics, or by some ideal future physics? Either gives problems: for present physics is incomplete and may be false in certain respects; yet who knows what is going to be the content of the ideal future physics? It looks as if physicalism is either obviously false (if physics is today's physics) or empty (since who knows what will be in the physics of the future).

This is a nice problem, but physicalism can solve it. Physicalism asks us to address the ontological question in this way: see what physics says there is, and then commit yourself to *that kind of thing* being all there is. As time develops, it may be that your commitments develop too. But this is just a reflection of the fact that you have no standard (other than physics) from which to answer the question of what there is.

This open-ended character does, however, limit what physicalists should permit themselves to say. They should not allow themselves to say, for example, that a physicalist *must* hold that there are no ghosts.[25] Certainly current physics holds that there are no ghosts, but if it were discovered that irreducible ghosts were needed to explain certain physical phenomena, then ghosts would be physical by this definition. Or consider parapsychology. If it turned out that there is good evidence that parapsychological phenomena—telekinesis, telepathy, and so on—were needed in order to explain certain physical effects, then these phenomena would have to become part of the realm of the physical. These possibilities are, of course, unlikely—not least because there is no uncontroversial, undisputed, solid evidence for parapsychological phenomena—but that does not affect the point of principle, which is that if we give 'physical' the meaning it has in 'physical science' then we cannot say *a priori* what the physical is, since we cannot say *a priori* what physical science is. But, I claim, physicalists can reasonably ignore the remote possibilities just discussed.

Someone could understand the physical in other terms. But none of these alternative understandings is satisfactory, since none can make any sense of the current disputes; in particular, the dispute we are considering about mental causation. For example, someone might say that the physical is what exists in space and time—but how would they then rule out the dualism considered above (§3) as being physicalism? Or they might say that the physical is the causal—but given the evident fact of mental causation, this makes mental phenomena physical by definition. Such definitions of 'physical' make physicalism virtually trivial; and while some may be happy with this, it certainly would not satisfy physicalists, who think of their doctrine as substantial and informative.

So what can physicalism say? If it is not an empty doctrine, devoid of all genuine content, what *meta*physical claim can physicalism allow itself to make? This is where the completeness of physics comes in. Physics, as it stands, and as it is likely to remain, attempts explanations of why things happen—things like the collision of particles, the motion of projectiles, and so on. Physicists claim that they can explain such events (often they say 'explain in principle') in terms of their dynamical equations and in terms of a small number of basic concepts—force, charge, momentum, acceleration, and so on. A metaphysical generalization of this is the completeness of physics.

What would it be, then, to deny the completeness of physics? It would be to hold that some physical effects—some effects of the same general kind as the kind of which physics treats—would not come about were it not for the presence of other causes, other causes which are non-physical in the sense of not being the subject-matter of physical science. This is something no physicalist—no one who shares the view that physics has a unique ontological and epistemological authority—can believe. I therefore claim that the completeness of physics must be an essential component of any physicalist view, a necessary condition for any non-trivial form of physicalism.

What has this got to with Fodor's second point? Fodor says that mental causation would violate the laws of the conservation of energy and mass. But it would be preferable to see Fodor's point as an expression of the completeness of physics: the reason that energy would not be conserved in a mental-physical interaction is that every physical effect must come about through purely physical causes. Mental causation would therefore have to introduce 'more energy' into the physical world, thus violating the conservation laws. The world of physical effects must be causally closed, according to physicalism.

13. The problem of mental causation for dualists

The completeness of physics is a necessary condition for physicalism, but it is not a sufficient condition. For one could hold the completeness of physics and still believe that there are mental things and properties, but that they have no effects. This is epiphenomenalism: the doctrine that mental states and properties have no physical effects.[26] But the dualist views we are considering deny epiphenomenalism: they are *interactionist* views. Given this, we can now state the problem of mental causation for dualism, which is one part of what is now known as the mind–body problem.

The problem comes from the conflict between the existence of mental causation and the completeness of physics. Assume:

(1) Mental phenomena have effects in the physical world;

add the completeness of physics:

(2) All physical effects have physical causes which are enough to bring those effects about;

and it is easy to see, in general outline, how the conflict arises. How can the mental cause bring a physical effect about if the physical cause is itself enough to bring it about?

It might seem as if one could answer by saying: the mental cause is just an *extra* cause. It is something added on to the physical cause. To see what might be wrong with this, we need to make explicit another assumption, which is the following:

(3) Mental and physical causes do not overdetermine their physical effects.

Causal overdetermination is when an effect has more than one cause, and each event would have caused the effect if the other one had not done so. Consider the assassination of a tyrant by two assassins. Each assassin shoots the tyrant, and so is a cause of the tyrant's death. But the assassination is set up in such a way that the shootings are independent: either would have killed the tyrant if the other had failed. The death of the tyrant is overdetermined by the shootings.

(Overdetermination in this sense must be distinguished from an event's having more than one cause. Consider the Second World War: one of its causes was Hitler's invasion of Poland, another was the invasion of Czechoslovakia. Moving further back, another cause might be thought to be the resentment felt by Germany after the Treaty of Versailles. All of these are plausibly among the many causes of the war, but of none of them is it true that any of them would have brought about the war if the others had not been there.)

Does the possibility of overdetermination make sense? Some would say that it does not. Those who believe in the counterfactual analysis of causation are committed to the following claim:

(C) If A caused B, then if A had not been the case, B would not have been the case.[27]

Applied to our example, we find that the counterfactual analysis entails that neither assassin's shot can be a cause of the tyrant's death! Because: of neither shooting is it true that if it hadn't been done, the death would not have occurred. We could either conclude that, despite appearances, overdetermination like that in the case of the tyrant's death cannot really happen; or we could conclude that the counterfactual analysis (C) is false.

This is an important issue in metaphysics; but fortunately, we do not need to settle it for present purposes. For even if overdetermination is possible in these very unusual circumstances, and (C) is strictly speaking false, it is nonetheless very implausible to suppose that this is the way mental and physical causes relate to each other. For if they did, then every time a mental state had some effect in the physical world, the completeness of physics guarantees that there would be a cause in one's brain which is itself enough to bring about that very same effect. It then looks like a coincidence that my body manages to co-ordinate so well, given these distinct causes of its motions.[28] Yet the idea that one's control of one's body is in this way coincidental is in conflict with everything we know about the causation of behaviour—either from our own experience, or from common sense. That is the justification for (3) above.

The problem of mental causation for dualism, then, is how to reconcile the existence of mental causation with the completeness of physics and the denial of the general overdetermination by mental and physical causes. This way of expressing the problem brings to light something very important which is sometimes overlooked: the problem does not arise because of something about the *mental*. It's because of a fact about the *physical* world: the completeness of physics. It's the assumed nature of the physical world which generates this aspect of the mind–body problem.

But didn't we assume substance dualism in setting up this problem? Yes, we did, since this is the way the problem has traditionally been formulated. But it turns out that this assumption was not essential. For all we are really assuming about the mental is that mental phenomena have physical effects, and that these mental causes are distinct from the physical causes of the same effects. Suppose that we rejected substance dualism, and accepted only a dualism of properties. Then, so long as we are thinking of the properties of things as causes (more on this below), the problem will still arise as above. The source of the problem is the conflict between the completeness of physics and causation by mental causes which are distinct from physical causes.

Since this problem is the focus of our discussion for most of the rest of this chapter, we can put the question of substance dualism to one side. As far as mental causation goes, substance dualism is a red herring. So rejecting substance dualism for the (admittedly weaker) property dualism will not help in solving this problem. For it still treats mental and physical causes as distinct. What obviously *would* help is to deny this: that is, to deny that there are two causes here. This would be to accept the *identity theory* of mental and physical causes:

(4) Mental causes are identical with physical causes.

This solves the problem. Since there are not two causes, but one, there is no risk of overdetermination. Mental causes are exactly the same entities as certain physical causes—in the brain, no doubt. This is the *identity theory* of mind and brain (or mind and body), and for a while it was the dominant physicalist theory of mind. I believe that the identity theory certainly solves the problem we have been discussing. But is it an independently plausible theory?

14. The identity theory

The argument just presented for the claim that mental entities are identical with physical entities needs two clarifications. First, the argument as it stands only gives us a reason for identifying with brain states those mental entities which are causes of physical events. If there are mental entities which have no physical effects (mental epiphenomena) then there is, as things stand, no reason to identify them with physical entities. Although there are those who hold that there are mental epiphenomena, many physicalists will say that all mental phenomena do have physical effects in one way or another, so we know enough to rule out epiphenomenalism. One approach which would guarantee this is the *functionalist* approach to mental phenomena, which says that mental phenomena are individuated—distinguished from one another—by their causal roles. The idea here is that the concept of a mental state is a causal concept: the concept of perception, for instance, is the concept of a state of mind which has certain typical causes (perceptible objects and events in the environment, say) and certain typical effects (the perception that it is snowing, say, typically causes the belief that it is snowing). Functionalism therefore holds that it is in the nature of certain mental states to have certain effects; therefore there can be no mental epiphenomena. Combining this with the completeness of physics and the denial of overdetermination yields the identity theory—and this is, in fact, how some functionalists have argued.[29]

The second clarification is that there are two ways in which causes can be conceived, and each way corresponds to a different kind of identity theory. Consider a simple causal interaction such as a brick breaking a window by being thrown at the window. Davidson has argued that causes and effects are events, where events are a kind of particular (see §10). According to Davidson, the event which is the cause of the window's breaking is the brick's hitting the window. This is a particular event which can be described in many ways: it could be described as 'the throwing of the brick' or as 'the throwing of a brick made in Walthamstow' or as 'the throwing of a red brick'. Each of these descriptions can be a description of the same event, and therefore of the same cause.

But there is another view of the ontology of causation, which holds that causes and effects have to be individuated in a more discriminating way. Take the case of the brick breaking the window. If we are to ask what made the difference to the window's breaking, then we could say 'the brick hitting it'; but we could be more specific: we could say that it was the brick's having a certain mass hitting the window at a certain angle, with a certain velocity, and so on. In this latter case, we are citing the properties of the brick, its features or attributes, as the properties which made the difference; that is, as the *causally efficacious properties* of the brick. We can of course still say that it was the event of the brick being thrown which caused the event of the breaking of the window, so long as we understand by this that there were certain properties which are efficacious in this transaction. I will call this view the view that *properties are causes*. (Some may prefer to say that it is *facts* which are causes, where a fact is something having a property; or that it is *instances* of properties which are causes; or that causes/events have their effects *in virtue of* their properties; but I do not distinguish here between all these formulations of the view.) The difference between this view and Davidson's is that this view counts different causally effiacious properties as different causes. So the same event or object can have a number of properties, not all of which are efficacious in bringing about the same effect.

I do not want to adjudicate here on which of these views is correct. My point is that corresponding to these distinct views is a distinct kind of identity theory. If causes and effects are events, then the identity theory which is motivated by the argument of the previous section is an identity theory of mental and physical events (i.e. particulars). This is in fact Davidson's view.[30] But if causes and effects are properties, then the identity theory we arrive at is the identity theory of mental and physical properties. This is the view of David Lewis and D. M. Armstrong. The latter view corresponds to property monism (there are only physical properties, and some of them are mental), while the former view is compatible with a property dualism (events have two kinds of properties, mental or physical). The contrast being drawn here is sometimes described as the contrast between 'type' (property) and 'token' (event) identity theories.

So, in the context of the present argument, whether one takes the argument to entail a property or an event identity theory depends on whether one thinks causes are events or properties. My own view is that causes are properties: when we look for causes, we are looking for the aspect of a situation which made a difference, and *aspects* are *properties* or *qualities*. I therefore agree with Hume when he says that, 'where several different objects produce the same effect, it must be by means of some quality, which we discover to be common among them'.[31] So I must reject the theory that events alone are causes—an event can be a cause, of course, but this is because it has some quality or property—and I will concentrate in the rest of this chapter on the property identity theory. (But I will talk for convenience simply of 'the identity theory'.) Given what was said in §10, we can move easily between talk of properties and talk of states.

The identity theory, then, says that mental properties are identical with certain physical properties. It is very important to realize that the identity theory does not deny the existence of mental properties. Its identity claims must be taken literally: a mental state M is the very same thing as a physical state P. This no more denies that M exists than the identity claim 'Cicero = Tully' denies that Cicero exists. (Or Tully, for that matter.) On the contrary: if any identity claim 'A = B' is to be true, then A and B must both exist.

Sometimes identity theories are described as the view that mental properties are 'really' physical or 'nothing over and above' physical properties. But this might mislead if it were understood as saying that something is being left out by making the identity claim. (As if someone had said: you think the mental property is a thing in its own right; but it's not! It's really dependent on something else!) Likewise, the identity theory should not say that non-physical things are really physical; for on this view, there are no non-physical things. Again, the matter is illuminated by looking at the comparison with other identity claims: is Cicero 'really' Tully, or is Tully 'really' Cicero? Is Cicero 'nothing over and above' Tully? One can perhaps construct possible stories in which these questions make sense—but in general it's better to avoid the questions altogether.

Of course, the identity theory does deny the existence of something: mental properties as conceived by the property dualist, or mental substances as conceived by the substance dualist. But the point of the theory is to say that denying this is not denying the existence of the mental. In this way, the identity theory must be distinguished from another kind of physicalist theory, eliminative physicalism. Eliminative physicalism is the view that there are no mental things at all: no properties, substances, events, or anything. The essence of the view is that the mental patterns of classification in the world are fundamentally misguided: we should not classify things in this way.[32] So while both the identity theory and the eliminative physicalist agree that everything is physical, they disagree about which physical things there are. That is, the eliminativist denies that any of the physical things there are are mental. (I shall not be much concerned with eliminative physicalism in this book.)

The distinction between the identity theory and the eliminative physicalist is sometimes expressed in terms of the idea of reduction. Identity theorists are *reductionists*; and reduction is distinct from elimination. The reduction of the gene to strands of DNA does not deny the existence of genes; but the elimination of caloric or phlogiston does deny their existence. The idea of reduction needs closer examination.

15. **Reductionism**

The identity theory says, not that non-physical things are really physical, but that insofar as it *appears* that there are non-physical things, these things are physical. A reduction is therefore the process or procedure of demonstrating that, and in what way, these things are physical. The terminology of reduction, though useful, can give rise to confusion. A reduction of X to Y suggests the idea of one thing being reduced to another. But of course, one *thing* cannot literally be *reduced* to another thing: either the one thing *is* the 'other' thing, or it is not. (Reduction should not therefore be thought of by analogy with reducing a sauce in cookery: for in this case, the cook starts off with a larger amount of material and ends up with a smaller amount.) Reductionism, like any theory, should give an account of what there actually is. It should not start off by affirming the existence of something which it then goes on to say is 'really' something else. For, to state the obvious: nothing is really something else.

What sense, then, can be made of the idea of reduction of entities? The best answer is given in terms of the idea of identity: a reduction (in Huw Price's phrase) 'identifies the entities of one domain with a subclass of entities of another'. Or, to put it another way: we start off with the 'target' entity, X, and find a reason for identifying X with Y. Our reduction tells us something we didn't know about X: that it is Y. Claims of reduction in this sense are identity claims, just as the identity theory of mind just described is an identity claim. This is why the identity theory is reductionist. The favoured non-mental parallel from the philosophy of science was the reduction of the temperature of a gas to the mean molecular kinetic energy of its constituent molecules: temperature is reduced to mean kinetic energy by being identified with it.

Understood ontologically, then, a reduction of A to B involves the claim that A = B. But identity cannot exhaust the idea of reduction. For identity is a symmetrical relation, but a reduction of A to B is not a reduction of B to A. And there are plenty of identity claims which are not reductions: it would be (at best) pointless to say that the discovery that Hesperus is Phosphorus is a reduction of Hesperus to Phosphorus. What reduction needs, in addition, is the idea that the 'reduced phenomenon' is made more comprehensible or intelligible by being shown to be identical with the 'reducing phenomenon'. We understand thermodynamical phenomena better when we are shown that they are (so the story goes) identical with certain kinds of mechanical activity. And we understand mental properties better when we are shown that they are (so the story goes) identical with physical properties of the brain.

These virtues of reduction—making sense of the phenomena, rendering them intelligible—are not ontological in the strict sense. That is, they are not virtues of how things are, in and of themselves, but of how things strike us, how they can be incorporated into our picture of the world. This recommends that we distinguish the identity claim just mentioned—the *ontological reduction*—from another idea, which I shall call *explanatory reduction*, which is that to which these virtues actually belong. Explanatory reduction is a relation between theories: for instance, when one theory explains why another theory is true, or gives us an insight into the underlying mechanisms which explain how the entities of the reduced theory work.[33]

Reduction can be explanatory and ontological, but it is not hard to see how one could have one without the other. An ontological reduction without an explanatory reduction would hold an identity theory of the entities in question without holding that the theories of these entities can stand in an explanatory relation. An example of such an approach is Davidson's anomalous monism, according to which all mental events are physical events but there is no explanatory link between the mental theory and the physical theory.[34] What about explanatory reduction without ontological reduction? What this means will only become clear when we examine so-called 'non-reductive' versions of physicalism below; but the basic idea is that there can be an explanatory relation of the appropriate kind between the theories of X and Y without having to identify Xs with Ys. To understand this better, we need to understand the idea of an 'explanatory relation'. I have nothing much to say on this matter, but we will return to the issue of explanation in (§27).

There is a general feeling in current philosophy of mind that reductionism is a Bad Thing, and it is more reasonable to be an anti-reductionist, even once the distinction between reduction and elimination if made. Insofar as reduction is understood as explanatory reduction—where this is conceived of as a kind of explanation—then this must be a mistake. Genuine explanations are advances in our knowledge, and faced with a possibility of advancing our knowledge it would be irrational to reject it merely on the grounds that it is 'reductive'. (Or rather, it makes little sense to do so, since 'reduction' is just a name for this sort of advancement of our knowledge.)

16. Against the identity theory: anti-reductionism

The identity theory, the ontological reduction of mind to body, certainly solves the problem of causal interaction. But the theory is widely rejected, because of a famous and simple argument of Hilary Putnam's. Putnam pointed out that the identity theory must say that any two creatures in the same mental state (i.e. who have the same mental property) must also be in the same physical state (i.e. they must have the same physical property). So if an octopus and I are in pain, we must share the same physical property. But given the diversity of organisms, all with their very different material constitutions, this is extremely hard to believe. It is surely very unlikely that all creatures capable of thought or experience or sensation *must* have their physical states in common. 'Thus', Putnam concluded, 'if we can find even one psychological predicate which can clearly be applied to both a mammal and an octopus (say "hungry"), but whose physical-chemical "correlate" is different in the two cases, the identity theory has collapsed.'[35]

Putnam's claim is not that the identity theory is impossible; it's rather that the theory is empirically unlikely: 'it is at least possible that parallel evolution, all over the universe, might *always* lead to *one and the same* physical correlate of pain. But this is certainly an ambitious hypothesis.'[36] His alternative suggestion is that mental states are not identical with physical states, but they are rather 'realized' by them. The realizations of the same kind of mental state can vary from creature to creature; hence this positive claim of Putnam's is sometimes called the thesis of *variable* (or *multiple*) realization.

There are various ways in which identity theorists can (and did) respond to this argument. One response is to say that the hypothesis which Putnam describes is certainly an ambitious one; to be sure, it is too ambitious to be believable. But the identity theory need not be committed to this strong thesis; all it needs to say is that the identities in question are relative to a species, or to a kind of organism. We should not identify pain with physical property P, but pain-in-humans with P, pain-in-octopuses with P*, and so on. Another response is to say that we should not take every mental predicate to pick out one uniform kind of mental state—for what counts as *thinking of Vienna* in my mind may be very different mentally from what counts as *thinking of Vienna* in your mind. For me, thinking of Vienna may conjure up images of Strauss waltzes, for you it may bring to mind the Emperor Francis Joseph. So the proper reduction of mind must first start with an accurate taxonomy of mental states, and this must await the discoveries of empirical psychology.[37]

However, it is hard not to see these responses as special pleading. Certainly it is reasonable to suppose that pain may be one thing in octopuses and another thing in humans, but what do these states have in common which make them all pain? If we say, with the functionalist, that it is the fact that they play the functional or causal role of pain, then why not call *this* property pain? And on the second response: maybe it is true that the common-sense classifications of mental states sometimes classify many diverse states as one. But all Putnam needs to make his point is one case where this does not happen: that is, one case where the common-sense classification does genuinely mark the sharing of a property. If this state is variably realized, then Putnam has established his point.

There are things that the identity theory can say in response to these points. But I will not pursue them here, since I believe that Putnam's argument must be accepted. So if the identity theory is false, then mental properties are not identical with physical properties. So mental properties are distinct from physical properties. Therefore property dualism is true after all. There is no way of avoiding this conclusion: if entities are not identical, then they are distinct, however else they may be related. There are two kinds of thing, not one: this is dualism, like it or not. One obvious consequence of this will be examined in the next section.

It is often emphasized in this connection that property dualism is not Cartesian dualism, and that it is consistent with a kind of physicalism, called *non-reductive physicalism*. Non-reductive physicalism denies what I call ontological reduction of properties, since it denies the identity theory. That's what makes it non-reductive; but what makes it physicalism? Sometimes it is described as a 'token identity theory' (or 'token physicalism'): mental and physical tokens (particulars) are identical, even if types (properties) are not. But this terminology is not helpful. For the 'token identity' claim is really just the denial that there are any non-physical particulars—that is, particulars with no physical properties—and this claim can be held by someone who denies the completeness of physics, which I have claimed is a necessary condition for physicalism. (An example of such a view will be given in §18.) So the token identity claim, though reasonable enough, is not an expression of physicalism in itself, if the completeness of physics is a necessary condition of physicalism. It is, quite simply, monism.[38]

A non-reductive version of physicalism which is worthy of the name, then, must be committed to the completeness of physics. What more must such a physicalism say? Although the doctrine denies the identity of mental and physical properties, it does not deny that mental properties depend on physical properties in the brain and elsewhere. If there were no such dependence, it would be hard to express the idea that the physical 'determines' everything, or that the physical is fundamental in the relevant sense. The dependence is often expressed in terms of the idea of *supervenience*: A supervenes on B when there is no difference in A without a difference in B. So, for example, it is sometimes said that the aesthetic properties of things supervene on their physical properties. This means that two things cannot differ in their aesthetic properties—grace, elegance, and so on—unless they differ in their physical properties in some way. Or, in other words, physical duplicates must be aesthetic duplicates too. The supervenience of the mind on the body is spelt out in obviously analogous ways.

Certainly a non-reductive physicalist should believe in supervenience. But this doesn't mean that supervenience plus the completeness of physics are all that is needed to express what a non-reductive physicalist should believe.[39] For consider an epiphenomenalist substance dualist, who holds the completeness of physics, and that mental properties supervene on physical properties, and yet mental properties are properties of a mental substance. The first and most obvious difference between this epiphenomenalism and non-reductive physicalism is that non-reductive physicalism typically asserts the causal efficacy of the mental, which the epiphenomenalist denies. In the next section we will consider this matter. The second difference, which I will dwell on here, may be expressed by saying (somewhat vaguely) that for the non-reductive physicalist, mere supervenience itself is not a 'close enough' connection between the mental and the physical. What this kind of physicalism needs is a connection which is closer than mere supervenience, but not as close as identity.

This idea of closeness is a little vague; but the general idea can be illustrated by considering the concept of *constitution*. We might say that a statue is constituted by the marble which makes it up. And it is plausible to say that constitution is not the same as identity—since identity is symmetrical and constitution not—but nonetheless constitution is a supervenience relation: there can be no intrinsic change in the statue without a change in the marble. Yet the relationship between the statue and the marble is not a mere correlation between distinct existences: if you took away the marble, you would take away the statue.[40] This looks like the sort of relationship between the mental and the physical which non-reductive physicalists want: dependence which is closer than mere supervenience. However, the physicalist is not entitled merely to take the idea of constitution and apply it to the relation between mental and physical properties. For we understood the idea of constitution in this example only as applied to a particular object: we think that the material parts of the statue, the bits of marble, constitute it. But the fact that we understand the idea of constitution when applied to particulars gives us no guarantee that we understand it when applied to *properties*. What is it, or what would it be, for one property to constitute another? A number of proposals have been offered, but as yet there is no settled consensus, so we can leave this as part of what needs to be spelt out in detail by the non-reductive physicalist.

However, if we were to understand what constitution of properties is, and there was good reason to think that mental properties were constituted by physical properties, then this would be an explanation of the supervenience of the mental on the physical, and this is part of what the physicalist wants. Supervenience is not sufficient by itself to characterize non-reductive physicalism, but if the supervenience were shown to be a consequence of some other physicalistic relation between mind and body, then a physicalist explanation of supervenience will have been given. This sort of explanation is what Terence Horgan has called 'superdupervenience'; I would prefer to call it an example of an 'explanatory reduction'.[41] Thus, as I said in §15, non-reductive physicalism can be seen to combine ontological non-reduction with explanatory reduction. There is some reason, then, to say that all versions of physicalism are reductive in one way or another—even the non-reductive versions![42]

17. The problem of mental causation for non-reductive physicalism

Non-reductive physicalism of the form just outlined has become something of an orthodoxy in the last few decades. But the view is open to the objection that it cannot solve the problem which the identity theory was introduced to solve: the problem of causal interaction of mind and body. This problem, remember, was the conflict between three claims:

(1) Mental phenomena have effects in the physical world.
(2) All physical effects have physical causes which are enough to bring those effects about (the completeness of physics).
(3) Mental and physical causes do not overdetermine their physical effects.

The identity theory resolves this conflict by identifying mental and physical causes:

(4) Mental causes are identical with physical causes.

Thus, depending on whether it is events or properties which are causes, we get an identity theory of events (the so-called 'token identity') or an identity theory of properties ('type identity'). Here we are concentrating on properties, so let us make that explicit:

(5) Properties are causes.

(Or, if we wanted to be more long-winded, 'causes have their effects in virtue of their properties'.) Now the distinctive thesis of non-reductive physicalism is its denial of the identity theory:

(6) Mental properties are not identical with physical properties.

It is the combination of (1)–(3) and (5)–(6) which creates the problem for non-reductive physicalism: for if properties are causes, then mental causes of certain physical effects are mental properties; but the completeness of physics guarantees that there is a purely physical cause of these physical effects. Adding that these effects are not overdetermined, and the causes are not identical, makes the problem explicit: one or more of (1)–(3) or (5)–(6) must go.

It should not really be a surprising discovery that non-reductive physicalism has this problem. For the identity theory was motivated by the need to explain mental causation: identifying mental and physical causes did this job. So it is not surprising that if you deny the identity of mental and physical causes, you have to find another way of solving the problem which the identity theory solved. The problem of mental causation, then, is not a side issue for non-reductive physicalism: it expresses a tension at the heart of the position.

The tension is understandable, from a physicalist point of view. For on the one hand, the argument against the identity theory from variable realization is very plausible. But on the other hand, the completeness of physics imposes a strong constraint on any account of the causal structure of the world: physical causes are enough to bring every physical event about (where 'physical', remember, refers to the subject-matter of physics). To deny the completeness of physics is to say that the purely physical story of the world is incomplete, not for reasons of explanatory convenience, but because it *leaves out some of the real causes of things*. This is not something any physicalist will want to say; but what should they say instead?

There are two strategies they can take in response to the conflict. Either they can detect some equivocation or ambiguity in one or more of these claims. Or they can add some extra assumption to try and render (1)–(3) and (5)–(6) consistent. An example of the first strategy is to say that there is not really a conflict because what matters here is the kinds of explanation we give of events.[43] The idea here is that we have scientific, physical explanations of events, whose aim is to fit the events into pre-understood patterns in nature; and we have mentalistic understandings of events whose aim is to show why people do what they do, that is, make sense of their actions in a way that shows them to be reasonable in the circumstances, given the person's point of view and state of information, and so on. And, the claim is, there is no reason to think that these two kinds of explanatory story must conflict. We can describe the cricket ball's hitting the wicket in physical terms, or in terms of the bowler's aims in attempting to win the game, and so on. There is no reason to think that these two explanations must conflict, and without such a conflict, there is nothing that requires that we identify the mental and physical entities to which we are appealing in these explanations.

The point is entirely correct; but it is irrelevant. For the problem as originally posed (§13) does not make any assumptions about the kinds of explanations we give of phenomena, and whether the same phenomenon—the cricket ball hitting the wickets—can be given more than one explanation. That is not the issue. The issue is one about causation, not explanation. There are many ways of explaining events and processes in the physical world; but if the completeness of physics is true, then there is one special kind of *cause*. To state the problem, then, requires us to distinguish between causation and explanation, since the completeness of physics is a claim about causation. If non-reductive physicalism rejects this distinction, then it must also reject the completeness of physics—since it is not reasonable to hold that there are only physical explanations of events. But without the completeness of physics, we don't have physicalism.

Another version of the first kind of strategy is to clarify the notion of causation involved in the argument. Some say, for example, that mental causes are causally *relevant* to physical effects, although not causally *efficacious*, or that mental causes 'programme' their effects without causing them in the physical sense, or that mental causes are 'structuring causes' not 'triggering causes' of physical effects.[44] But a difficulty with these approaches is that it is hard to see them as more than *ad hoc* responses to the problem in hand; it can seem as if a specific notion of mental causation is being tailored simply to solve the problem.

The second kind of strategy is more promising. This takes causation for granted, but adds another claim to clarify the idea of non-reductive physicalism. The additional claim is a supervenience thesis, to the effect that the physical *metaphysically necessitates* the mental. Frank Jackson expresses this idea in terms of possible worlds: any (minimal) physical duplicate of our world is a duplicate *simpliciter*.[45] The physical thus necessitates the mental in the following sense: given the way things actually are physically, the mental facts could not have been otherwise. This is not to say that physicalism is a necessary truth: there could be possible worlds where physicalism is false, but these are not possible worlds where things are as they *actually* are physically. So this thesis is distinct both from the thesis that physicalism is a necessary truth and the thesis that supervenience is a mere contingent relation.

If we now assume that causation is counterfactual dependence between events or facts, then the problem of mental causation can be addressed in the following way. A mental cause M counts as a cause of a physical effect E because if M had not been there, E would not have been there. That is just to apply the counterfactual criterion. But the simultaneous physical cause P upon which M supervenes (M's 'supervenience base') also counts as a cause of E because if P had not been there, E would not have been there. This is not overdetermination, because if M had not been there, its supervenience base P would not have been there either. P both causally determines E and metaphysically determines M. Therefore: if M were not there, E would not be there, because if M were not there, P would not be there. In other words, if the mental supervenes on the physical, then whenever a physical cause brings about some effect, a mental cause comes along for the ride. But the mental cause is a cause in the same sense as the physical cause: causation on this picture is essentially counterfactual dependence.[46]

By appealing to this idea of necessary supervenience, or metaphysically necessary determination, non-reductive physicalists attempt to solve the problem of mental causation without the need of the identity theory. In fact, it is not surprising that both identity and necessary supervenience can solve this problem. Since they are both necessary relations, neither the identity theory nor the necessary supervenience theory allows that the mental can 'float free' or vary independently of the physical (so necessary supervenience can perhaps play the role of Horgan's 'superdupervenience': see §16). This is how the mental and physical causes can act in harmony.

But there are two problems with the necessary supervenience theory, which make it hard to believe. The first is that while we have a relatively good understanding of the idea of identity, and why it should be a necessary relation, we have no such understanding of metaphysical necessities which are not identities but mere dependencies between one thing and another. Why should it be that certain relations between distinct phenomena are metaphysically necessary? Is there anything we can say to explain this further? If not, metaphysical necessities begin to look somewhat mysterious.

Accusations that views are mysterious are, however, rather hard to evaluate, and so the objection just voiced is rather inconclusive. But the second objection is clearer: this is that the metaphysical necessity of psychophysical supervenience rules out the very possibility of a physical replica of a person which lacked mental properties (e.g. a 'zombie' in David Chalmers's sense).[47] As we shall see in §29, this is a very strong commitment. If there were a way of solving the mental causation problem which did not have this commitment, then we should prefer it.

18. Emergence

For these reasons, I reject the necessary supervenience theory. And I have already rejected the identity theory, because of variable realization. So how should I solve the problem of mental causation?

Let us put to one side epiphenomenalism and the view that there is massive overdetermination (i.e. the denials of (1) and (3)). These are simply incredible. The denial of (5) is a reasonable view: this says that events are causes, so we can identify mental and physical events without having to identify their properties. In effect, this is Davidson's anomalous monism.[48] This view certainly solves the problem, but at the price of denying that the properties, features, or aspects of events have nothing to do with what those events cause. This price is easy to pay in Davidson's metaphysics, since talk about the properties of things is understood as talk about the ways things are described, and who would want to say that the way an event is described has anything to do with what it causes? But, for reasons that cannot be pursued in depth here, I am not willing to pay this price.[49]

This leaves (2): the completeness of physics. Does it make sense to deny such a doctrine? Two points must be noted initially. The first is that to deny the completeness of physics is not to return to substance dualism, Descartes's view. For one could hold a monistic view about substances—that all substances have physical properties, so all substances are physical—and yet deny the completeness of physics, by denying that *all* physical effects are entirely fixed by purely physical causes: in some cases, mental causes are needed as well. This latter claim is entirely consistent with the idea that each substance is a physical substance. Denying the completeness of physics amounts to accepting what has been called 'downward' causation: causation from the 'higher' level of the mental to the 'lower' level of the physical. Whatever the problems with downward causation, an inevitable commitment to Cartesian dualism is not one of them.

The second point is that such downward causation is not inconsistent with the laws of mechanics, the science of motion, for reasons that have been well explained by Brian McLaughlin. Suppose for the sake of argument that what downward causation requires is what McLaughlin calls 'configurational forces': forces that can only be exemplified by matter which has a certain complexity, or a certain kind of structure. Configurational forces are therefore unlike the gravitational force, which holds between any two particles. To illustrate McLaughlin's point, let's consider the case of the laws of classical mechanics: Newton's laws of motion.[50] When a body acts on another body to produce acceleration, it must conform to these laws. These laws are, in C. D. Broad's words, 'general conditions which all motions, however produced, must conform to'.[51] That is, they do not tell us everything about *how* motions are produced, or why things move. When a particular force is exerted on a given object, say the force exerted by a body's electric charge, then the acceleration of the body will be fixed by the laws governing electric charge—for example, Coulomb's law—and any other forces acting upon the body, in accordance with the general laws of motion, to produce the resultant acceleration. The laws of motion themselves do not place any limit on what kinds of forces can operate on bodies; so if there are forces which can only come into being when matter achieves a certain level of complexity, all that classical mechanics requires is that the motion produced by these forces should *conform* to Newton's laws. So if we understand downward causation in terms of configurational forces, then the existence of downward causation is not incompatible with the laws of mechanics. (Actually, I do not think we should conceive of causation in terms of forces, but that is another matter.)

The position we are envisaging here, one which denies the completeness of physics and upholds monism, has strong affinities with the doctrine which was once called 'Emergence' or 'Emergentism'. On this view, mental properties are emergent properties, they are properties which 'emerge' out of the properties of matter when that matter achieves a certain degree of complexity. Traditionally, not all properties of macroscopic, complex matter are emergent in this sense: some properties, like (say) weight or mass, are a direct result of the weight or mass of a thing's parts. The mass of an object whose ten parts each weigh one gram can easily be seen to be a simple product of the masses of its parts. These properties were called 'resultants'. The contrast between resultants, like the weight of a macroscopic object, and emergents, like an object's colour, seems intuitive enough; but on examination, it is very hard to make precise. Sometimes, for instance, it is defined in terms of the idea that the presence of emergents cannot be 'predicted' from knowledge of the thing's parts. But this would answer the question about which properties are emergent in terms of what can be predicted, and this is a question about our state of knowledge—a flimsy ground on which to rest an ontological distinction.[52]

But we do not need to define emergence in this way. All we need to mean by calling mental properties emergent is what has been given to us by our line of inquiry so far: that is, mental properties are distinct from physical properties, though they may supervene on those properties; and they have their own causal efficacy. What this last claim means may be best brought out by example. Take a standard case of mental causation: your headache causes you to go to the cupboard to get an aspirin. The headache is distinct from the brain property B which is also a cause of you going to the cupboard. To say that the headache is a cause of the action, then, is at least to say this: if you hadn't had the headache, you wouldn't have gone to the cupboard. It may also be true that if you hadn't had B, you wouldn't have gone to the cupboard either. The central point is that if your having the headache is a necessary condition for going to the cupboard, in the sense that if you had not had the headache, then in the circumstances you would not have gone to the cupboard, then how can a purely physical cause be enough on its own—sufficient, in the purely physical circumstances—for your going to the cupboard? The short answer is: it can't be. A longer answer is that a physical cause might be sufficient, in the circumstances, to make you go to the cupboard, if the circumstances included the mental cause too. But then the mental cause could be sufficient, in the circumstances, for your going to the cupboard, if the circumstances include the brain property B. (This is not overdetermination, but rather the harmless phenomenon of one effect having many causes, as described in §13.) So one way to deny the completeness of physics is to allow that a physical cause *can* be sufficient in the circumstances for an action, so long as the circumstances include a mental cause.

But there is another way too. For we have been considering a specific, particular example of a causal interaction, where the following counterfactuals are true:

(M) If I had not had the headache, then I would not have gone to the cupboard to get the aspirin.
(P) If I had not had brain state B, then I would not have gone to the cupboard to get the aspirin.

According to David Lewis's theory of counterfactuals, a counterfactual 'If A were the case, B would have been the case' is true just in case the closest possible worlds where A is true are worlds where B is true.[53] If we understand the counterfactuals (M) and (P) in Lewis's way, then we would express their truth-conditions as follows:

(M*) In the closest possible worlds where I did not have the headache, then I did not go to the cupboard to get the aspirin.
(P*) In the closest possible worlds where I did not have the brain state B, then I did not go to the cupboard to get the aspirin.

Now while it is fairly clear that (M*) is true, given our commitment to mental causation, it is not so clear that (P*) is true. Brain state B is a particular brain state. Given variable realization (§16), we allow the possibility that another slightly different brain state might 'realize' the headache in a different situation. So the question about whether (P*) and (P) are true turns on whether a world where a different realizer realizes the headache and I still go to the cupboard is *closer* than a world where there is no headache-realizer at all, and I do not go to the cupboard. That is, if the closest world in which I did not have B is a world where I have a very similar brain state to B, which realizes my headache, then M has more right to be called a cause than B does (even if B is 'sufficient in the circumstances' for my action).[54]

If this view of the counterfactuals were right, then one would have another reason for denying the completeness of physics: B may be sufficient for the action, but M should be regarded as the cause. The view could certainly be challenged; but it is plausible and I will leave it here for the reader's consideration. I conclude that whatever view we take of the causal process here, it remains true that if emergentism is true, the completeness of physics is false: there are some effects which would not have come about if mental things were absent from the world. But if one really believes that there is mental causation, then I think this is exactly what one should expect to say. (There is a sense in which an ontological reductionist can say this too!)

Is the denial of the completeness of physics something which a reasonable person, well-informed about the current state of scientific knowledge, can contemplate? Opinions differ. For some philosophers, to deny the completeness of physics is to be somewhat in the position of Cardinal Bellarmino refusing to look down Galileo's telescope: it is a plain refusal to countenance the known scientific facts.[55] But for others, the completeness of physics is a not a scientific fact, but rather a philosophical principle invented to fit what physical science has discovered into a particular metaphysical vision of things. It could then be argued either that we should reject the metaphysical vision without rejecting any scientific theory, or that the metaphysical vision does not need the completeness of physics.[56] My attitude is the last of these; but here I am content to point out the main moral of this chapter: that if ontological reductionism is denied, and the price to pay for the non-reductive physicalism described at the end of §17 is too high, then the only alternative for one who believes in mental causation is to deny the completeness of physics.

One final point needs making about emergentism. One characteristic claim of the traditional emergentist is that there is a sense in which the relation between emergent properties and their 'bases' cannot be explained; or at least, that we should not necessarily expect to be able to explain this relation. The relation between mind and brain is something which we should accept, in the words of Samuel Alexander, with 'natural piety'. The attitude of natural piety is the attitude we should have to nature when we have reached the end of our explanations, when we accept certain phenomena as 'brute facts'. We can then express the further difference between emergentism and non-reductive physicalism as follows: while they both hold that the mental supervenes on the physical, the non-reductive physicalist believes that this supervenience must be *explained*, while the emergentist is willing to accept the supervenience as a fact of nature. In other words, non-reductive physicalism holds that there must be an explanatory reduction; emergentism holds that whether there is such a reduction is an entirely empirical question, and not one to whose answer we should commit ourselves in advance of enquiry.

19. **Physicalism as the source of the mind–body problem**

We have almost come to the end of our survey of the mind–body problem. We have been considering the problem of causal interaction between mind and body, and physicalism as a solution to that problem. But to complete the picture, we need to consider briefly the idea that physicalism is not the *solution* to the mind–body problem, but the *source* of the problem. (Obviously we must be talking about more than one problem here, since the same view cannot be both the source and the solution to the same problem.) Thus Shoemaker writes:

In common with many other contemporary philosophers, I see the mind–body problem, not as the problem of how a nonphysical mind can interact with a physical body, but rather as the problem of how minds can be part of a fundamentally physical reality. In part this is the problem of how certain widespread 'Cartesian' intuitions about mind can be either explained away, i.e. shown to be illusions, or else shorn of their apparent dualist implications. More generally, it is the problem of how distinctive features of the mental—intentionality, consciousness, subjectivity etc.—can have a place in a naturalistic worldview which sees minds as a product of biological evolution and as having a physico-chemical substrate in just the way other biological phenomena do.[57]

The question here is one which has been pursued in detail by many physicalist philosophers. We might be persuaded that everything is physical, and that human mental life consists in the activity of millions of brain cells. But we still might wonder about how the phenomena of *consciousness* fit into to this whole story. How can a brain be conscious? How can mere grey matter be responsible for the *richness* of my conscious life (the philosopher says, proudly displaying the richness of his conscious life)? Surely this presents an insuperable obstacle to physicalism, the fact that we cannot understand how anything physical can be conscious?

It is, of course, easy to be amazed by the fact that mere matter is capable of sustaining conscious experience. But in itself, the kind of point just made is of little philosophical value. (Our suspicions ought to have been aroused immediately by the fact that it would hardly be an answer to this kind of worry to say that consciousness inheres in a non-physical thing!) What is really wrong with this way of making the point about consciousness may be brought out by making an analogy with a famous story about Wittgenstein.[58] Wittgenstein is said to have asked his students why people used to think that the sun went around the earth. One replied: 'because it looks as if the sun goes around the earth.' To which Wittgenstein is said to have responded: 'and how would it look if the earth went around the sun?' The obvious answer—'exactly the same!'—can be given to the analogous question about mind and brain: why did people use to think that the mind was not the brain? Because it seems as if the mind is not the brain? And how would it seem if the mind were the brain?

So one cannot say, in response to a theory which says, for example, that a mental state like pain is a brain state: 'but how can pain be a brain state? Doesn't this leave out the subjective character of the pain, how it feels?' For the proper physicalist answer to this is that, in itself, it begs the question. As Lewis says:

Pain is a feeling. To have pain and to feel pain are one and the same. For a state to be pain and for it to feel painful are likewise one and the same. A theory of what it is for a state to be pain is inescapably a theory of what it is like to be in that state, of how that state feels, of the phenomenal character of that state ... Only if you believe on independent grounds that considerations of causal role and physical realisation have no bearing on whether a state is pain should you say that they have no bearing on how that state feels.[59]

However, many philosophers believe that independent grounds are provided when we consider the question, not of *what* it is like to be in a conscious state, but how we *know* what it is like to be in such a state. This is the 'knowledge argument' made famous by Frank Jackson and others.[60] I will outline the argument briefly, explain why it does not beg the question against physicalism, and then put it to one side until we return to it in §28.

The argument starts with a thought-experiment. Consider Mary, who has spent all her life in a black-and-white room, has never seen any colours other than black and white. Now imagine that Mary has made an intensive study of the science of colour in all its aspects—physics, physiology, psychology, and so on. In fact, let's suppose that she knows all the physical facts about colour. Now suppose that one day Mary leaves her black-and-white room, and the first thing she sees is a red tomato. It is natural to say that she now knows something which she did not know in the black-and-white room: what it is like to see red. Yet this thing she now knows is not a physical fact, since by hypothesis she knew all the physical facts in the black-and-white room. So if objects of knowledge are facts, then Mary learns a new fact in the black-and-white room.

The knowledge argument does not beg the question against physicalism. This is clear if we represent its premises and conclusions as follows:

(1) Mary knows all the physical facts about colour in the room.
(2) Having left the room, Mary learns something new about colour.
(3) Therefore: not all facts are physical facts.

That, in essence, is the argument—though some extra assumptions might be needed to fill it out properly. But it is clear that neither premise (1) nor premise (2) obviously beg any questions against physicalism. A physicalist could hardly object to the idea of someone learning all the physical facts (1), and (2) is a simple and intuitive thing to say about the story as described above. Maybe, when these premises are scrutinized, they will come to show some deep incoherence, or beg some important question. But this is not obvious; we shall return to the argument in §28.

The conclusion the knowledge argument suggests is that to accommodate all the facts about conscious experience—knowing what it is like—physicalism must be rejected. So if the knowledge argument is sound, the hope which Shoemaker expressed, that consciousness could come to be shown to be part of a 'fundamentally physical reality', is a lost one. In effect, then, the contemporary mind–body problem is a dilemma: If the mind is not physical, how can it have effects in the physical world? But if it is physical, how can we explain consciousness?

20. What does a solution to the mind–body problem tell us about the mind?

Returning to our main theme, three main strategies have emerged for explaining the causal place of the mind in the physical world—the first horn of the above dilemma. The first is the identity theory or ontological reductionism. The second is non-reductive physicalism, the metaphysically necessary determination of everything by the physical. The third is emergentism. Which should we choose?

The tension here is between the completeness of physics, which seems to make mental causation problematic, and the variable realization of mental states, which seems to make identity of mind and body impossible. But in one way, very little is solved when this tension is resolved. For suppose we had an answer to the question: we knew decisively that physics was causally complete, and we were persuaded then that mental states were not variably realized in a way that challenged the identity theory. How much would we know about the mind? Well, we would know that mental properties are physical. But knowing that they are physical is not *ipso facto* knowing which physical properties they are, and what the characteristics of these properties are. On the other hand, we might be persuaded that the completeness of physics is false, and that the evidence for variable realization is overwhelming. This might incline us, then, to non-reductive physicalism or emergentism. How much would we know about the mind? We would know that mental properties are non-physical properties or even emergent properties, but we would not *ipso facto* know what kind of non-physical or emergent properties they are, and what their characteristic features are.

So although it might solve the first part of the mind–body problem to be told that mental properties are physical (or non-physical or emergent) properties, there is more to the understanding of the mind than the mind–body problem. An analogy: all matter is made up of the same basic constituents.[61] All flesh is grass, in the words of the prophet Isaiah. But vegetarians believe that some of this matter should not be eaten. And insisting that all flesh is grass does not go any way towards explaining why some people are vegetarians and some are not. Similarly, saying that the mind is physical (or emergent) does not tell us very much about which of the many physical (or emergent) things it is. The rest of this book attempts to investigate the nature of these mental properties, physical or not.

3

Consciousness

21. The conscious and the unconscious

In Chapter 1, I proposed that the essence of our idea of mind can be expressed by talking in terms of a subject's perspective or point of view. It is natural to think of the subject's point of view as the subject's *conscious* awareness of the world in perception, thought, imagination, and so on. This is certainly part of what I mean. But we need also to recognize unconscious mental phenomena, and several important distinctions among unconscious mental phenomena and how those phenomena can be brought into consciousness. We need to distinguish between the sense in which one may have a belief or an intellectual commitment which one does not currently 'have in mind'—that is, in one's conscious mind—and the sense in which one may have a deeply unconscious desire, urge, or drive, which can only be brought to consciousness by some special technique or therapy. The first kind of unconscious mental state is the kind we try to discover by asking ourselves what we think or want. It is the second kind of unconscious mental state which Freud is often said to have discovered[1]. Whatever the truth in this claim, it is fairly clear that the theory and practice of psychoanalysis have provided many more ways in which the ordinary concept of mind has accommodated the idea of unconscious thought, desire, and mentality generally.

The topic of consciousness touches most of the other areas of the philosophy of mind. Thought and its relation to consciousness and the unconscious will be discussed in the next chapter; perception and its relation to consciousness will be discussed in Chapter 5. This chapter is concerned with the essence of consciousness itself: its nature, its explanation, and its relation to this book's main theme, intentionality. Certain forms of consciousness have been thought to be problematic for an intentionalist theory of mind: in particular, the so-called qualitative conscious properties or *qualia* of sensation are widely considered to be non-intentional. So if intentionality really is the mark of the mental, intentionalism needs to give an account of consciousness. This chapter will first attempt to give an intentionalist account of those aspects of consciousness which have traditionally been considered to be most problematic for intentionalism. Then it will return to the problems of consciousness raised for physicalism in §19.

What I am pursuing here is not a definition of consciousness, in a sense which would distinguish it from unconsciousness, since if someone were puzzled about what we were talking about here, it is unlikely that they would be illuminated by any definition. However, what will be important in what follows is the precise characterization of the phenomena under discussion. So we do need something like an initial taxonomy of kinds of states of consciousness, or events in consciousness.

The first distinction we need is between the consciousness involved in merely being aware of the world, and the *self-consciousness* involved in being somehow aware of oneself when one is aware of the world. One can be, for example, seeing the world outside one's window go by, and then one can become aware that one is seeing the world. What exactly this amounts to, and the extent to which the first kind of consciousness depends on the second kind, is controversial. Kant thought that consciousness in general depends for its possibility on self-consciousness (or as he called it, 'apperception'). Some contemporary writers, by contrast, think that a creature could be conscious in the first sense without needing self-consciousness; in fact, some believe that this is what the consciousness of some animals is actually like. In this chapter I will remain neutral on this question.

More pertinent to my concerns here is the distinction between being conscious, and being conscious *of* something (or conscious *that* something is the case). Some conscious states are described in terms of what the subject is conscious of: one can be conscious of a knock on the door, conscious of a sudden drop in the temperature. Similarly, one can be conscious that the room has become darker, and so on. Contrasted with this is the idea of being conscious *simpliciter*, which is sometimes predicated of creatures (as in 'the patient is conscious') and sometimes of states ('pains are necessarily conscious'). Some philosophers have said that *consciousness of* is the more fundamental notion—according to Sartre, for example, 'all consciousness, as Husserl has shown, is consciousness of something'[2]—but others think that the fundamental notion is the notion of simply being conscious. The distinction is sometimes called the distinction between 'transitive' and 'intransitive' consciousness, for the obvious reason that '*x* is conscious of . . .' takes an object, while '*x* is conscious' does not.[3]

A more theoretical distinction is Ned Block's distinction between access consciousness and phenomenal consciousness. Phenomenal consciousness, Block says, 'is experience; what makes a state phenomenally conscious is that there is something "it is like" to be in that state'.[4] The quoted phrase refers to Nagel's well-known claim that 'an organism has conscious mental states if and only if there is something that it is like to *be* that organism'.[5] There is something it is like to be a goat, I believe, something it is like to be a bat, but nothing it is like to be a lump of rock or a daffodil. The conscious states of the creature for which there is something it is like to be that creature, then, are states of phenomenal consciousness. Block gives examples to illustrate the idea of phenomenal (or 'P-') consciousness:

we have P-conscious states when we see, hear, smell, taste and have pains. P-conscious properties include the experiential properties of sensations, feelings and perceptions, but I would also include thoughts, wants and emotions . . . differences in intentional content often make a P-conscious difference.[6]

So some intentional states are P-conscious. This means that when Block says P-consciousness 'is experience' he is employing the word 'experience' in a broad sense to include thoughts, wants, and emotions as well as sense-experiences. What we have then are a bunch of closely related synonyms: *experience, phenomenal consciousness, what it's like.* There is little cause for concern here; anyone who understands one of these terms will understand all three. (But in the next section we will introduce other terms—'qualitative' and 'qualia'—whose meaning is less well understood.)

Block's broad application of the word 'phenomenal' is apt. For the English word 'phenomenon' derives from the Greek for *appearance*, and thoughts, intentions, and desires are certainly part of the appearance of mind (§§1–2).[7] Kant's concept of the phenomenal world is the concept of the world as it appears to be, as contrasted with the world as it is in itself. It would be (at best) a misleading change of terminology to insist that there is nothing phe-nomenal about intentional states—indeed, the idea of intentionality was introduced in Chapter 1 in terms of ideas like *how things seem to the subject* and the *subject's perspective on the world*, and these phrases are meant to pick out thoughts as well as sense experiences. The question for this chapter, rather, is whether there are non-intentional phenomenal states too.

Block distinguishes P-consciousness from Access (or 'A-') consciousness: 'A representation is A-conscious if it is poised for free use in reasoning and for direct "rational" control of action and speech . . . An A-state is one that consists in having an A-representation.'[8] The basic idea is that a phenomenon is access-conscious (A-conscious) when is accessed (or accessible) to be used by a subject or cognitive system. So, for example, my belief that London is the capital of England is A-conscious because I can report my belief and it can govern my actions. Since the same state may be available for use at one time but not at another, it follows that being A-conscious is not a property of states as such, but is dependent on the state's relation to the accessing mechanisms. This is not so with P-consciousness: some *states* are P-conscious and some are not. And as Block makes clear, the A/P distinction is not the same as the transitive/intransitive distinction, since many P-conscious states (e.g. percep-tions) are states where one is conscious *of* something.

Block argues that it is possible for A- and P-consciousness to come apart:

phenomenal states which are not access conscious, and access consciousness of states which are not phenomenally conscious. I will not be greatly concerned with this, since my chief concern in this chapter is with phenomenal consciousness. There are two reasons for this concern: first, as Block notes, it is phenomenal consciousness that has been the focus of discussions of the traditional problem of consciousness (to be discussed below: §§26–9). The second reason has to do with the main theme of this book. The defence of intentionalism requires that all conscious states are intentional. Now Block claims that the paradigmatic access-conscious states are propositional attitudes such as beliefs and desires.[9] So these states are intentional by definition. Could there be non-intentional states which are A-conscious? It is hard to see how there could be, since Block defines an A-state as one that 'consists in having an A-representation'. So all A-conscious states are representational by definition. Therefore the states which an intentionalist should be concerned with are the supposed phenomenally conscious but non-intentional states.

I will not, then, be making much of Block's distinction throughout this chapter. This is not because I reject the distinction. In fact, I think it is partly based on an intuitive phenomenon, which any theory of consciousness has to accommodate. This is the phenomenon of becoming aware that something is now in consciousness. We are all familiar with trying to describe something that was in some sense in our awareness yet we only 'became conscious' (as we say) *of* it after a while. Block's A-consciousness must be further distinguished from the notion of higher-order thought (HOT), which has been used by some philosophers as the most basic (or simply a basic) form of consciousness. On this view a state is conscious when it is the object of a higher-order thought: a thought is conscious when it is being thought about, a sensation is conscious when it is being thought about, and so on. If a state is the object of a higher-order mental state, it does not follow that that state is A-conscious, simply because it does not follow that *it* is poised for use in reasoning. (How could a sensation, for example, take part in a process of reasoning?) Yet one thing one could mean by saying one is conscious of one's sensation or perception is that one is thinking about them. So it is a perfectly good use of the term 'consciousness'.

We have got a number of notions here—phenomenal consciousness, access consciousness, self-consciousness, transitive and intransitive consciousness, higher-order thought. The relations between these concepts will prove important as we go along, but my focus in the first part of this chapter is intentionalism, and the idea that certain phenomenally conscious states of mind raise a problem for intentionalism. Our main concern, then, must be with phenomenal consciousness as such.

22. The distinction between the intentional and the qualitative

It is often said that there are two basic kinds of mental state or property, the intentional and the qualitative. Bodily sensations, for example, are qualitative in nature, and qualitative mental states are not intentional. This is one way of stating the doctrine I call *non-intentionalism*: the doctrine that not all mental states are intentional. Thus David Rosenthal:

There are two broad categories of mental property. Mental states such as thoughts and desires, often called propositional attitudes, have content that can be described by 'that' clauses. For example, one can have a thought, or desire, that it will rain. These states are said to have intentional properties, or intentionality. Sensations, such as pains and sense impressions, lack intentional content, and have instead qualitative properties of various sorts.[10]

Here intentional states are described as those with a propositional content and qualitative properties are properties which are characteristic of sensations, states of mind which lack propositional content. Now no one should deny that some states of mind have propositional content and others do not. But this does not imply that intentionalism is false. It would only imply this if *being intentional* were the same thing as *having propositional content*. But as I argued in §8, it is not. Since not all intentional content is propositional content, then the fact that some mental states are not propositional attitudes does not refute intentionalism. Intentionalism need not be the thesis that all mental states are propositional attitudes.

But what are 'qualitative' mental states, or mental properties, supposed to be? In a passage which is representative of a non-intentionalist orthodoxy, Jaegwon Kim says that qualitative states are those

that involve sensations: pains; itches; tickles; afterimages; seeing a round, green patch; hearing screeching car tires against pavement; feeling nausea and so on. These mental states are thought to have 'phenomenal' or 'qualitative' aspects—the way they *feel* or the way things *look* or *appear*; thus, pains are thought to have a special qualitative feel that is distinctive of pains—they hurt. When you look at a green patch, there is a distinctive way the patch looks to you: it *looks green* and your visual experience involves this green look ... Each such sensation has its own distinctive feel ... The expressions 'raw feel' and 'qualia' are also used to refer to these qualitative mental states.[11]

Kim, like Rosenthal, classifies perceptual experiences (Rosenthal's 'sense impressions') as among the states with qualitative character. The reason for this is presumably because there is *something it is like* to see, hear, smell, or touch something, just as there is something it is like to have a sensation. But it is equally plain that perceptual experiences also have propositional content: one sees that a bus is coming, smells that someone is cooking goulash, or hears that the glass broke.[12] So it seems that perceptual experiences are propositional attitudes which also have qualitative character. Therefore the distinction between the qualitative and the intentional is not exclusive: some propositional attitudes have a qualitative character.

But saying this does not yet tell us what qualitative character *is*. We can say that perceptions and sensations 'feel' a certain way, to be sure; but it does not take much reflection to realize that the way a visual perception 'feels' is different from the way a bodily sensation feels (this will be defended further in §24). So whatever qualitative features are, we should not think of them as being the same in perception as in bodily sensation.[13] In fact, it is somewhat hard to see what is added to the claim that sense perceptions are conscious by saying that they have qualitative features. So perhaps we should construe 'qualitative' in the following way: qualitative states of mind are conscious states of mind, and consciousness comes in many forms.

But if we say this, then it seems that not just perception, but many other propositional attitudes can have qualitative features, since (as Block points out) many propositional attitudes can be phenomenally conscious. So if the qualitative is just the conscious, then there are many propositional attitudes that are qualitative. And the fact that some propositional attitudes are not conscious just means that we have to distinguish between conscious mental states and non-conscious ones. But this was something which we already knew, before having to appeal to the idea of the 'qualitative'.

So either 'qualitative' simply means 'phenomenally conscious' in Block's sense, or it does not. If it does, then sensations, perceptions and other propositional attitudes are qualitative. But then the important distinction among mental states is between the conscious and the non-conscious, not between the qualitative and the intentional. If 'qualitative' does not just mean 'phenomenally conscious', then what does it mean? If we take Kim's lead, then we might say that a state of mind is 'qualitative' when it has qualities which are like those of sensation, or which are sensory (this is not the same thing, as we noted when distinguishing perception from sensation). But in this sense of 'qualitative', many conscious propositional attitudes or episodes are not qualitative, as we saw above: conscious thoughts do not have a sensory character. It follows that qualitative states are one variety of conscious state, but there are others. So to understand consciousness, it is not enough to understand the qualitative. Once again, the important distinction seems to be that between the conscious and the non-conscious.

In an attempt to impose some clarity on this confusing terminology, I shall use the word 'qualitative' in this second sense: to describe those mental states whose conscious character is either sensory or like that of bodily sensations.

And following Block, I shall use the word 'phenomenal' to describe those states—whether intentional or not—for which there is something it is like to be in them. Phenomenal character is thus the broader notion: conscious thoughts, perceptions, and other propositional attitudes, plus sensations and emotions, all have a phenomenal character. The phenomenal character of a state of mind is its conscious character, and an account of the phenomenal character of a state of mind is an account of what it is like to be in that state of mind.

23. Qualia

As Kim says, qualitative mental states are also called 'qualia' (singular: 'quale'). But as with 'qualitative' and 'phenomenal' the term 'qualia' is used in many ways. Some writers use the term as I am using the term 'phenomenal': so a state has qualia if and only if there is something it is like to be in it. In this sense, there can be no sensible debate about the existence of qualia. But other writers use the term to pick out the 'intrinsic' properties of experience, where intrinsic properties are contrasted with intentional properties. Thus Block: 'qualia realism . . . is the view that there are intrinsic mental features of our experience.'[14] To avoid confusion, I will adopt this latter usage: qualia are non-intentional conscious properties.

This use of the term 'qualia' is a departure from Kim's claim that qualia are qualitative properties: for I am using the term 'qualitative' for those properties which are sensory or characteristic of bodily sensation, whether or not these properties are intentional. I use the term 'qualia' for non-intentional conscious properties. So the relations between the ideas of the phenomenal, the qualitative, and 'qualia' can be displayed as follows:

- *Phenomenal states* = all phenomenally conscious states/acts/properties;
- *Qualitative states* = sensory states; those phenomenal states/acts/properties with a sensory phenomenal character;
- *Qualia* = non-intentional properties whose instantiation explains (or partly explains) the phenomenal character of qualitative states.

So, according to this terminology, it is not tautological to say that one can give an account of qualitative properties or states in terms of qualia; and it is not contradictory to say that one can give an account of qualitative properties or states in terms of intentionality. Both are substantial theses. In §§24–5 I shall be concerned with the conflict between them—the debate between intentionalist and non-intentionalist accounts of the qualitative. But first I must say a little more about qualia.

Qualia are non-intentional conscious mental properties. What is a non-intentional mental property? If we accept my definition of intentionality given in §8, then a non-intentional mental state is one which has no intentional structure: it is not directed on anything, it has no intentional object, no aspectual shape, and no distinction can be made between anything like *mode* and anything like *content*. But what are qualia properties of? Here we need to make an important distinction. For some philosophers, qualia are properties of subjects of experience, and hence they are mental states (in the sense in which I introduced that term in §10). For others, they are properties of mental states or events, and hence higher-order properties (i.e. properties *of* properties). So, for example, the first view would call a particular toothache a quale, or one could call the naggingness of the toothache a quale.

This distinction is important because, although intentionalism must reject qualia in the first sense—obviously, since intentionalism is the view that all mental states are intentional—it need not reject qualia in the second sense. A version of intentionalism—*weak intentionalism*—maintains that all mental states have some intentionality, but that some of these states have qualia-properties. On this view, the experience of a toothache, for instance, has intentionality (it involves directedness upon a tooth), but on top of this it may have specific qualia which account for its particular feeling. The stronger form of intentionalism, however, says that no mental state has any non-intentional mental properties. We will return to this distinction in §25.

The instantiation of qualia is what is supposed to explain (or partly explain) the phenomenal character of qualitative states. No one supposes that the instantiation of qualia is what explains the phenomenal character of *all* conscious states, for reasons we have already touched upon. The phenomenal character of the realization that now is the time to write to one's mother is not explained in terms of qualia. The phenomenal character of conscious thought and propositional attitudes will be discussed in the next chapter.[15] Our concern here will be with qualitative states: bodily sensations and perceptual experiences. Of these, perceptual experiences—seeing, hearing, touching, and so on—are perhaps the more controversial examples of states with qualia. So since my concern is with whether qualia provide a refutation of intentionalism, it is appropriate that I deal first with the *least* controversial example of qualia, which provide the best case for non-intentionalism: these are bodily sensations—pains, itches, and so on. For even if there were no qualia in perceptual experience, intentionalism would still have to explain the qualitative character of bodily sensation. So an intentionalist must examine the supposed cases of qualia in bodily sensation and show that they have been mistakenly classified as non-intentional. This will occupy us for the next few sections.

24. The intentionality of bodily sensation

In our talk about pain and other sensations, we can distinguish between the state of being in pain, and the pain that one feels when in that state. When I say that Vladimir is in pain, for example, 'x is in pain' is a one-place predicate which predicates a property of Vladimir. But when I say that Vladimir feels a pain in his toe, it appears that I am relating Vladimir to an object, a pain, by using the three-place predicate 'x feels a y in z', where the y place could be filled in with other sensation-words, and the z place could be filled by words for other parts of the body. When there is a danger of ambiguity between these two ways of talking, I will use the term 'pain-state' for the state of being in pain, and the term 'pain-object' for the object (apparently) related to the subject when that subject feels, or is aware of, or is conscious of a pain.

Now it is tempting to think that the intentionality of sensation is revealed by the fact that, in the second kind of case mentioned, we can describe the consciousness involved in pain as a kind of *transitive* consciousness: one is conscious of a pain in one's leg. Transitive consciousness seems at first sight to be a form of intentionality: when one is conscious of the bus approaching, the approaching bus is the intentional object of your consciousness. It is natural to conclude that since claims of the form 'X is conscious of Y' are ways of talking about the intentionality of conscious states, so claims of the form 'X is conscious of a pain' express an intentional relation between X and a pain-object.

Unfortunately, this is too fast. Searle, among others, has denied that the transitive 'conscious of' always expresses intentionality:

The 'of' of 'conscious of' is not always the 'of' of intentionality. If I am conscious of a knock on the door, my conscious state is intentional, because it makes reference to something beyond itself, the knock on the door. If I am conscious of a pain, the pain is not intentional, because it does not represent anything beyond itself.[16]

But Searle's objection is not decisive, since 'I am conscious of a pain' can mean at least three things. First, being conscious of a pain might mean that one is aware of being in a pain-state. If so, then it is a 'higher-order' awareness of another mental state, and is as intentional as any other higher-order mental state. For higher-order mental states have lower-order states as their intentional objects: a belief that one believes that p has one's *belief that p* as an object.

Second, if being conscious of a pain is being aware of a pain-object, then the analogy with a knock on the door holds: the pain-state is as intentional as being conscious of a knock at the door. For the fact that the pain-object (if there is such a thing) is not itself intentional is no more relevant to the intentionality of the awareness of the pain-object than the non-intentional nature of the knock is relevant to the intentionality of the consciousness of the knock. We will return to the question of pain-objects at the end of this section.

Third, and finally, being conscious of a pain may simply mean *being in pain*. But it is the intentionality of this which is at issue. So Searle cannot object to the intentionalist's thesis by saying that 'I am conscious of a pain' simply means 'I am in pain'. He needs another reason, and he gives one: pains are not intentional because they represent nothing beyond themselves. As it happens, this is not obvious: a number of philosophers have defended the thesis that pains represent damage to the body.[17] But even if we don't accept this thesis, there is a better way of defending the intentionality of sensation.

The better defence of the intentionality of sensation comes from a correct understanding of their felt location. It is essential to bodily sensation, as we normally experience it, that it feels to have a location in the body. Pains and other sensations feel to be located in parts or regions of the body. To attend to a sensation is to attend to the (apparent) part or region of the body where the sensation feels to be. The location of a bodily sensation need not be felt to be precise; and it can involve the whole body. A feeling of nausea can overwhelm the middle of one's whole body, and a feeling of physical exhaustion can pervade one's whole body. The point is not that a sensation must be felt to occupy a non-vague relatively circumscribed location, but that it is felt to be somewhere within one's body. The necessity of this would explain why we find it so hard to make sense of the idea of a sensation of one's own which has a location (say) ten inches outside one's left shoulder. Phantom limbs are not such cases: what subjects feel in a phantom limb pain is not that they have a pain at some distance from the point at which the limb was severed; rather, they feel that their body extends further than it actually does.[18]

That bodily sensation has an apparent location may be uncontroversial; that its location is *felt* may be less so. The non-intentionalist might say that the 'felt' location really involves two things: a sensation (a *quale*) and a belief that the sensation is located in a certain part of the body. On this view, the location of a sensation is not part of the feeling of a sensation; rather it is the content of a *belief* about where the sensation is. But this cannot be right. Belief is a state of mind which is revisable on the basis of other beliefs and evidence. When rational subjects come to have a reason which tells decisively against a belief, then they revise the belief. So if the apparent location of a sensation is explained by a belief about its location, one would expect the belief to be revised when a subject comes to have a reason to think that the sensation does not have that location. But this is not so. Someone who becomes convinced by the physicalist arguments for identifying sensations with brain states will come to believe that sensations are really located in the brain. But having this belief does not change the apparent location of the sensation in the body. Moreover, this person is not irrational—that is, does not have a contradictory belief—when they claim that a sensation is in the brain but it seems to be in the leg. Feeling a sensation to be located at a certain place is not the same as believing that one has a sensation located at that place.

So why does the felt location of sensation mean that sensations are intentional? In §§5–6 I outlined the two essential features of intentionality: directedness and aspectual shape. These features generate what I call the relational structure of intentionality: intentional states involve relations to intentional contents (e.g. propositions) by intentional modes (e.g. belief). The nature of an intentional state is given by giving the intentional mode and the content. Every intentional state has an intentional object, in the sense that it is directed on or at something. The relation between object and content was explained in §8.

So if pains and other sensations are genuinely intentional, we have to be able to distinguish the intentional object, the mode, and the content. Take the example of a pain in one's ankle. The first thing to note is that this is a form of awareness; and it is not a 'mere' awareness, or 'bare' awareness. It is a transitive form of awareness: an awareness *of* one's ankle. It is for this reason that it is natural to say that the ankle is the object of the state. Being in this state of pain is a matter of the ankle being presented to one in a certain way. Remember that, in general, the intentional object of a state S is what is given in an answer to the question, 'what is your mind directed on when in S?' For example, the correct answer to the question, 'what is your thought about?', gives the intentional object of your thought. Now pains are not naturally said to be 'about' things; instead one asks 'what hurts?' or 'where does it hurt?' and the answer gives the intentional object of a pain: my leg, my arm, and so on. That there is a relational structure here is shown by the fact that there is a distinction between the subject of the experience and the object or region which hurts; that there is an intentional object is shown by the fact that the subject's mind is directed on that object. And as with other intentional objects, there are cases where the intentional object of a sensation does not exist; for example, in phantom limb cases.

The intentional object of the pain—the ankle as perceived by sensation—is presented to the subject of the pain in a certain way. One's ankle is a part of one's foot, it is made up of bones and muscle, but it may not be presented as such in the state of pain. One may have a pain in one's liver, but not have any idea that the liver is where the pain is—one could have a pain which one can only identify as being 'over here' without even knowing that one has a liver. Thus bodily sensations exhibit aspectual shape: their objects are presented in certain ways, to the exclusion of other ways. Two sensation-states could, as it were, converge on the same object, presented in two different ways. The content of the sensation-state is how it presents the part of one's body as being: the content of a phantom limb pain 'in' a leg might be *my leg hurts.*

What about the intentional mode? When one has a pain in one's ankle, the intentional mode is a mode of feeling: it is a way of feeling one's ankle. The intentional content is the content of the feeling: that is, one must feel, in a case of pain, that one's ankle hurts. To draw an analogy with outer percep-tion, we can say that pain is a kind of feeling, just as seeing is a kind of perceiving. There are of course many other kinds of bodily feeling; and each of these ways in which one can feel one's body are the intentional modes which have parts of the body as their intentional objects. It might be objected that this proliferates modes unnecessarily. But the same kind of objection could be raised against a theory which explained differences in consciousness purely in terms of differences in qualia: there would be as many distinct qualia as there are distinct types of bodily sensations. It is not clear why this should be a problem for the intentionalist view any more than it is for the qualia view.

On the approach just outlined, the intentional object of a pain-state is a part or region of the body, not a pain-object. Real parts of the body are straightforward real things—we have a good idea of their nature, how to distinguish one from another. But pain-objects are obscure entities: if we were to take them seriously, we would have to construe them as entities with an existence somewhat like particular objects (since they can 'move' and return) and somewhat like events (since they take time). What kind of entities are these? Moreover, paradoxes arise when we try and take talk about pain-objects seriously. Block has pointed out that the following argument is invalid:

1. The pain is in my hand.
2. My hand is in my pocket.
3. Therefore: the pain is in my pocket.

But if pains were objects, then what would be wrong with the conclusion? What would be wrong with the idea that an object inhabiting some space would also inhabit the space which contained that space?

Block's example is puzzling in any case, for all the inference 1–3 seems to depend upon is the transitivity of the relation *x is in y*; and this seems like a very natural assumption to make. Block himself diagnoses the problem as deriving from an ambiguity in the word 'in'. Michael Tye disagrees, claiming that the problem arises because 'The pain is in my hand' is an intensional context (see §4 for the idea of an intensional context).[19] He draws the parallel with other intensional contexts containing psychological verbs by showing how they create apparently similar invalid inferences:

4. I want to be in City Hall.
5. City Hall is in a ghetto.
6. Therefore: I want to be in a ghetto.

But Tye's explanation is not convincing. The invalidity of 4–6 is obviously due to the fact that one can represent the object of one's desire in one way, while not representing all the facts about it. That's the obvious explanation of the invalidity, and Tye is right to say that we do not need to say that 'in' is ambiguous in this case. But what is Tye's parallel explanation of the invalidity of 1–3? There is no object being presented as one way but not as another, as in the City Hall case. It will not do merely to point out that there are cases of intensional contexts where 'in' is not ambiguous, like 4–6, if we have no explanation of what creates the intensionality in 1–3.

Indeed, that intensionality is not the explanation of why 1–3 is invalid is supported by an example of Roberto Casati's:

7. The hole is in my trousers.
8. My trousers are in the cupboard.
9. Therefore: the hole is in the cupboard.

This is straightforwardly invalid, and it looks like the same sort of argument as 1–3; but there is no intensional context.[20] Casati proposes that the *in* of 'the hole is in my trousers' expresses the causal or ontological dependence of the hole on the trousers; and the *in* of 'my trousers are in the cupboard' does not express such a dependence. If this is so, then Block's account would be right about this case: 'in' is ambiguous in 7–9.

Could the same explanation apply to the case of 1–3 too? That is, could the '. . . in . . . ' in 'the pain is in my hand' express a causal or ontological dependence of the pain on my hand, and could this fact, plus the fact that my hand does not have this dependence on my pocket explain why 1–3 is ambiguous? This is along the right lines, but it cannot be correct as it stands. For if there can be phantom pains in the hand, then a pain cannot be ontologically (and *a fortiori* causally) dependent on one's actual hand. A phantom limb patient, under the misapprehension that he has a hand, could rehearse the premises of the argument of 1–3.

The right thing to say, I believe, is that while the pain is not causally or ontologically dependent on the hand for the reason just given, the pain-state is *intentionally individuated* by the hand. That is to say, any pain-state needs an object to 'complete' it, to make it the state it is. Just as my thought of Napoleon is individuated by Napoleon, he is part of what makes it the thought it is, so my pain in my hand is individuated by my hand; that is part of what makes it the pain it is. And just as I can think about Pegasus even when it does not exist, I can have a pain in my hand even when I have no hand. (If you think this usage is not proper English, then you can replace it with ' . . . seem to have a pain in my hand' or ' . . . have a pain in what seems to be my hand'. This amounts to the same thing.) 'In' expresses intentional individuation.

Unlike causal or ontological dependence, intentional individuation is not relational: X can intentionally individuate Y even when X does not exist. Frank Jackson is right, then, when he says that 'if sensation statements essentially related persons to parts of their body, they could not be true in the absence of appropriate parts of the body. But the phantom limb phenomenon shows that they can be'.[21] But Jackson is wrong to conclude that this tells against a view which analyses away the apparent reference to mental objects in terms of mere awareness of the body. For all that has been shown is that such awareness is not a relation to a body-part; but if awareness were a form of intentionality, it would not be relational in this sense (§8).

An advantage of this explanation is that it allows us to talk of pains being 'in' parts of the body without taking talk of pain-objects literally. For if what it means for a pain to be *in* a body part is that the pain-state is intentionally individuated by the body part, then we can agree that pains are in the body without admitting that there are really pain-objects. (Another reason for suspicion about pain-objects is that not all languages talk about pains as if they were objects. Talk of pains as objects may be an artefact of English idiom; but I cannot pursue this here.)

These are my reasons for thinking that pains and other bodily sensations are intentional states. Sensations involve awareness of the body: they present parts or regions of the body by means of intentional modes, and they have a certain aspectual shape.

25. Strong intentionalism and weak intentionalism

Suppose these points about bodily sensation were accepted. And suppose, for the sake of argument, that it was accepted that all other mental states—including perceptions and emotions—are intentional. Even so, one could still accept that certain mental states have qualia, in addition to their intentional properties. This is the view I call weak intentionalism: all mental states are intentional, but some have non-intentional conscious properties, qualia. The weak intentionalist holds that qualia are higher-order properties of states of mind. So qualia are properties of properties. Another way to express weak intentionalism is to say that the intentional nature of certain mental states does not exhaust their phenomenal character; two experiences could share their intentional nature and differ in their phenomenal character. Yet another way to express the view is as follows: not every phenomenally conscious difference in states of mind is an intentional difference. One could be a weak intentionalist about perception, about emotion, about sensation, or about all three. My concern here is with sensation.[22]

I shall suppose that a weak intentionalist view of pain says that having a pain is an intentional state: it is an awareness of something happening in a part or region of your body. But this is not the whole story about the phenomenal character of pain. For there are also qualia which contribute to how pain feels. Thus, the conscious nature of the sensation-experience is determined by two things: the part of the body the experience presents as its object, and the qualia. We can illustrate this by considering two pains, one in the right ankle and one in the left, which feel to be in different places and yet in some sense feel the same. The sense in which they feel the same is given by the qualia which the pain-states share. The sense in which they feel different is given by their intentional objects (their locations).

What are these non-intentional qualia properties of? A natural answer is that they are apparent properties of the part of the body which hurts. But this cannot be the right answer for the weak intentionalist. For pain-qualia are supposed to be properties of mental states: the naggingness of a toothache is a property of the toothache, while the toothache itself is a (partly intentional) state of a conscious subject. A non-intentionalist, by contrast, holds that certain conscious mental states (call them 'pure qualia') have no intentionality at all. So if it is to distinguish itself from non-intentionalism, weak intentionalism must deny that there can be pure qualia: qualia cannot be instantiated *except* as properties of properties: that is, intentional state types. If qualia were properties of body parts, then they would not be properties of properties. But they must be properties *of properties*, because otherwise there could be instantiations of pure qualia. I will assume then that according to a weak intentionalist theory of sensation, the qualia involved in pain are properties of the intentional state of being in pain. This parallels what is said by a weak intentionalist theory of visual perception, according to which visual qualia are properties of visual experiences: that is, properties of mental states.

But is it really true to say that being aware of pain involves being aware of properties of one's mental state? The pain in my ankle seems to be going on in a part of me: it seems to be the *ankle* which is hurting me. It is not as if I am aware of the location of my ankle, and (in addition to this) I feel that *my being so aware* has a quale. The intentionality and the qualitative character of the pain do not seem to be separable in this way. So when one has a pain in one's ankle, there do not seem to be two things going on—the intentional awareness of the ankle, and the awareness of the pain-quale. Rather, the awareness of the ankle seems to be *ipso facto* awareness of its hurting. The hurting seems to be in the ankle. How the ankle feels seems to be a property of the ankle. It does not seem to be an intrinsic property of the intentional awareness of the ankle.[23]

A standard objection to the idea of qualia in visual perception is that when one pays attention to one's experience, 'all one finds is the world'—in J. J. Valberg's phrase.[24] One looks at the redness of a glass of wine, looking for non-intentional properties of experience, and all one finds is an apparent property of the wine: its redness. This fact about experience has come to be called the 'transparency' of experience (see §43). My objection to weak intentionalist views of sensation is similar: when one pays attention to one's pain, one pays attention to the *object* of one's pain, not to features of the experience. One pays attention to the ankle, and its hurting. Neither of these are, on the face of it, higher-order features of an experience. Weak intentionalism about sensation must therefore be rejected. If we accept intentionalism about sensation, we must accept strong intentionalism.

Strong intentionalist theories of sensation say that the phenomenal character of a sensation consists purely in that state's intentionality. There are three ways this can be understood. It can be understood as locating the conscious character of a mental state in features of the *intentional content* of the state; differences in conscious character must be differences in content. Second, the theory could locate the conscious character of a mental state in features of the *intentional mode*—the subject's relation to that content. And third, differences in content can consist in some combination of differences in content and differences in mode. This threefold distinction is just a result of the fact (outlined in §8) that intentional states can differ in their modes, their contents, or both.

Tye has recently advanced a theory of the first sort; this is what I call his *representationalism.*[25] Tye claims that pain (for example) is a representation of damage to the body, or disturbance in the body. The conscious state is a representation of a certain state of affairs, and the consciousness is located in the state of affairs represented. The theory's treatment of pain, however, is not very convincing. It seems clear that there are many varieties of pain, not all of which the suffering subject would be aware of as representing *damage* to the body.[26]

Tye's theory locates differences in the phenomenal or conscious character of a sensation in the representational content of the state alone. The alternative strong intentionalist view says that the phenomenal character of a state is fixed not just by the content, but by the content and the intentional mode. This is the third view mentioned above, and it is the view I want to defend. (The second view, that the phenomenal character of the state of mind is fixed purely by the mode, has little to be said for it: obviously, any plausible intentionalist view must allow that the intentional content contributes to phenomenal character.)

I call this theory the 'perceptual theory', since it treats bodily sensation as a form of perception, the perception of things going on in one's body.[27] To make the connection with perception clear, consider first a strong intentionalist theory of perception, and what it would say about the phenomenal character of (say) visual experience. The phenomenal character of a visual experience of an aeroplane flying overhead is given by giving its content—the aeroplane, its shape and size, and so on—and by giving the experience's intentional mode: seeing. The phenomenal difference between seeing an aeroplane overhead and hearing one is partly a matter of the content—*what* is experienced—but also a matter of the mode of apprehending this content, the intentional mode in Searle's sense. Certain properties of objects (e.g. colours) can only be apprehended in certain modes, so cannot figure in the content of certain modes (you cannot smell colours). But others are not mode-specific: thus, for example, the difference between seeing shapes and feeling them is partly a matter of the intentional mode in question. According to a strong intentionalist theory of perception, the phenomenal character of a perception is fixed by two things: mode and content.

I say the same thing about bodily sensations. The consciousness involved in bodily sensations is a result of two things: the intentional content of the sensation, and the intentional mode. Consider a pain in one's ankle. I said that the ankle is the intentional object of the pain-state. Like the intentional objects of many outer perceptions (e.g. aeroplanes), the ankle need not itself be a conscious entity. In perception and in sensation, consciousness need not reside in the intentional *objects* of awareness in order for the *state of awareness* to be conscious.[28]

However, when investigating the phenomenal character of an intentional state or act, we are interested not just in the objects of awareness, objects that might be the objects of many intentional states or acts, but in intentional content. It's not just ankles, but how things are with them, which fixes phenomenal character. The intentional content of a pain might be something like this: *my ankle hurts.* (This makes the content propositional for simplicity; but remember that I am not committed to all content being propositional.) Moreover, we have not fully specified the phenomenal character of this state until we have said in which intentional mode it is presented. Compare: we have not fully specified the phenomenal character of a perception of an aeroplane overhead until we have said whether the aeroplane is seen or heard.

The perceptual theory presents pain, and the other bodily sensations, as involving intentional modes. How can the theory accommodate the fact, which we raised as a problem for weak intentionalism, that pain seems to be *in* the part of the body, that it seems to be a *property* of the body? When we attend to our pains, as I said above, we attend to the part of the body in which we feel the pain. But haven't I said that pain is a way of being aware of one's ankle, and therefore something more like a relation and not a property?

The way to answer this question is to understand the special nature of the concepts which we apply when we talk and think about sensations. The content of a pain in one's ankle might naturally be put into words as 'my ankle hurts'. On the face of it, this sentence seems to be saying that there is a property of hurting which my ankle has. But on reflection, it is clear that the concept of *hurting* contains a covert relation to a subject. Something cannot hurt unless it hurts *someone*; and a part of one's own body cannot hurt unless it hurts *oneself*. We can make no real sense of the idea that a part of one's own body might hurt, without its hurting oneself. Hurting is therefore not just a matter of a part of one's body having an intrinsic property, but rather a matter of that body part and its properties apparently affecting oneself. Hurting thus has a relational structure: the content of the sensation is that one's ankle hurts, and the mode is the feeling. This captures the sense in which the part of one's body which hurts is *doing something* to oneself, that there is something about the body part which is responsible for one's feeling in this way.[29]

To pay attention to a pain is to pay attention to the place which hurts. But one cannot pay attention to the place which hurts without paying attention to the hurting, and the hurting, I have claimed, is the way the body part or location is (so to speak) forcing itself upon oneself. Therefore, in being aware that one's ankle hurts, one is aware that it is hurting oneself. This is why I say that according to the perceptual theory, the phenomenal character of the pain is given by two things: the content of the experience and the intentional mode.

Finally, I need to return to the question of how, on this view, one can have a pain in one's ankle even if one does not have an ankle. The account of the relational structure of intentionality described in §8 makes intentionality a relation, not to an actually existing object, but to an intentional content. Part of the point of the idea of content is to express or capture the aspect under which the object of the intentional state is presented; the other part is to distinguish different states in the same mode. And these can be distinguished even when the intentional object does not exist. This is why we cannot say in general that intentional states are relations to intentional objects. As noted in §24, phantom limbs show that someone can feel a pain in a part of their body even when this part does not exist. So an intentionalist cannot say that pain is a relation to a body part. Rather, pain is a relation to an intentional content, where the intentional content is the way things seem to the subject. It seems to the subject that they have a limb, and this is compatible with them knowing that the limb does not exist.

It could be said, in opposition to this, that pain is always a relation to an existing intentional object, but the intentional object is the *cause* of the pain in the body or brain. But since the cause could be something of which the subject was utterly unaware, this would break the connection between the idea of an intentional object and the phenomenology, the idea of how things seem to the subject. What the perceptual theory is trying to capture is how things seem. The cause of the sensation in the body may be another matter.

So it can be true, then, that someone can feel a pain in their foot even when they have no foot. And this is compatible with its being appropriate to tell someone 'it's not your foot that hurts, there's no such thing; it's an effect of the amputation'. Compare: it could be true that someone thinks that fate is against them, and this is compatible with its being appropriate to tell them 'it's not fate, there's no such thing; it's just bad luck'. The cases are, in the relevant respects, parallel.

One thing which is novel about this view is that it locates the phenomenal character of the state partly in the intentional mode. It might be objected that I am simply assuming the phenomenal, stipulating it into existence by my assumption that some intentional modes are conscious and some not. This objection is confused. Of course I am assuming that some mental states have phenomenal character and some do not. But so do those who talk in terms of qualia. Rather than assuming that certain intentional states are by their nature conscious, they assume that there are certain non-intentional properties which are by their nature conscious. If I assume consciousness, so do my opponents. But we have no alternative, since there are no prospects for anything like a *definition* of consciousness in other terms.

Having the elements of a general account of conscious sensation in place, we now must return to the issue which we left unfinished in §19: whether physicalism can give an account of consciousness.

26. Physicalism, consciousness, and qualia

It is often said that it is the qualia of conscious experience which give rise to the hard part of the mind–body problem. For many of those who distinguish between conscious states and intentional states, the problem of giving a physicalist account of intentionality is perceived to be much less difficult than the problem of giving a physicalist account of qualia. Indeed, the whole mind–body problem is these days often posed as follows: how can a physicalist account for qualia? It might seem, therefore, that if the intentionalist account of consciousness is correct, and consciousness can be understood without having to appeal to qualia, then the force of this aspect of the mind–body problem is diminished. For if there are no qualia, then physicalism does not have to explain them. The only problem that remains is the physicalist explanation of intentionality, and this is something which is less deeply problematic than the explanation of qualia.

This line of thought assumes two things. First, it assumes that if there are no qualia, then there is no problem (or less of a problem) about consciousness for physicalism. And second, it assumes that giving a physicalist account of intentionality is less problematic than giving a physicalist account of qualia. Both assumptions are mistaken. The second assumption is undermined by the fact that, despite the optimism of some recent manifestos, little progress has been made with dealing with the fundamental problems of misrepresentation and error which have dogged physicalist reductions of intentionality.[30]

The first assumption is mistaken because it turns out that, insofar as there is a problem of consciousness for physicalism, it does not depend on the existence of qualia in the sense discussed above. No matter what consciousness is, no matter which version of intentionalism is true, the real problem of consciousness remains. Furthermore, the real problems for physicalism are problems not just for physicalism but for any theory which attempts to explain consciousness in a certain way. I shall now defend these claims.

What is the problem of consciousness for physicalism supposed to be? As I argued in §19, we cannot generate a philosophical problem merely from our sense of wonder that the wet stuff in the brain can give rise to consciousness. This *is* an amazing fact; but some facts are amazing, and sometimes that's all that can be said. I said in §19 that a different problem is posed by what Jackson calls the 'knowledge argument': it seems that physicalism cannot account for what we *know* when we know what it is like to be in a conscious state. The knowledge argument is one of a trio of arguments—including the 'zombie argument' and the argument from the 'explanatory gap'—which have been used to articulate the problem of consciousness.[31]

The zombie argument begins by asking us to imagine the existence of zombies: creatures exactly like us in all physical respects, but lacking phenomenal consciousness.[32] They may have as many mental states as you wish, as long as none of them are phenomenally conscious. Then it is argued that what is imaginable or conceivable is metaphysically possible. It follows that zombies are metaphysically possible: call this claim *the zombie hypothesis*. Physicalism, remember, asserts either that mental states are identical with brain states, or that they are metaphysically determined by (necessarily supervene upon) brain states. Either way, the relation between mind and brain has to be a metaphysically necessary one, since identity and metaphysical determination are necessary relations. So according to physicalism, it is not possible for a brain exactly like mine to exist without mental states exactly like mine existing. But this is what the zombie hypothesis is supposed to show. So if the zombie hypothesis is correct, physicalism is false.

While the zombie argument raises a problem for physicalism's metaphysical claims about the relations between mind and body, the explanatory gap argument raises a problem for physicalism's *understanding* of consciousness.[33] According to this argument, physicalism requires that all phenomena be susceptible in principle of a physicalistic explanation.[34] There is a general pattern of explanation we have found in the physical world, where the properties of macroscopic objects are explained in terms of the properties of microscopic objects. For example, we can explain the fragility of certain crystals in terms of the lattice structure of the molecules which make them up; and once we understand the lower-level structure, we can understand how it can give rise to the higher-level structure. But we have very little idea of how this explanation can apply to the relation between phenomenal consciousness and the brain. What is needed, it is claimed, is an account of this relation which enables us to understand, in Joseph Levine's words, 'why when we occupy certain physico-functional states we experience qualitative character of the sort we do'.[35] Here the situation seems different in the case of consciousness than it is in the case of the propositional attitudes. For according to functionalism, beliefs and other propositional attitudes are functional states realized in the physical material of the brain. It is the brain's having the causal structure it does which makes it realize the propositional attitudes it does. Therefore if one fully understood the brain's causal structure one would understand how it sustained the propositional attitudes: there would be no gap between a full understanding of the brain's structure and an understanding of the causal structure of the propositional attitudes. Once we understood that these brain states were playing these causal roles, we could not fail to see them as realizing the propositional attitudes, on the functionalist view. Whether or not one accepts the functionalist theory, it is not hard to see that such an explanation at least makes sense. No such possibility is visible in the case of the phenomenal consciousness involved in seeing red; for seeing red does not have a functionalist analysis (sometimes the inverted spectrum hypothesis is invoked in support of this claim: see §44). Therefore physicalism is inadequate because it cannot give the right sort of explanation of consciousness.

Finally, let us briefly recapitulate the knowledge argument. The idea is, remember, that someone could have complete knowledge of the physics, physiology, and psychology of colour vision, but not know what it is like to see red. Therefore this person comes to know something new when they see red for the first time, and therefore there is something to know which is not a physical fact. So not all facts are physical facts: facts about what it is like to be in certain conscious states are not.

Notice that at no point do these arguments make use of the concept of qualia in the sense in which I am using this term. I described all three arguments without talking about qualia. All I assumed was phenomenal consciousness: the zombie argument asks us to imagine a physically identical creature without phenomenal consciousness, the explanatory gap argument asks us about the explanatory relation between brain states and phenomenal consciousness, and the knowledge argument assumes that there is such a thing as knowing what it is like to be in a certain kind of phenomenally conscious state. There is no need to mention qualia in the sense in which they were dismissed above. So the intentionalist's dismissal of qualia cannot help in addressing these arguments. Intentionalism gives no extra comfort to physicalism. (If all one means by 'qualia' is *phenomenal consciousness*, then that's fine; but this is equally irrelevant since no one will deny qualia in this sense.)

Here we have three arguments, then, purporting to show how consciousness is the source of a problem for physicalism. Despite the similarities in the arguments, they involve some very different claims and assumptions. In the next three sections I will examine the arguments, in what I consider to be the ascending order of plausibility.

27. The explanatory gap

It is fairly obvious that there is an explanatory gap, in the sense that not very much is currently known of a systematic nature about how the brain causes, sustains, or constitutes states of consciousness. This much is common ground. But the explanatory gap argument claims further that no matter what we found out about the causation of states of consciousness, this would not close the explanatory gap. In fact, it could be true that all mental states are physical states and yet physicalism would still not be established. Why? Because physicalism must not only 'provide a physical description for mental states and properties but also . . . provide an *explanation* of those states and properties'—in Levine's words. This looks like a version of the doctrine of the explanatory adequacy of physics, which in §12 I claimed physicalists ought to reject as excessively ambitious. It seems possible that one could hold that all entities are physical, or exhaustively determined by physical entities, and that every event has a physical cause which is enough to bring it about—*without* holding that there can (even in principle) be an explanation of phenomenal consciousness in physical terms. In fact, this is the position championed by Colin McGinn.[36] McGinn is inspired by Nagel's belief that we must believe that physicalism is true, but there is a sense in which we cannot understand *how* it can be true. Levine and other proponents of the explanatory gap argument think this is an unhappy resting-place. They say that physicalism is unsuccessful until it has *explained* phenomenal consciousness. Assuming that an unsuccessful theory can hardly be a true one, then the conclusion is that physicalism cannot be true if it cannot explain consciousness.

As I said in §12, I think this requirement on physicalism is too strong (even speaking as a non-physicalist). To see why, let us return to the motivation for physicalism: the problem of mental causation (§13). The clearest and simplest physicalist solution to that problem, I claimed, is to identify mental and physical causes. Suppose one made such an identification of a mental property M with a physical property P: M = P. Does this identity claim need to be explained? But how can one explain an identity claim? How can one *explain* the claim that Cicero = Tully? One can explain how one person came to have two names, but having done that there is nothing left to do. Similarly, one can explain perhaps how mental state M came to be called 'M' and how P came to be called 'P'; but what more is to be explained if M really is the same entity as P?[37]

However, even if physics *did* have to be explanatorily adequate (as well as ontologically and causally adequate) it is not clear that the possibility of a physical explanation of consciousness must be as bad as Levine thinks—if, that is, we take the word 'explanation' in its normal sense. For in its normal sense, one may have explained the presence of a certain sensation, say, when one has located its causes in the body and the brain. And nothing in the explanatory gap argument says that we cannot find the causes of conscious phenomena. But this is not the sense of explanation they have in mind. For Levine, 'explanation is supposed to involve a deductive relation between explanans and explanandum'.[38] One has an explanation of P when one can deduce P from a statement of the explanans. Causal explanation is not explanation in this sense—unless every causal explanation is nomological (invokes laws) and determinism were true. But plainly not every causal explanation is nomological, so causal explanation is not the kind of explanation Levine has in mind.

The relevant kind of explanation is where one can deduce the nature of the explanandum from information about the explanans—as when one can supposedly deduce the knowledge that water is a liquid from information about its molecular structure.[39] If two propositions are deductively related then this is a necessary relation; but there is no such necessary relation between any true propositions about the brain and propositions about phenomenal consciousness. How do we know this? Because the truth of any set of physical propositions about a creature is compatible with the absence of phenomenal consciousness in that creature. And how do we know *that*? Essentially, because we can imagine it. So this particular part of the explanatory gap argument rests on something very like the zombie hypothesis.

So there are three assumptions underlying the explanatory gap argument: first, that physicalism entails that physics must be explanatorily adequate, not just ontologically and causally adequate; second, that explanation in the relevant sense must be deductive, and therefore a necessary relation; and third, that zombies are metaphysically possible.[40] The first two assumptions are either very strong claims, or they are uninteresting stipulations about the meanings of the terms 'physicalism' and 'explanation'. Taking physicalism as the view which I described and motivated in §12, it seems to me that there is no reason why a physicalist should accept these stipulations. The zombie hypothesis will be examined in §29 below, after we have tackled the notorious knowledge argument.

28. The knowledge argument examined

The knowledge argument rests on much less controversial assumptions than the other two arguments. These are the premises and the conclusion of the argument:

(1) Mary knows all the physical facts about seeing red without ever having seen red. (This is the black-and-white room thought experiment.)
(2) Mary comes to know something new when she sees red for the first time.
(3) Therefore: not all facts are physical facts.

The argument as presented relies on the idea of a *physical fact*. Both 'physical' and 'fact' need clarification.

First, 'physical'. What we are asked to imagine is that the knowledge which one acquires about colours inside Jackson's black-and-white room is stated in the language of physics. But it would not help Mary if she learned things in the room which were in the language of psychology and physiology. Nor would it help her if she learned a fully developed dualist psychology (if there were such a thing), talking about states of consciousness while explicitly acknowledging their utterly non-physical nature. None of these theories would help tell her what it is like to see red. The point is not that the kind of knowledge she gains in the black-and-white room is physical knowledge; rather, the point is that it is the sort of knowledge that can be stated in some form or another. (It's 'book-learning'.) As David Lewis puts it, the 'intuitive starting point wasn't just that *physics* lessons couldn't help the inexperienced to know what it is like. It was that *lessons* couldn't help.'[41]

So although physicalism—the view that all facts are physical facts—is one of the targets of the argument, it is really an instance of a more general target: the view that all knowledge of the world is the kind that can be imparted in lessons, without presupposing any particular kind of experience. Thus if emergentism (§18) were committed to this view of knowledge, then it too would come within the knowledge argument's range. Likewise with Cartesian dualism—one could not know what it is like to see red, the argument says, even if one learned the complete Cartesian theory of the mind. So in the discussion below, bear in mind that when I say 'physical' I also include all these other kinds of knowledge.

Second, 'fact'. Philosophers disagree both over the nature of facts, and over whether there are such things. Some say that facts are true propositions, others that they correspond one-to-one with true propositions, and others say that they are what make true propositions true (they are 'truth-makers').[42] I shall not enter these debates here: all the knowledge argument needs to mean by 'fact' is: *object of propositional knowledge*—where a state of propositional knowledge is one described in claims of the form 'X knows that p' where X is a knower and 'p' is replaced by a sentence. So for something to be a new fact is for it to be a new piece of knowledge, an advance in someone's knowledge, some piece of knowledge that they did not have before. This might seem to be a fairly commonsensical idea; but as we shall see below, it has been regarded as problematic.

The validity of the argument has been challenged, as has the truth of the argument's premises.[43] Those who challenge the argument's validity normally claim that it involves an equivocation on 'know'. In the first premise, 'know' is used to express propositional knowledge, but (they say) in the second premise it is used to express knowledge-how or ability knowledge. We should agree that Mary learns something new, but what she learns when she first sees red is how to recognize red, to imagine red, and remember experiences of red things.[44] Having seen something red, she can now recognize the colour of fire engines, she can consider whether she wants to paint her bedroom red, and she can remember this decisive encounter with a tomato. These are cognitive abilities, not pieces of propositional knowledge, and it is a widely held view that there is no reduction of ability knowledge to propositional knowledge. So Mary can learn something new—in the sense of gaining an ability—but it is not a new piece of propositional knowledge. Knowing what it is like to see red is know-how. So the knowledge argument is invalid because it involves a fallacy of equivocation: 'know' means something different in the two premises. Since it is only in the case of propositional knowledge that the objects of knowledge are facts—if I know how to ride a bicycle, *how to ride a bicycle* is not a fact—it is concluded that Mary does not come to know any new facts and physicalism is saved.

This response, known as 'the Ability Hypothesis', presupposes two things: first, that knowledge-how or ability knowledge is completely different from, and irreducible to, propositional knowledge; and second, that regardless of the abilities she acquires, Mary does not come to know any new propositions whatsoever. The first claim is a general theoretical claim about the relation between know-how and propositional knowledge. The second claim is one about the specific case of Mary and the room. Both claims are questionable.

The first claim is questionable because the frequently invoked distinction between propositional knowledge and know-how has never been satisfactorily articulated. Certainly there are abilities; and there are states of propositional knowledge. But why suppose that having an ability is never a state of propositional knowledge, or that having some propositional knowledge is never an ability? The reason cannot be found in our ordinary ways of ascribing knowledge. There are plenty of cases in which we describe people as knowing how to do something, where that knowledge can also be expressed—without remainder, as it were—in propositional terms. Someone who knows how to get to the Albert Hall from Paddington Station might know, among other propositions, that the Albert Hall is ten minutes walk from Kensington High Street tube station, that this station is on the same underground line as Paddington, and so on. There is no reason to suppose that anything is left out when one has stated all the propositions the person knows.

To repeat: I am not denying that there is such a thing as ability knowledge. But if ability knowledge is what is expressed when we say someone knows how to do something, then nothing rules this out from being propositional knowledge too. As A. W. Moore says,

The thesis that some knowledge is non-representational cannot be proved just by appeal to the fact that people know how to do things. It is absurd to suppose that knowledge how to spell 'comma', for instance, is non-representational, or indeed anything other than knowledge that it is spelt 'c', 'o', double 'm', 'a'.[45]

The relevance of this to the knowledge argument is as follows: unless it can be shown that an ability is never a state of propositional knowledge, then the Ability Hypothesis fails. For unless this were so, then for all the Ability Hypothesis says, Mary's abilities to recognize, imagine, and remember red things could also be states of propositional knowledge.

But (more importantly) even if it *could* be shown that states of ability knowledge are never states of propositional knowledge—say, for example, that one's knowledge of how to ride a bicycle is not a state of propositional knowledge—it is still not obvious that in the story as described, Mary learns no new propositional knowledge. The second claim described above is dubious too. This claim is dubious because there is a very natural way for Mary to express her knowledge of what it is like to see red: 'Aha! Red looks like this!'. (Let's suppose that Mary knows that tomatoes are red, and she knows that she is seeing a tomato; these are innocuous assumptions.) Now 'Red looks like this' is an indicative sentence; in a given context, it surely expresses a proposition; and in the context described, the proposition is true. (It could have been false. Suppose Mary were shown a joke tomato, painted blue; the proposition expressed by 'Red looks like this' would be false; red doesn't look like that.) And it is a proposition that Mary did not know before. So *even if* Mary did acquire lots of know-how, and *even if* know-how is essentially different from propositional knowledge, then there is still something that she learns which she couldn't have known before. And that is enough for the argument to succeed.

Further support for the view that there is a proposition which is learned is provided by Brian Loar's observation that someone can reason using the sentence 'Red looks like this': they could say, 'If red looks like this, then either it looks like this to dogs or it doesn't'. On the face of it, this is a conditional of the form 'If P then Q'; the substituends for P and Q are bearers of truth-values and therefore possible objects of propositional knowledge.[46] The Ability Hypothesis has a lot of explaining away to do to support its conclusion that nothing propositional is learned.

I therefore reject the Ability Hypothesis; the argument is valid. But what about the premises? Few physicalists wish to challenge the first premise, that in the story as told, Mary knows all the physical facts about colour vision (with 'physical' and 'fact' understood as above).[47] For suppose a physicalist did deny this. Then they would have to accept that there are some physical *facts* which in principle cannot be known without having certain experiences. It may be true that having knowledge in general requires having experiences of some kind. Yet how can physicalism, which bases its epistemological outlook on physical science, allow that science must require us to have certain *specific* experiences? The suggestion has little plausibility.

Most responses to the argument have challenged the second premise instead, and claimed that Mary does not learn any new fact. What is rather going on is that she apprehends or encounters in a new way something she already knew. One way to understand this takes 'new way' to mean a new Fregean mode of presentation of the objects and properties already known. On this interpretation, the puzzle about the argument is of a piece with other puzzles about intensionality (§4). Vladimir might know that Hesperus shines in the evening but not know that Phosphorus shines in the evening. We do not conclude from this that Hesperus is not Phosphorus since, as is well known, 'X knows that p' is not an extensional context. (Cf. the famous 'masked man' fallacy: 'I know my father; I do not know this masked man; therefore this masked man is not my father.') On this view, the fact that Hesperus shines in the evening is the same fact as the fact that Phosphorus shines in the evening—after all, they are the same star, the same shining, the same evening! So although Mary knows that red looks like this, this is not a new fact that she has learned but, analogously, a new mode of presentation of a fact she knew before.

But which fact is this? We need to identify something which can be referred to in more than one way, the relevant fact concerning which can be learned about in the black-and-white room. One way of putting it might be like this. When she leaves the black-and-white room, Mary judges that seeing red is like *this*. The physicalist says that seeing red is being in brain state B, so let's suppose Mary knew this in the black-and-white room. Mary can therefore infer that being in brain state B is like this. We therefore have two terms, 'seeing red', 'being in brain state B', which pick out the same thing, and a predicate 'like this' which can only be fully understood when one is having the experience. But nonetheless, the experience is the brain state.

Furthermore, one might be sceptical on independent grounds about whether there is a *fact* corresponding to the proposition that *red looks like this*, on the grounds that there are not indexical or demonstrative facts in addition to what make indexical and demonstrative statements true. Suppose, for example, Vladimir is lost in the forest; he consults his compass and a map and remarks with relief 'I am here!', pointing to a place on the map. Surely, the fact that he is expressing here is not different from the fact that Vladimir is on the bridge on the bend of the river, even if he uses different words to express this fact? Given that Vladimir is on the bridge at the bend of the river, how can there be a further 'here'-fact on top of this?[48] There are no indexical facts; just indexical sentences which are made true by non-indexical facts. So perhaps the same kind of thing could be said about Mary's knowledge that red looks like *this*?

There is an important truth in this point which I will deal with shortly. But it is important to repeat the point that no substantive notion of fact was assumed in setting up the knowledge argument. 'Fact' simply means *object of knowledge*. So if Vladimir has learned something new in the forest, he has learned a new fact by definition. One might want to say that this notion of fact is not relevant to physicalism, but then one needs to provide an account of facts and knowledge of them. In fact, this is not necessary, for this whole line of response is flawed, as I shall now explain.

The distinction between different modes of presentation of the same thing is supposed to show that the second premise of the argument is false: Mary does not learn anything new. But it cannot show this. For if this construal of Mary's case and the case of Hesperus and Phosphorus are really parallel, then this entails that someone who comes to believe that Phosphorus shines in the evening because of their belief that Hesperus is Phosphorus does not learn anything new, but only comes to appreciate a previously known fact under a new mode of presentation. And this cannot be right: the original point of the distinction between sense and reference was to do justice to the fact that the discovery that Hesperus is Phosphorus can be a significant advance in someone's knowledge. It was a *discovery* about the heavens that Hesperus is Phosphorus, it was a new piece of knowledge that the Ancients gained. So, similarly, the knowledge that Phosphorus shines in the evening is a new piece of knowledge. Given that all the knowledge argument means by 'fact' is *object of knowledge*, then the normal approach to the distinction must say that what the Ancient astronomers learned when they learned that Hesperus is Phosphorus is a new fact.

Of course, there is *something* which is the same before and after the discovery: how things are in the world, the reference of the terms, the entities. No one disputes this. There is a sense of 'fact' according to which 'Hesperus shines in the evening' and 'Phosphorus shines in the evening' express the same fact, to be sure. But the relevant question is whether anything is learned when someone learns that Hesperus is Phosphorus, whether there is any new knowledge at all. This is very hard to deny—at the very least, there is new knowledge that two modes of presentation are modes of presentation of the same thing.

It would be fruitless for the physicalist to try and draw some principled difference between the Mary case and the case of Hesperus and Phosphorus (after all, they introduced the parallel!). So either physicalism says that nothing new is learned in either case—which is a hopeless thing to say—or it says that something is learned in both cases. This is the only plausible thing to say. But then Mary does learn something new, the argument's premises are true, and we already decided it was valid. So is physicalism refuted?

According to the knowledge argument's conception of physicalism, the answer has to be *yes*. Remember that the argument takes physicalism to be the view that all facts are physical. Given what is meant by 'fact', this means that all propositional knowledge is physical. And given what is meant by 'physical', this means that all knowledge is the kind of knowledge which can be learned inside a scenario like the black-and-white room—that is, without having to have any particular kind of experience.

But why should physicalism have to say that all *knowledge* is physical in this sense? Indeed, why should physicalism be a thesis about knowledge at all? As we introduced it in §12, physicalism is a view about what there is, and its strongest defence derives from the fact that it explains mental causation. To be the kind of view which will do this, physicalism, I claimed, must be at least committed to the causal completeness of physics. But it need not be committed to the explanatory completeness of physics. And it need not be committed to the view that all knowledge must be expressible without the expresser having to have any particular experiences. Physicalism does not need to say that physics must state all the facts. (The idea that it *must* may derive from the image of the book of the world, with all the ultimate truths written down in the one true story of reality. But the image is misleading; if what I say here is right, there could never be such a book.)

The analogy with indexical knowledge introduced above can help make this point clear. When Vladimir exclaims 'I am here!' pointing at the map, this is something he learned. He now knows where he is, and he didn't before. In a classic paper, John Perry describes himself following a trail of sugar around a supermarket, intending to tell the shopper from whom it came that he was making a mess.[49] When Perry realized that *he* was making a mess he learned something, that he expresses by saying 'It's me! I am making a mess!' And this piece of knowledge is distinct from the knowledge he would express by saying 'The shopper with the leaking sugar bag is making a mess'.

Both examples of new pieces of knowledge require one to have a certain position in the world: Vladimir and Perry cannot learn what they learn without occupying certain positions, or being the person that they are. But it is plain that this is compatible with every object and property involved in these stories being physical, in the sense of §12. The fact that these pieces of knowledge are only available from certain perspectives does not entail that there are some further non-physical entities involved in the these situations. To appreciate this point, we do not need to enter the debate about the nature of facts or decide how to 'individuate propositions'.[50] All we need is to recognize that there is knowledge which can only be had from certain points of view. This knowledge will not be physical knowledge in the knowledge argument's sense. So, surprising as it may seem, a physicalist can sensibly deny that all knowledge is physical knowledge.[51]

It turns out, then, that the knowledge argument, though valid, has the same weakness as the explanatory gap argument: both arguments define physicalism in what are ultimately epistemological terms. The explanatory gap argument assumes that physicalism must be capable of giving physicalist explanations of everything, while the knowledge argument assumes that physicalism must say that all knowledge is physical. A number of writers have drawn attention to this feature of the arguments.[52] But they have not located the problem in the definition of physicalism; doing so shows why a physicalist need not be worried by the arguments. So long as a physicalist does not hold that all knowledge is physical, or that physics must be explanatorily adequate, then these arguments pose no problem.

29. Zombies

But the zombie argument is different. Although the argument uses an epistemological premise—the premise about how we know what is possible—physicalism itself is defined purely in metaphysical terms. Physicalism, for this argument, is just the claim that the physical metaphysically determines the mental—either because mental phenomena are physical, or because the mental necessarily supervenes upon the physical. This is a purely metaphysical conception of physicalism, and what is more, it is the most widely accepted conception these days.[53]

The zombie argument is simple in structure, so all the interest is in the premises:

(1) Zombies are conceivable.
(2) If zombies are conceivable, then zombies are metaphysically possible.
(3) If zombies are metaphysically possible, then physicalism is false.
(4) Therefore: physicalism is false.

The argument is plainly valid. So what about the premises? Premise (3) we shall take as unexceptional: the clearest versions of physicalism outlined in Chapter 2 are identity theories, and identity is a necessary relation; but even if one thought of physicalism in terms of determination or supervenience, these relations would have to be metaphysically necessary if they are to be used in formulating physicalism. The existence of zombies would be a clear counter-example to this metaphysical determination. So premise (3) stands.

Premise (1) is also fairly uncontroversial, with one clarification. What we are supposing to be absent in the zombie's mind is just phenomenal conscious-ness. Sometimes it is said that zombies have the usual array of intentional states, including perceptions, but no qualia. Even from a weak intentionalist perspective, this is hard to make sense of. It's as if one started off by imagining a perceptual awareness of the world, and subtracted something, which left the intentional representation of the world intact but without the consciousness. But anyone who agrees with the claim made above that purely intentional states can be phenomenally conscious will not be able to imagine a zombie in this sense. Does this mean that the zombie hypothesis is incoherent?

No. For the hypothesis needs to appeal only to the absence of phenomenal consciousness. There are different theories of what phenomenal conscious-ness consists in—some think it involves awareness of qualia, others think it is intentional—but that is a different question. Whatever the correct account of phenomenal consciousness is, all premise (1) requires is that one can conceive of a physical replica of any phenomenally conscious creature which lacks it. This is clearly conceivable.

All the controversy about the zombie argument, then, resides in premise (2): what is conceivable is possible. This claim is certainly controversial, partly because it is widely held that questions about conceivability are questions about what *a priori* possibilities our concepts allow, but questions about possibility are questions about how modal reality is—which possible worlds there are. Therefore there can be situations which are in some sense conceiv-able but not truly possible. (And conversely, situations which are possible but not conceivable; but these need not concern us here.) For example: it might be said that one could conceive of a situation where water is not H_2O, but what one is conceiving is impossible because water is necessarily H_2O. An analogous claim in response to the case of the zombie hypothesis would be to say that zombies may be conceivable, but this doesn't mean they are possible, since the relationship between mind and body may be, contrary to appearances, necessary.

But this response to the hypothesis is inadequate, for reasons which Kripke famously made clear. One explains away what one is conceiving when one conceives that water is not H_2O by saying that one is conceiving of something which only *seems* like water but isn't. But when one imagines the zombie, one cannot be imagining something for which it only *seems* like it lacks the feeling of pain (say), but really it is in pain: for anything which is really in pain can never seem to lack the feeling of pain![54] This is because anything which is pain feels like pain, so we cannot imagine or conceive of something that is really pain but does not feel like it. But we can conceive of the zombie not being in pain; this can't just be a matter of it *seeming* lack the feeling of pain. But it is physically identical to me when I am in pain. So physicalism is false.

The argument is familiar, and has been debated in great detail by many.[55] There are many ways to respond, but it seems to me that none of the responses are adequate. Physicalism fails as a theory of consciousness. Since we have already rejected physicalism as a theory of mental causation (§§18–19) this should not be a great surprise. I will end this chapter with some remarks about how to fit consciousness into the emergentist framework I prefer.

30. The prospects for explaining consciousness

The three anti-physicalist arguments have a common assumption: that there is no *conceptual* or *analytic* connection between the concepts of consciousness and the physical/non-mental concepts in terms of which consciousness is being explained/reduced.[56] If there were such a connection, then it would not be possible to imagine a phenomenal zombie, any more than it would be possible to imagine an unmarried bachelor. And clearly, if there were a conceptual connection between the functional states of the brain and any given state of consciousness—for example, if one could give a conceptual analysis of seeing red in terms of its functional role—then there would not be an explanatory gap. And if there were a conceptual connection between the physical truths and the mental truths, then it would possible for someone in Jackson's black-and-white room to learn all the physical facts and then simply infer knowledge of what the mental facts are like. This lack of a conceptual connection is what fuels all the thought-experiments mentioned; to deny it is an uphill struggle, which would require explaining all the thought-experiments away.[57]

If the connection between consciousness and the brain is not a conceptual necessity, and it is not a Kripkean *a posteriori* necessity, then what is the nature of the connection? The answer suggested by emergentism is that it is a natural, lawlike (nomological) connection. Consciousness (and the mental generally) supervenes upon the physical state of the brain. This supervenience is contingent. The mental is distinct from the physical but nomologically supervenes on it. The alternative to this is to hold that this supervenience holds as a matter of metaphysical necessity. But if the zombie argument is sound, this view should be rejected.

4

Thought

31. Thoughts and beliefs

The term 'thought' can be used to apply to particular acts of thinking, or to the intentional content of such acts. So two people can 'have the same thought' in the sense of instantiating the same intentional property, or performing the same mental act (mode plus content), or they can 'have the same thought' in the sense of standing in some intentional relation (mode) to the same content (e.g. a proposition). For example: two people could be wondering whether it will rain, and in that sense have the same thought; alternatively, we could call the proposition they are wondering about *the thought that it will rain*. This second way of talking about thoughts is perhaps more of a philosophical use of language—Frege called the content of a judgement a *Gedanke*, translated as 'thought'[1]—though it has a natural enough everyday use in sentences like 'the thought that some people are naturally more intelligent than others has been debated throughout history'. This latter usage corresponds to an ordinary use of 'idea': one can have an idea, just as one has a thought. Two people can have the same idea in the sense of thinking about something in the same way, or in the sense of having the same attitude to the same content.

If we are not to confuse all these notions, we need to impose some terminological clarifications. So: I will use the term 'idea' generally to mean content of an intentional state or act, bearing in mind, as always, that this need not be a proposition (that is, a candidate for evaluation as true or false). And since I have reserved the term 'content' for *what is thought* in acts of thinking (*mutatis mutandis* for other intentional states), I will generally use the term 'thought' for acts of thinking (using 'act' in the technical way specified in §10).

In recent philosophy less attention has been paid to the concept of thought as such. More attention has been paid to the *propositional attitudes*: belief, desire, hope, and the rest. Part of this chapter will be about the propositional attitudes, but I think that we have not completed our inventory of intentional states if we focus only on the attitudes. I reject, therefore, something I call the *Propositional Attitude Thesis*: the thesis that all intentional states are propositional attitudes. One reason for this rejection emerged in Chapter 3: conscious sensations are intentional but they are not propositional attitudes. But the category of *thought* needs to be included in our inventory too, since, as we shall see, not all thoughts are propositional attitudes.

Thoughts are mental acts, in the terminology introduced in §10, but not all thoughts involve the same intentional modes. Wondering is a kind of thinking, imagining is too, and so is considering something. So a case of *thinking about something* may be a case of considering it, or contemplating it, or imagining it. The concept of *thinking*, then, seems to be a *determinable* concept, of which considering, wondering, and so on are *determinates*.[2] A paradigmatic determinable concept is the concept of being coloured. Something cannot be coloured without being a particular colour, and cannot be that particular colour without being a particular shade of colour. Yet *being red* should not be analysed into *being coloured* plus something else, in the way that *being square* can be analysed as *being quadrilateral* plus *being equilateral and equiangular*. Being red is rather a way of being coloured. So if the concept of thought is a determinable concept, we should say that wondering, contemplating and so on are ways of thinking.

We need to distinguish between thoughts and beliefs. Although the expression 'I think ... ' can be used to express what one believes, this does not mean that 'thought' is just another term for belief. Wondering is not a way of believing, nor is imagining or considering. One can wonder whether *p* is true, and this is a matter of being undecided as to whether to believe it. But there is a deeper difference: thoughts and beliefs belong to different metaphysical categories. Thoughts are mental acts (and therefore events), whereas beliefs are dispositions, and therefore states. This ontological difference is the clue to an important thesis about belief, which I shall now defend: there is no such thing, strictly speaking, as a conscious belief.[3] This thesis runs counter to an orthodox view about belief, according to which some beliefs are conscious and some are not. But once the right distinctions have been made, the thesis should be quite unexceptional. I will start with some truisms about belief.

Belief is a state: it is a property instantiated by a believer. It is not an event: it is not something which *happens* or has temporal parts (see §10 for this distinction). Belief is the paradigm propositional attitude. Beliefs are commonly attributed in sentences of the form 'S believes that p' where p is a sentence and S a term for the believer. The sentence which, together with the complementizer 'that', forms the so-called 'that-clause', is normally assessable as true or false; in other words, it expresses a proposition. What is distinctive of the intentional mode *belief* (the attitude) is a certain kind of commitment to the truth of this proposition. This commitment is sometimes called 'holding true': to believe something is to hold it to be true or to take it to be true. This is little more than a synonym for 'belief', but nonetheless it turns out that belief's relation to truth is the key to its nature, as we shall see.

Two mental acts which bear a close relation to belief are judgement and assertion. Judgement is the formation of belief.[4] Not all beliefs need be the products of judgements—some beliefs are the relatively automatic products of perception, some may be the products of unconscious inference, and some may be innate. All these possibilities of belief without judgement make sense. We might say that judgement stands to belief as decision stands to intention: decision is a mental act which is the formation of an intention. Assertion is the linguistic expression of a belief, and is also a mental act.

The relation between belief, assertion, and truth is what lies behind the phenomenon known as 'Moore's paradox'.[5] G. E. Moore was interested in sentences of the form, 'I believe that p, but not-p'. This is not a paradox in the strict sense of the word (i.e. an unacceptable conclusion drawn by apparently sound reasoning from apparently true premises). And what it expresses is not necessarily a contradiction: if some proposition p that I believe is false—as some surely are—then it is true of me that I believe that p, but (in fact) p is not the case. However, the interesting thing is that, if I am rational, I would never *say* anything of this form; although such a sentence could be true, I would never rationally be in a position to assert it. Whatever the ultimate explanation of this phenomenon, it must appeal at least to the fact that assertion is the expression of belief. In asserting that not-p, I am *expressing* my belief that not-p, and this conflicts with my assertion that I believe that p.

Notice that this is not the case with the other attitudes. There is nothing wrong with saying 'I want it to be the case that p, but not-p'. Indeed, it could be said to be necessarily true of wants that a rational person would judge what is wanted not to be the case. What is distinctive of belief, though, is that it 'aims' at truth, in the sense that the truth of a belief one holds cannot be an independent question for one—independent, that is, of whether one believes it. Someone who wonders whether a particular belief of theirs is true is *ipso facto* wondering whether to hold on to that belief.[6]

Now assertion is one kind of mental act in the technical sense, and it is also an action—in the non-technical sense that it is something under the control of the will. But belief has an intimate relation to all rational actions, not just assertion. What an agent does is partly a result of what they believe, what they want, and what they intend. When a person acts, they are trying to achieve some end or goal, however modest. But in order to do this, they must make assumptions about how the world is. Those who are rational do not try to achieve their goals if they think that, because of the way the world is, they are unlikely to achieve them. So an agent's beliefs have an impact on which of their goals they try to achieve; indeed, they also have an impact on what the agent's goals are.

I will express this familiar thought by saying that beliefs have *actual and potential consequences*. Nothing could be a belief that does not have the actual or potential consequences of belief. However, it is important to emphasize, if it is not obvious already, that I do not mean by this that there is any one particular consequence associated with a given belief. There can be no such thing. The consequences of a belief are its consequences *given* other states of mind, especially desires.[7]

The idea that belief has these kinds of relations to desire and action is an idea which is associated with the functionalist theory of mind. The functionalist theory of mind says that mental states are individuated by their causal roles, that is, their distinctive patterns of causal relations to other mental states, and to actions.[8] But as I have described it, the idea is independent of the functionalist thesis, for two reasons: first, functionalism typically attempts a *reductive definition* of mentalistic notions, and second, functionalism sees the mind as a *causal* mechanism; neither idea is essentially contained in the idea that what people do is the result of what they believe and what they want.

Now, for beliefs to have the actual and potential consequences they do, it is not necessary that everything that you believe should be in your conscious mind, in the stream of consciousness. Of course not. In fact, it makes little sense to suppose that everything you believe—everything you take to be true—could be in your stream of consciousness. But nor do the beliefs that are currently guiding your action at the moment need to be in your stream of consciousness. This suggests that, for belief to play this action-guiding role, it need not be conscious at all. But it is sometimes said that there is a distinction between 'dispositional beliefs' and 'occurrent beliefs', where occurrent beliefs are the beliefs which are in your consciousness at a given moment. Since occurrences are events, this would suggest that some beliefs (the occurrent, conscious ones) are mental acts or events, and some (the non-conscious ones) are mental states. There would therefore be two kinds of belief: the state kind and the event kind. That there are belief states should not be doubted; but are there are also conscious belief-events?

32. Consciousness and belief

It might seem obvious that there are. Consider a conscious process of reasoning, where one draws a conclusion from premises one believes. Coming to a conclusion, we may suppose, is an event—a judgement—but when one has come to a conclusion, the conclusion can then be in your conscious mind. This is something you believe, it is an event in consciousness—so it might seem that this is a conscious belief-event. However, a little reflection shows that this is not right. For we need to distinguish between *being conscious of what you believe*, and *consciously believing*. The latter is what we are supposed to be looking for, but so far, it is not obvious that we have yet discovered anything other than the former.

To see this, consider those intentional phenomena which can, it seems, be both states and events. Worry is an example. Suppose you are worried about your finances. This can be a general state that you are in, which manifests itself in various actions and reactions of yours: caution when spending money, frustration when shopping, moments of irritation in the presence of profligate friends, and so on. In this sense, your worry about your finances is a state you are in, which has various manifestations or consequences. But there is also the phenomenon of consciously worrying about your finances—an episode in your mental life, an event. This is something which takes time, which is something you can be said to *do*: worrying in this sense is something which can be described in an answer to the question, 'what are you doing?' or 'what are you thinking about?' You can answer, 'I've been worrying about my finances for the last half hour'. 'Worry about your finances' can therefore name a state, but it can also name a conscious event.

Contrast belief. When one draws the conclusion of an inference, or when one tries to figure out what one believes on some topic, then one is *conscious of believing p*, or *conscious that one believes p*. But this is not the same as *consciously believing p*, in the same way that one could be consciously worrying about something. For consciously worrying is not the same as being conscious *that* one is worrying. One could become conscious that one is worried about one's finances by discovering something about one's behaviour, say; and one could do this without undergoing the kinds of inner events which constitute conscious worrying. Similarly, then, one could become conscious that one believes something, without consciously believing it. So we can make sense of the idea of being conscious that one believes something without this involving an appeal to a conscious belief-event.

On reflection, the idea of such an event is actually rather hard to understand. Remember that one sign that worry can be an event was that one could say 'I have been worrying about X for the last half hour' or 'I worried about X for a few hours last night, then I was distracted by the television'. But it makes little sense to say 'I have been believing p all morning'; or 'I believed p for a few hours last night and then I was distracted by the television'. This is good evidence about the nature of the phenomenon under consideration. For, given what was said above about the consequences involved in believing something, it is not really surprising that a single event could not have the consequences of believing something. An event could be an event of worrying, though, even if it disappeared after a while. Worry can be short-lived, and disappear for no reason; belief cannot.

This point is connected to the common idea that belief has 'no phenomenology'; there is nothing it is like to believe something. Scepticism about the phenomenology of belief sometimes arises from the plausible thought that even if belief has a phenomenal character, its phenomenal character cannot individuate belief. For things seeming to be a certain way, perceptually or not, can often be insufficient for believing that things are that way. And one can believe something unconsciously; that is, without things seeming any way at all.

This is sometimes given as a reason for thinking that phenomenology is irrelevant to intentionality in general. The idea is that, even if intentional states do have phenomenological features, these are not essential to their individuation. For example, Braddon-Mitchell and Jackson make the following claim about desire: 'The desire for food based on the belief that you will die unless you eat is exactly the same *desire* as the desire for food based on pangs of hunger. The desire *per se* has no special feel or phenomenology.'[9] But whatever is the case about desire, it would be premature to draw the conclusion that phenomenology is irrelevant to intentionality in general. For these considerations only show that *belief and desire states* have no phenomenal character; they do not show that no intentional states or acts have phenomenal character. And it is clear that this conclusion cannot be true in general; since, as we have already seen, it is undeniable that perceptual experiences have phenomenal character (their intentionality will be further discussed in Chapter 5). So, for all these considerations show, there could be other kinds of intentional mental event or act—and in particular, other kinds of thought—which do have phenomenal character. The conclusion that thoughts lack phenomenal character is premature.

I have said that we should distinguish being conscious of what one believes from consciously believing. What is it, though, to be conscious of one's beliefs? One must, of course, be conscious of the propositional content of the belief, but this is not sufficient. For in most cases, one can consciously consider a proposition, or 'entertain' it, whether or not one believes it. The exceptions are when merely reflecting on some proposition is enough to make one believe it: for example, 'I exist' or 'I am here now'. But, in all the other cases, we can ask: what needs to be added to one's consciousness of the content of one's belief, to make a case where one is conscious of the belief? Does one have to be conscious *that one believes* the proposition too? Of course, one can ask oneself about one's own belief that p, 'do I really believe p?' But, as Gareth Evans has argued, answering this question is normally carried out by the same procedures which one would put in place by asking oneself whether 'p' is true:

In making a self-ascription of belief, one's eyes are, so to speak, or occasionally literally, directed outward—upon the world. If someone asks me 'Do you think there is going to be a third world war?', I must attend, in answering him, to precisely the same outward phenomena as I would attend to if I were answering the question, 'Will there be a third world war?'. I get myself in a position to answer the question whether I believe that *p* by putting into operation whatever procedure I have for answering the question whether *p*.[10]

If I want to find out whether I believe that p, then all I *need* to do is to attempt to answer the question whether p. In other words, being conscious that one believes that p need involve no more than being conscious that p. But then we must conclude that being conscious *that* p is distinct from being conscious *of* p; one could be conscious of p when one is considering or wondering whether p. But one could not be conscious *that* p if one were merely considering it.

The conclusion I draw is that, although there is such a thing as being conscious of one's belief, that does not mean that there is such a thing as consciously believing. 'Occurrent belief' is a myth. But there is such a thing as occurrent thinking; or, in other words, thinking is an occurrence or an event. But what kind of event? In particular, are all episodes of thinking propositional attitudes? To answer these questions, we need to look more closely at the idea of a propositional attitude.

33. Propositional attitudes

Bertrand Russell invented the term 'propositional attitude' for those states which can be ascribed in sentences of the form 'S øs that p', where S is a subject, ø a psychological verb, and p a sentence.[11] In my terminology, a propositional attitude is an intentional state or event whose intentional content is assessable as true or false. (Some propositional attitudes are states, some are events: the belief that p is a state, while noticing that p is an event.) In the next section I will examine the propositional attitude thesis, the thesis that all intentional states are propositional attitudes. Before examining this thesis, we should clarify the idea of a propositional attitude.

First, something about propositions. This will lead us back into the difficult area of *intensionality* discussed in §4. 'Proposition' is a technical term, or a term of art, whose main theoretical role is to be that which is expressed by a statement, an utterance of a declarative or fact-stating sentence, and what is believed or held to be true. When we say that two people make the same statement, or that they believe the same thing, the proposition is what is stated or believed. And when a belief or a statement is true or false, this is because the proposition believed or the proposition expressed in the statement is true or false. This is what is meant by saying that propositions are susceptible of 'non-derivative' classification as true or false: the possession of truth-values does not derive from the possession of truth-value by something else.[12]

Now some philosophers have argued that certain linguistic contexts create 'truth-value gaps', where a sentence apparently appropriate for the expression of a proposition says something which is neither true nor false. Statements which contain names which have no reference, for example, have been said to give rise to truth-value gaps. So have borderline uses of vague terms. Suppose we accept this thesis. Do such sentences fail to express propositions, or is it rather that not all propositions are capable of being true or false? If we say the former, then we need another notion other than *proposition* to express the sense in which someone who asserts such a sentence *says something*—someone might utter some words and in doing so make a claim about the world, but the claim is neither true nor false. The person has not said nothing, has not spoken nonsense, so we need some 'proposition-like' notion to describe the kind of thing that they have said. If one were to accept truth-value gaps, then, there is a certain simplicity in saying the second thing instead: the person did express a proposition, but not all propositions have truth-values. If one said this, then one would need another way of saying what all the contents of propositional attitudes have in common, other than that they are all either true or false. One possible approach is to say that a proposition is what is expressed in a complete indicative sentence. Then we need an account of what makes a sentence indicative, which does not rest on the idea of its being (or expressing something) true or false. Another, more metaphysical, approach is to say that all propositions purport to represent facts or *states of affairs*, where a state of affairs is something (or things) having a property (or properties) at a time (or during a period of time). Then we have to explain states of affairs independently of the idea of propositions being either or true or false.[13]

So long as the basic idea of a proposition can be understood without having to be committed to the idea that all propositions are either true or false, then we need not be concerned here with the idea of truth-value gaps. I will put the idea to one side. What is more important for our purposes is the *constituent structure* of propositions. This connects with our earlier discussion of intensionality in §4.

Standard semantic treatments of propositional attitude sentences (including sentences of the form 'S says that p') take their logical form to express a relation between the subject of the attitude and a proposition.[14] But there is a fundamental disagreement over whether propositions should be individuated simply in terms of the objects and properties on which their truth depends, or whether the individuation should take into account the *ways* in which those objects and properties are represented by the subject of the attitude. The first approach is often called the Russellian (or neo-Russellian) approach, the second is known as the Fregean. As noted in §6, Frege thought that a correct semantics should attribute *sense* to words as well as *reference* (when they have reference). For a Fregean, a propositional attitude ascription like 'Vladimir believes that the Pope is infallible' relates Vladimir to a proposition whose constituents are senses, modes of presentation of worldly referents. The proposition (or in Frege's terminology *Gedanke/*'thought') that the Pope is infallible is therefore a different proposition from the proposition that John XXIII is infallible, just in case 'the Pope' and 'John XXIII' differ in sense. This is because senses are distinguished by a principle of cognitive significance: if it can be informative for a rational thinker who understands the words 'A' and 'B' to learn that A = B, or if it is possible for such a rational thinker to doubt that A = B, then 'A' and 'B' have different senses.

The Russellian, by contrast, would say that if A = B, then sentences of the form 'A is F' and 'B is F' express the same proposition. The driving force behind these Russellian theories is based on two very plausible (even undeniable) ideas: first, that whether what is expressed by a sentence is true depends on whether things are as the sentence says they are. Whether 'A is F' is true depends simply upon whether A is F. Second, that the contribution made by a word to the truth-conditions of a complex sentence must be same as the contribution it makes to the truth-conditions of a simple sentence which is embedded in the complex. So since the contribution made by 'A' to the truth-conditions of 'A is F' is the same as the contribution made by 'B' when A = B, so the contribution made by 'A' and 'B' must be the same in the complex sentences 'Vladimir believes that A is F' and 'Vladimir believes that B is F'.

This is not true on the Fregean approach. On the Fregean approach, the contribution made by a part of a sentence to the truth-value of the sentence containing a propositional attitude verb depends on the sense of that part of the sentence. So 'Vladimir believes that the Pope is infallible' may differ in truth-value from 'Vladimir believes that John XXIII is infallible' if the words 'John XXIII' and 'the Pope' differ in sense. For the Fregean, it is not just the ordinary references of terms (say, as they occur in simple, non-propositional attitude sentences) which determine the truth-conditions of a propositional attitude sentence. This means that Fregeans have a more complex task ahead of them to explain the *compositionality* of propositional attitude sentences: how the truth-conditions of such sentences depend on the meaning or significance of their parts.

(A variant on the Russellian approach is to treat propositions as sets of possible worlds. The proposition expressed by sentence 'S' is the set of all those worlds in which 'S' is true. So if there is a possible world in which A is F but B is not, then the two sentences 'A is F' and 'B is F' express different propositions; if there is not, then they do not. This does not significantly alter the landscape.)

The Russellian derives a conception of propositions from the requirements on compositionality, but then has difficulty explaining our intuitions about propositional attitudes. What I mean by this is that the Russellian has to say that if A = B, and Vladimir believes that A is F, then it follows that he believes that B is F, even if he sincerely denies this. Applied to Frege's famous example, then, it turns out that the ancient astronomers who would have been reluctant to affirm that Hesperus shines in the morning *did* nonetheless believe it—

since Hesperus is Phosphorus, and they believed that Phosphorus shines in the morning.[15]

Whatever merits the Russellian theory has for displaying the semantic structure of certain attitude attributions, it is fairly clear that if the notion of a proposition is going to be used in a theory of intentionality such as the one I am proposing here, then the Russellian theory cannot be the fundamental theory. This is because intentional states have aspectual shape (§6). The theory of sense is an attempt to express how aspectual shape is involved in propositional attitudes. This is not to deny that Russellian propositions may be useful for certain kinds of attributions of attitudes (for more on attitude attributions, see §35). There may be contexts when it is right to express certain similarities and differences between mental states by appealing to Russellian propositions. But this cannot be the right method in general. For Russellian propositions are extensional, while Fregean propositions are intensional. And, as I claimed in §6, when ascriptions of mental states are intensional, this is a reflection of, or an expression of, their intentionality. So an ascription of a propositional attitude which attempts to capture the subject's point of view must be an ascription of an attitude with a Fregean content.

The approach of this book requires that, if they are to capture the essential aspects of intentionality, propositions must be individuated in the Fregean style. What about attitudes to propositions? Anything which it makes sense to insert into the ø place in the schema 'S øs that p' is an attitude to a proposition; so 'thinks', 'hopes', 'believes', 'wishes', and so on are all attitudes. There are other cases where the natural schema is slightly different, but coming from the same corner, so to speak: ' . . . wonders whether p', ' . . . speculates whether p', and ' . . . considers whether p' are examples. Indeed, these might be the same example underneath—I do not take a stand here on the question of which propositional attitudes are reducible to (or paraphrasable in terms of) others.[16]

Sometimes talk of the propositional attitudes is abbreviated to talk of 'beliefs and desires'; but reflection shows that desire is a little harder to fit into our schema. 'Vladimir desires that he will swim the Channel' is perfectly grammatical, but 'Vladimir wants to swim the Channel' is more idiomatic. However, 'to swim the Channel' does not express a proposition, and nor do many of the complements which we find it most natural to put after verbs of desire: Vladimir wants *a bottle of wine* or he wants *world peace*. Swimming the Channel is an event, a bottle of wine is an object, and world peace is presumably a state of affairs. It is a relatively simple matter to formulate a proposition corresponding to each of these things Vladimir wants: 'he swims the Channel', 'he has a bottle of wine', 'world peace exists'. For the moment, we will assume that such paraphrases are adequate and always available; given the existence of such a paraphrase, desire is a propositional attitude. (Or, to put it more pessimistically: to the extent that such a paraphrase is possible, desire should be thought of as a propositional attitude.)

How should the attitudes be distinguished from one another? The familiar proposal I shall endorse here is that the difference is, broadly speaking, functional or dispositional. That is, the attitudes differ in the different relations, or potential (dispositional) connections, in which they stand to one another. We have already seen that beliefs and desires have a special relation to action: one does what one does because of what one wants and how one takes the world to be. So if you believed that this was a bottle of wine in front of you, and you wanted a bottle of wine, and you did not believe that there was any obstacle to getting this bottle of wine, then this would lead you to act so as to get yourself this bottle of wine. (Functionalists will say that 'lead you' must mean 'cause you', and I agree—but as I said above, the mere idea of these relations between the attitudes does not entail this further thesis.) The different attitudes, then, may be individuated by how they relate to and depend on one another: if one hopes that p, then one desires that p, and one believes that at this moment not-p.

34. The propositional attitude thesis

The propositional attitude thesis says that all intentional states (or acts) are propositional attitudes. In §6 I argued that it is not essential to the idea of intentional content that it be propositional. But this is consistent with all intentional states being, as a matter of fact, propositional attitudes. However, we came across some counter-examples to this thesis in §24: there I argued that bodily sensations involve directedness upon an object, without being propositional attitudes. But the intentionality of sensation is controversial; can we make a strong case against the propositional attitude thesis without assuming it? Can the thesis be undermined on less controversial grounds?

The obvious, uncontroversial counter-examples to the thesis come from the apparently object-directed emotions, most obviously love and hate. (There are other clear examples too, like worship; but I shall here focus on love and hate.) Loving a place or person or thing is most naturally understood as being a relation between the lover and the thing loved. Hate likewise. These states of mind are patently intentional: they have intentional objects and they involve intentional modes. But their contents are not propositional, and they are not reported in the 'S øs that p' style.

What should defenders of the propositional attitude thesis say about these examples? They could always deny the existence of the phenomena of love and hate, of course; but this is surely a desperate path to take, simply to defend a philosophical thesis. Love and hate (and their milder variants, affection, fond-ness, distaste, and irritation—all object-directed) seem to be fundamental elements of normal mental lives. What merit can there be in a theory which denies these apparently patent phenomena simply to preserve a theory?

Defenders of the thesis may instead deny the existence of love and hate on the grounds that these concepts are vague, or that their identity conditions are unclear. But it is not obvious why this point, even if it were true, should tell particularly against these object-directed states, and not against all intentional states, and particularly the propositional attitudes. It can often seem to be vague whether someone really desires something, in exactly the same ways in which it is vague whether someone loves someone; the problems here seem to be with vague concepts, not with love and hate. Furthermore, questions can be raised for believers in propositional attitudes about how to distinguish or count beliefs and desires, about how many beliefs there are. If there is a problem with the identity conditions for states of love and hate then similar problems could presumably be raised for beliefs and desires. (So, if it is obvi-ous to you that love doesn't 'really exist', then ask yourself whether it is so obvious that desire 'really exists'.) The right approach, it seems to me, is not to follow Quine and reject the reality of the attitudes as well, but rather to try to find the clearest description of the phenomena as they strike us.

An alternative approach is to give a *reduction* of love and hate: an account which gives necessary and sufficient conditions for all truths of the form 'A loves B' and 'A hates B' in terms of propositional attitude ascriptions of the 'A øs that p' style in a way which preserves the content of the original truths. Attempts to do this have been without success, and it is hard to see where one should begin in attempting it. However, perhaps reductive translation is not necessary. A weaker approach would be to say that statements about love and hate, although not translatable into propositional attitude formulations, are nonetheless made true by the existence of propositional attitudes. So it can be literally true that A loves B, but the only facts that are needed to *make* this true are facts about the beliefs and desires of the lover.

This claim might just amount to the idea that the truth of ascriptions of love and hate supervenes on the truth of ascriptions of belief. But by itself this does not show that love and hate are 'really just' propositional attitudes, any more than the supervenience of the mental on the physical shows that the mental is 'really just' the physical (see §18). So, if there are such phenomena as love and hate, then they may supervene on beliefs and desires or they may not. Why should this show anything about the propositional attitude thesis? On the other hand, if there are no such phenomena, then the approach is simply a variant of the eliminative approach which I have just dismissed. So the appeal to supervenience is either irrelevant or simply a version of eliminativism about love and hate.

We have considered three approaches to the apparently object-directed emotions which may be made by a defender of the propositional attitude thesis: elimination, reduction, and supervenience. Elimination is no more plausible for the object-directed emotions than it is for other intentional states; no plausible reduction has ever been proposed; and the supervenience approach is either a version of elimination or its truth is not relevant to the propositional attitude thesis. Given the failure of these attempts to defend the thesis, and the apparent phenomenological facts, the question arises as to why anyone should have believed the propositional attitude thesis in the first place.

One possibility is that defenders of the thesis were thinking of intentionality purely in terms of the role of intentional states in explaining and rationalizing behaviour. In order to explain a piece of behaviour, one needs to cite only beliefs and desires of the agent, and since the only functional or causal role for intentional states is in rationalizing and causing behaviour, the only intentional states one needs to cite are the beliefs and the desires of agents. Anything else should be explained away or reduced to beliefs and desires (plus, maybe, some other propositional attitudes).

But two premises of this argument are mistaken. First, it is not right to think of intentionality purely in terms of the explanation of behaviour. We also have to understand the subject's *point of view*, and often our understanding of this is not formed just by how the subject's point of view figures in understanding their behaviour. Second, it is not true that the only states which one needs to appeal to in explaining behaviour are the propositional attitudes. Once we are freed from the paradigm of the propositional attitude thesis, then it is easy to see that one may explain why someone behaved in a certain way towards a particular person because they hated them. Love, hate, and the other object-directed attitudes have as much of a role in explaining behaviour as the propositional attitudes.

35. *De re* and *de dicto* attitudes

Thoughts and the propositional attitudes are in many ways the paradigmatic intentional states. My purpose in this chapter is not, of course, to defend the intentionality of thought—that idea would hardly be necessary, given what I mean by 'intentionality'—but to clarify it. So far I have distinguished thoughts from beliefs; I have argued that beliefs are never conscious, but one can be conscious of one's beliefs; and I have rejected the propositional attitude thesis. We now need to look more closely at the nature of the intentionality of thought belief, and other attitudes.

The essential features of intentionality are directedness and aspectual shape. The aspectual shape of the propositional attitudes is well expressed by individuating the propositional contents of the attitudes in the Fregean style, in terms of the mode of presentation of the intentional objects. In the case of thoughts which are not propositional attitudes, the aspectual shape of a thought could also be captured in a somewhat similar style, in terms of the potential informativeness of propositions containing the sub-propositional content constituents. The directedness of a thought consists in the fact that it has an intentional object, in the sense of 'object' introduced in §5. But it is consistent with all this to say that intentionality can be ascribed in a transparent style, as when we say that Oedipus wanted to marry his mother. This ascription of desire is surely true—even though Oedipus would not have put it this way himself (even if he had spoken English). The ascription of an intentional state, as we learned in §§5–6, *can* be extensional; the point I tried to defend in §§5–6 is that when ascriptions are *intensional*, this is an expression of their intentionality.

It is crucial, therefore, to distinguish between the content of someone's intentional states and the conditions for, and circumstances of, the *ascription* of those states. Of course these issues are related; but nonetheless they must be clearly distinguished. We cannot say that the only way to *ascribe* a thought is in the intensional manner, or that thoughts should *never* be ascribed extensionally. Since our practice of ascribing thoughts involves both intensional and extensional ascriptions, there is no reason to reject one for the other, and a theory of the ascription of intentionality must make room for both.[17] (So, in particular, it must make room for both Russellian and Fregean propositions.) But taking this liberal view of ascription of thought is consistent with taking a more stringent view on the contents of intentional states: what is actually going on in a thinker's mind. So this distinction enables me to say that it can be true that Oedipus wanted to marry his mother, even though no such thought was going through his mind.

One way to express this conclusion is to say that the existence of *de re* ascriptions of thoughts and attitudes does not entail the existence of *de re* intentional states. The term *de re* is usually contrasted with the term *de dicto*, and we may explain the contrast with reference to belief in the following way (applying this contrast to other attitudes is then straightforward).

In many cases, we ascribe beliefs to thinkers by following the name or a description of the thinker with 'that' followed by a complete indicative sentence (this is the so-called 'that-clause'). So we might say,

(1) Oedipus believes that the old man in the road is a nuisance.

Here the sentence relates Oedipus to the proposition expressed by the sentence 'the old man in the road is a nuisance'. This kind of belief-ascription is called *de dicto*; we could think of this label as a shorthand for the idea that the ascription is relating Oedipus to what is expressed by a saying, a *dictum*. These ascriptions, *de dicto* ascriptions, are the familiar and (I shall argue) the fundamental form of belief ascriptions.

But we also ascribe beliefs in another kind of way. Imagine yourself to be in the situation where you are assessing Oedipus's situation from the outside, and you say:

(2) That old man in the road: Oedipus believes he is a nuisance.

Here the ascription relates Oedipus not to a complete proposition or *dictum* ('he is a nuisance' does not as such express something true or false). Rather, what one is doing, it seems, is relating Oedipus to a thing (the old man) and something predicated of him (being a nuisance). It is because such ascriptions relate a thinker to a thing (*res*) that *de re* is a good term for them; they have also been called 'relational' belief ascriptions.[18] And since these ascriptions postulate a relation between a thinker to the object thought about, they are extensional in both senses described in §4. From (2), we can infer:

(3) There is someone whom Oedipus believes is a nuisance.

(After all, why should any ascriber use the expression 'that old man' unless he thought there was an old man?) And if the old man is Oedipus's father, then if (2) is true, so is this:

(4) That old man, Oedipus's father: Oedipus believes he is a nuisance.

And for this to be true, Oedipus does not have to know or believe that the old man is his father. So *de re* or relational ascriptions license existential generalization and allow substitution of co-referring singular terms. So when we say that Oedipus wanted to marry his mother, this is similarly a *de re* ascription; we might put it rather cumbersomely as follows:

(5) Concerning Jocasta, Oedipus's mother: Oedipus wanted to marry her.

While the corresponding *de dicto* ascription is not something we would say, if we want to express what is really in Oedipus's conscious mind (let's ignore controversial ideas about the unconscious for the time being):

(6) Oedipus wanted it to be the case that he marry his mother.

Saying this amounts to saying that Oedipus would give an affirmative answer to the question, 'do you want to marry your mother?' And this is clearly not what we mean when we say that it is true that Oedipus wanted to marry his mother.

As anyone with the slightest acquaintance with this area will know, the ascription of beliefs and the other attitudes is a complex subject, involving many difficult and subtle questions which need not concern us here. Our main theme is the psychological reality of the states and events ascribed. How does the *de re/de dicto* distinction relate to this question? Some philosophers have claimed that 'belief' is ambiguous; or, what amounts to the same thing, that there are two kinds of belief, *de re* belief and *de dicto* belief.[19] But it is important to emphasize that this does not follow from what we have said so far; other assumptions would be needed to draw this conclusion. All that we have established is that there are ways of ascribing or attributing beliefs which relate the believer to the object of belief, creating an extensional context. But it is consistent with this to say that the belief which is ascribed is nonetheless a relation to a complete and Fregean proposition. The fundamental reason for maintaining this derives from the conviction that, in any state of mind, its intentional object is presented (thought about, desired, etc.) under some aspects, to the exclusion of others. So a full description of such a state must attempt to capture these aspects.

In defence of this way of reading the *de re/de dicto* distinction, we can note that a central feature of *de re* ascriptions is that the object of a *de re* belief ascription is mentioned *outside* the scope of the 'believes . . .' clause. Certain kinds of *de re* ascription may have the following form:

There is an object *x*, such that *x* = a, and S believes of *x* that it is F.

And here the variable '*x*' is bound by the quantifier outside the scope of 'believes . . .', and 'a' is a name for *x* which may or may not be a name which S knows. Since the ascriber mentions *x* outside the scope of the psychological verb, they are entitled to give it whatever names they like. The natural metaphysical picture of what is going on, then, is that someone is reporting someone else's state of mind, from the outside, by relating them to the object they are thinking of, maybe by describing that object in a way that the other person would not accept or recognize. But this does not mean that there are *de re* relational beliefs, a distinct kind of state of mind from *de dicto* beliefs.

36. Internalism and externalism

So the idea that there are *de re* ascriptions of thoughts and attitudes does not imply that there are *de re* intentional states and acts, which necessarily involve relations to real existing objects. That was one of the morals of the previous section. But this talk of intentionality involving relations to real existing objects will recall our earlier discussion in §7 about whether intentional states (and acts) are *broad* or *narrow*. An intentional state is broad only if its existence entails the real existence of its intentional object, narrow when it doesn't. We cannot infer the existence of broad intentional states, then, from the existence of *de re* ascriptions of such states; so what other reasons could be given for believing in the broadness of the intentional?

This is a question which has been the subject of intense debate over the past twenty-five years, the debate between *internalists* and *externalists* about mental content. My own sympathies in this debate are with internalism; but I cannot hope to settle this huge debate in the short space of this chapter. Instead my task in the next few sections of this chapter will be a more modest one: to establish the *coherence* of internalist intentionality. I will not argue here that intentionality *must* be understood in an internalist way, only that it *can* be.

Initially, one might think that internalist intentionality is an essentially more problematic idea than externalist intentionality. For externalists typically say that thoughts come to be about their objects by being related to them, causally or otherwise. This is the way in which they typically understand the idea that thoughts are *individuated in terms of* the objects and properties in the world that they are about: it is the existence and identity of the objects and properties thought about that determine the existence and identity of the thought. Put this way, it can seem that externalism about thoughts is inescapable. For how could there be a thought which was not individuated in terms of its objects? If there were such a thing, then surely it would lack any intentionality and would scarcely deserve the name *thought*.

However, this line of thought is mistaken. For what it ignores is that the idea that thoughts are individuated in terms of the things they are about *is just the idea of intentionality*. This was the heart of the idea of intentionality before the doctrine of externalism was invented. So externalists cannot lay any special claim to this idea. Internalists too can say that narrow thoughts are individuated in terms of the objects they are about; but they will have to deny that this 'individuation' is a relation. This is because they hold that certain of one's thoughts could be the same even if their objects did not exist. That is to say, internalism is a thesis about the identity conditions of thoughts and other intentional phenomena across possible worlds or counterfactual situations: it says that a thought about X would be the same state or act of mind even if X did not exist. Normally, an internalist will hold that many or most of the objects one thinks about actually exist. Of course: internalists are not committed to saying that there is no world outside our ideas! What they say is that a thought would remain the same even in possible worlds where its objects did not exist.

So it is a mistake for externalists to think that only they are entitled to say that thoughts are individuated by what they are about. Internalists just need to make sense of the idea that 'individuate' can be used in an essentially non-relational way. This is the difficult task which lies ahead of internalists.

In order to show how there can be such a thing as internalist intentionality, internalists invite us to reflect on the case of thought about the non-existent (see §7). Externalists might reply that thought about the non-existent is necessarily an exception: the normal situation must be thought about actual existing entities. This is surely correct; but the internalist's point was not that most objects of thought do not exist, only that by paying attention to these cases, we can understand how there can be such a thing as intentionality without a real existing object.[20]

To develop their case, internalists can appeal to the idea that the 'real structure' of the content of thoughts might not be what it initially seems to be. An traditional way to do this has been to appeal to Russell's *theory of descriptions*, according to which the logical form of sentences containing definite descriptions is that of a quantified sentence: a sentence 'The F is G' is to be understood as having the form 'There is exactly one F which is G'. Since the meaning of the sentence is the proposition it expresses, we can extrapolate to the propositional content of thought, and say that when someone (say) believes a proposition which they might express by saying 'The F is G', the proposition believed is really a quantified proposition to the effect that there is exactly one F which is G.[21] In the case of thought, we do not distinguish between its surface form and its real form, as we do with language; rather, we distinguish between the surface form of the expression of a thought, and the proposition which is the thought's content. Of course, it may be that the words used for the expression of the thought 'run through your mind'—so you might consciously say to yourself 'the pineapple in the fridge must be rotten by now', and yet according to Russell, the propositional content of your thought is that there is exactly one pineapple in the fridge and it must be rotten by now. However, it is not essential to the application of Russell's theory to states of mind that this distinction can be made; for the application is supposed to apply to beliefs too, and to believe that p it is not necessary that any sentence (or anything else) runs through your mind (see §32).

The point is rather about the truth-conditions of the belief, under what circumstances the belief is true or false. The appeal of Russell's theory for internalists is that it makes good sense of many kinds of thought or belief about the non-existent. Russell showed how his theory managed to give truth-conditions to statements containing non-referring descriptions, as in the famous example, 'The present king of France is bald'. Here the meaningfulness of this sentence does not depend on whether the expression 'the present King of France' has a reference; only the truth of the sentence depends on this. In defending the theory of descriptions, Quine writes:

It is awkward, in general, to let questions of meaningfulness or meaninglessness rest upon casual matters of fact which are not open to any systematic and conclusive method of decision. We may never know whether Jones loves none, one or many; and it is best not to have to wait for that information in order to decide whether to accord the expression '$(\imath x)$(Jones loves x)' a place in our language. The truth or falsehood of expressions must indeed wait, in general, upon inquiries which lack any systematic and conclusive technique; but the meaningfulness of an expression—the eligibility of an expression to occur in statements at all, true or false—is a matter over which we can profitably maintain control.[22]

The same applies to the truth-conditions of the belief: equipped with Russell's theory of descriptions, we can say that a belief that the present King of France is bald is true just in case there is exactly one bald King of France, and false otherwise. In a world like this one where France is no longer a monarchy, the belief is false, but it is still thinkable: the existence of the *belief* does not depend on the existence of the king. Nor does it depend on the reality of a non-existent king, or a 'subsistent' king, whatever that might be (see §7). John McDowell puts this point well, when he says that

the point of the theory of descriptions is exactly to avoid an apparent need for nonexistent real objects as relata for intellectual acts. Where a relational conception of intellectual acts would require them to stand in relations to possibly non-existent objects, Russell instead takes their content to include *specifications* of objects. If no objects answer to the specifications, that does not threaten the contentfulness of the acts.[23]

The theory of descriptions thus provides us with a model for internalist intentionality, in the sense that it clearly describes cases where the 'thinkability' of a belief about a particular object—the availability of its propositional content—does not depend on the existence of a specific object, and therefore does not entail a relation to that object. Rather, the content of a Russellian descriptive belief specifies the conditions that the intentional object must meet in order for the proposition to be true. When there is no such object, then the proposition is false. In these cases, as McDowell puts it, 'an illusion of a relation to an ordinary real object does the work that seemed to require an actual relation to a merely subsistent object'.[24] An illusion of a *relation*, not an illusion of *content*: that is exactly the idea behind internalist intentionality. And this is how an internalist can say that such a belief is 'about' the present King of France, since the king is the intentional object of the thought, even though there is no such thing. The internalist assumes that 'X is about Y' does not express a relation either.

It might be objected that Russell's theory is not properly internalistic, since a specification of the existential propositions involved will inevitably include reference to *properties* and *relations* (e.g. being king, being bald), and unless these references can be paraphrased away, the thoughts end up involving relations to properties rather than objects.

There are a number of things that an internalist could say to this, ranging from a less committed response to a more committed response. The less committed response would be to say that the appeal to the theory of descriptions was only intended to make room for the internalist conception of thought or belief about *particular objects* (or particulars in general). Someone could be an internalist about thought about particulars but not about properties. Such a view would say that none of our thought is constitutively dependent on any particular *object* in our environment, but it is nonetheless dependent on the existence of certain properties.

The more committed response would be to say that, just as terms for particulars can fail to refer, so can terms for properties: there can be empty property terms.[25] One way, though not the only way, to treat such terms is to think of reference of predicates being explained in terms of an interconnected network of predicates that form a theoretical structure. These predicates can then be replaced by variables which can in turn be bound by quantifiers, in the style of the Ramsey–Carnap–Lewis method for the definition of theoretical terms.[26] In this way, the predicates of the theory can still be meaningful even if there are no properties corresponding to the predicates. We can leave this well-known sort of approach here, since it may be granted that there is some internalist intentionality, but there are more fundamental forms of intentionality which cannot be given any internalist treatment at all.

37. **The argument for externalism**

Nonetheless, to say that we can make sense of internalist intentionality is not yet to say very much. For externalists do not have to argue that internalism is so superficially incoherent; and typically they do not. Rather, they typically employ a form of argument, invented by Hilary Putnam, which has become known as the Twin Earth argument.[27] The Twin Earth argument aims to show that the content of a thought or attitude is not determined by, or does not supervene on, the intrinsic properties of the body or brain of thinkers; or, as it is sometimes put, that the content of thought is not 'in the head'. If thoughts and attitudes are individuated by their contents, then they too are not in the head. Thoughts are not in the head, according to externalists, because they are partly constituted by the objects and properties they are about.

These kinds of argument usually involve a thought-experiment in which two physical duplicates ('Twins') occupy environments which are different in some significant respect. For example, we can imagine an environment just like this one, except for the fact that the stuff which fills the lakes and rivers is not our water, that is, H_2O, but some other chemical substance, whose chemical formula we can call XYZ. This is Twin Earth. Now suppose that each of the Twins says to themselves, 'water, water everywhere, nor any drop to drink!' Assume that neither Twin knows of the difference between H_2O and XYZ. It is then argued that the Twins are talking about different things when they use the word 'water' and that they are therefore thinking different thoughts. But since they are physical duplicates, this difference in their thoughts cannot consist in any difference in their internal physical (or psychological) structure, since these are the same. So they have different thoughts even though their heads are the same; so their thoughts cannot be in their heads.

This striking argument has been through many versions, and has been challenged in many different ways. As Putnam presented it, it was tied up with views about linguistic meaning and natural kinds which are not relevant to the lesson of the argument for externalism.[28] There are also a number of hidden assumptions in the argument, which need to be made explicit. But it is nonetheless a straightforward matter to strip the argument down to its essence.[29] Assume the coherence of the Twin Earth story, and argue as follows:

(1) The content of a thought determines what the thought is about/what it refers to.
(2) The Twins are referring to different things when they use the word 'water'.
(3) Therefore their thoughts have different contents. (This follows from (1) and (2): if A determines B then a difference in B implies a difference in A.)
(4) Therefore the Twins are thinking different thoughts, since thoughts are individuated by their contents.
(5) Since the Twins are physical duplicates, but differ in their thoughts, their thoughts are not determined by the physical nature of their bodies and heads.
(6) Therefore their thoughts are not 'in their heads'.

So where are their thoughts, if not in the head? The normal externalist answer is that the actual objects thought about are partly constitutive of the thoughts in question. The real objects thought about partly constitute a subject's thought.

So an internalist conception of intentionality has to do more than assert that Twins are psychological or intentional duplicates; it has to answer the Twin Earth argument. The argument as presented above is valid; the question then is whether the premises are true. It seems to me that there are only two plausible places for an internalist to challenge the premises. Internalists could deny premise (2), that the Twins are thinking about/referring to different things; or they could deny premise (1), that the content of a thought determines what it refers to/what it is about.

The first option might look plausible when we are considering the particular example Putnam uses: water. For after all, what is wrong with saying that the Twins are talking about the same thing, water, since they do not know the difference between XYZ and H_2O, and why can't there be two kinds of water? In many cases, our words for natural kinds or substances pick out kinds of things which can differ in various superficially undetectable ways—to use another example of Putnam's, our word 'jade' picks out two distinct substances, jadeite and nephrite. The natural thing to say here is that there are two kinds of jade. Why shouldn't we say the same about water? Indeed, we talk of heavy water (D_2O) as water, and there seems no non-stipulative reason not to do so. At the very least, it can be argued that our intuitive linguistic judgements do not settle the question of whether XYZ is water; if, for example, it were discovered that what we pre-theoretically regard as water had many different underlying microstructures, maybe three or four, maybe more, what should we conclude? That only one of them is water (say, the one we first interacted with)? Or that they are all kinds of water? Or that there is no such thing as water? It is implausible to suppose that our linguistic practices must dictate an answer *a priori*, so that we already know *now* what we would say about this case. So why should we so willingly accept that the stuff which on Twin Earth they call 'water' is not water? Why not say that H_2O and XYZ are both water, and say that the Twins have a single, common concept, which they express with the word 'water'? That would enable internalists to short-circuit the Twin Earth argument by characterizing the sense in which the Twins share mental states.

But plausible as this may be in certain cases, this 'common concept strategy' cannot work in general. For to show that it works in general, the internalist would have to show that there *could not* be a case where everything seems the same to the Twin subjects, and yet the things referred to in the thoughts of each Twin are different. And it seems impossible to show this.[30] For since we recognize that the underlying reality of something can be something above and beyond its perceptual appearance, externalism only needs a case where an aspect of the reality of something is stipulated to be something hidden from the way it appears to the Twins. The externalist point can be made particularly vividly where thought about particular objects is involved. I may be thinking about Vladimir, and my Twin is thinking about Twin-Vladimir. Vladimir and Twin-Vladimir are different people. But they are qualitatively indistinguishable, in the sense that if I were confronted with Twin-Vladimir, I would not be able to tell him apart from Vladimir. The argument above applies just as much to the case of thoughts about Vladimir as it does to Putnam's example of water. All the externalist needs to do is to give an example where some kind of thing can have a qualitatively indistinguishable doppelgänger which differs from the original thing in some essential way, and run the Twin Earth argument with that. How could an internalist establish that there could *not* be such a case?

So, even if it is a plausible thing to say in certain cases, the common concept strategy cannot be used by internalists across the board. If they are going to undermine the Twin Earth argument, then, the internalists must therefore deny premise (1) of the Twin Earth argument. Let us call premise (1) the *Content Determines Reference* principle. Is it plausible to deny this principle?

The first thing to notice is that the Content Determines Reference principle is a relatively theoretical assumption, not something (like the point just discussed, concerning the availability of doppelgängers in general) which falls out of our ordinary way of thinking about the world. The idea behind the Content Determines Reference principle is that the content of a thought 'reaches out' to its reference, in the sense that, if the reference had been different, so would the content. The content of the thought that Vladimir is hungry concerns Vladimir, and there is, as it were, enough in the content itself to fix that this is so. The idea is a version of Frege's idea that sense determines reference. In Fregean terms, since sense is a mode of presentation of reference, grasping a sense is a way of putting you in touch with a reference. Less metaphorically: sense is tied to reference, in the sense that different reference means different sense.

But can this principle be true in general—true, that is, for all kinds of thought? The case of indexical thoughts—thoughts expressed using indexical pronouns such as 'I', 'here', and 'now'—suggests not. For in these cases, it is at the very least not obvious that the content of the thoughts, in the sense of what is grasped when one understands the expression of the thought, is what alone determines their references. Suppose two people, Alice and Bob, in two distinct places, think to themselves *it's really hot in here*. According to the Content Determines Reference principle, the *here* component of their thought must be different in content, since it differs in reference. But what could this difference in content amount to? Both Alice and Bob are thinking about where they are in the 'here' way; so isn't there a case for saying that their thoughts have the *same* content, even if their *here* thought-components refer to a different place? If one holds on to the Content Determines Reference principle, one has to say that their *here* thought-components have different contents. But this is somewhat implausible; for while there is obviously a difference between these thoughts—Alice and Bob are thinking about different places—there is equally obviously a similarity. Should we say that the content is different or the same?

In one sense, this is a purely terminological question about how to use the word 'content'. Should we say that Alice's and Bob's thoughts differ in content, or that they share content? In one way, it doesn't matter; 'content' is a quasi-technical term which we can use how we like, so long as we are consistent and clear in our usage. But in another way, it does matter. For we have admitted that Alice's and Bob's thoughts are similar in the sense that they are thinking about where they are in the same kind of way. And the idea of thinking of something in a certain kind of way ties up with our earlier discussion (§6) of content as the aspectual shape of an intentional state or act. Given that there is this plausible sense of content—the *way something is being thought about*—in which Alice's and Bob's thoughts share content, then the

Content Determines Reference principle begins to lose any general applicability that it may have had. For consider: to maintain that the Content Determines Reference principle applies to indexical thoughts, one would have to maintain that whenever two thinkers are thinking about a different place, person, or time, in an indexical way, then these thoughts differ in their contents. But if this is the only notion of content we are allowed to have, then we are not allowed to say that all 'here'-thinkers or 'now'-thinkers have any aspect of the content of their thought in common. And this is implausible.

If the Content Determines Reference principle does not apply in certain cases, then there is room for the internalist to say that it does not apply in the Twin Earth argument. For remember that this principle played a role in that argument by supporting the step that if the Twins are thinking about different things, their thoughts have different contents. The case of indexicals shows that this is not a generally valid move for all plausible uses of the word 'content'. So it is open to the internalist to say that this is not valid in the Twin Earth case too: the internalist can say that Twins' thoughts do share content, even though they differ in reference (H_2O and XYZ). What is needed, according to the internalist, is a modification of the Content Determines Reference principle: content determines reference, *relative to a context*. Twins' thoughts share content, but because they are in different contexts, they differ in reference.[31] This is not an *ad hoc* principle, since we need it in the case of indexicals too. The content of the thought expressed by 'It's hot here' determines the reference of 'here' only when situated in its context, the place of thought or utterance.

The defender of the Content Determines Reference principle may admit that in the indexical case, there is a notion of content according to which Alice and Bob's thoughts have the same content. This is certainly the right thing to say; but notice that saying it seriously weakens the application of the principle in the Twin Earth argument. For unless the defenders of the principle can show why the Twin Earth case is significantly different from the indexical case, then they are forced to admit in addition that there is a notion of content according to which Twins' thoughts have the same contents too. And if this is admitted, then the conclusion of the Twin Earth argument seems to be that, *in one sense of thought*, the Twins' thoughts are not in their heads, but *in another sense* the Twins' thoughts are in their heads. If this is the situation, then the debate can start about which sense of 'thought' or 'content' is the best one, and for what purposes. The Twin Earth argument, on this reading, is not a knock-down argument against internalism; it just introduces us to the idea of broad or externalist states, via the unrestricted Content Determines Reference principle. If we reject the general applicability of this principle, then we do not yet have a reason to accept the general truth of externalism.

The intentional states shared by Twins are called 'narrow states' (§7). The content of these states can then be called 'narrow content'; but it is important to realize that this is not supposed to be a peculiar or novel kind of content, a strange kind of content that is all 'in the head' or 'lacking full-blooded intentionality' or 'inexpressible'. Narrow content is just what thoughts share when we abstract from the features of context which the Twin Earth argument asks us to consider as relevant (e.g. the difference between XYZ and H₂O). As such, it is not more peculiar than the content which Alice and Bob's thoughts share.

The upshot, then, is this. The Twin Earth argument does not refute internalism, since it depends on the Content Determines Reference principle, which internalists can legitimately reject. The rejection of this principle is not *ad hoc*, but has an independently motivation in the case of indexical thoughts. The principle should be modified: content determines reference relative to a context. However, just as the Twin Earth argument does not show that there cannot be narrow intentional states, the response to the argument does not show that there cannot be broad intentional states. There may be other reasons for believing in broad states; the next section will consider some.

38. Demonstrative thought

As I noted in §7, someone could think that the intentionality of certain thoughts is internalistic, while that of others is not. In particular, they might claim that *descriptive* thought and belief (thought expressed in terms of descriptions, expressions of the form 'the F') is internalistic, but that thoughts characteristically expressed in terms of *demonstrative* expressions ('that' or 'that F') cannot be. As in the previous section, my aim here is not to try to settle this debate, but just to indicate why an internalist conception of these kinds of thoughts cannot be ruled out at the outset.

Consider the case of perceptual demonstrative thought. These are thoughts or judgements whose canonical expression is in terms of a demonstrative pronoun, 'this' or 'that', used to refer to some object in the perceived environment. (I shall talk generally about thoughts, though I mean this to include judgements.) So, for example, one might express one's thought that a certain perceived pineapple is rotting by saying 'that pineapple is rotting'. It is generally agreed that such demonstrative thoughts are irreducible to purely descriptive thoughts; that is, there cannot be a purely descriptive (and hence, following Russell, quantificational) thought which has the same content as the thought just mentioned. No thought to the effect that a pineapple which satisfies a certain purely descriptive condition—being in a certain place, a certain shape and size, and so on—is rotting, could be equivalent in truth-conditions and cognitive significance to the thought that *that pineapple is rotting*. One reason for this is that, given any purely descriptive condition of no matter how complex a content, it seems possible that a rational thinker may still have reason to doubt whether it is *that pineapple* which satisfies the condition.

Moreover, it is also plausible that, unless there were some demonstrative thoughts of these kinds, then nothing makes it the case that we are thinking about the objects that we are. This is a conclusion one can draw from P. F. Strawson's argument that, if all reference were in terms of pure descriptions, then nothing would make it the case that one was talking about the objects in this world as opposed to a qualitatively identical duplicate or replica world (assuming such a thing is possible).[32] If one were just restricted to thoughts of the form 'the F (etc.) is G', and the only constraint on thought was that the objects have to meet the descriptive conditions set by these propositions, then our thoughts would be equally true of the duplicate world as they are of ours. Therefore genuine singular reference, in terms of names or demonstratives or other singular referring expressions, is needed to anchor our thoughts to the world we are in.

These two plausible claims about demonstrative thought may be summarized as follows:

(1) No purely descriptive or quantificational thought is equivalent in content or cognitive significance to a demonstrative thought.
(2) Unless there were some such demonstrative thoughts about the perceived environment, then not even the descriptive or quantificational thoughts which we do have could be 'anchored' to this world.

I shall not dispute these claims, nor say much about what 'anchored' means. The question is what they have to do with externalism and internalism.

Given the irreducibility of demonstrative thought to purely descriptive thought, claim (1) would refute a global internalism about thought—a thesis to the effect that all thoughts are narrow—only if there could not be an internalist account of demonstrative thought. And claim (2) would similarly refute a global internalism, by showing the priority of demonstrative over descriptive thought; but again, only if there could not be an internalist account of demonstrative thought.

As noted above, my ambition here is not to defend a global internalism, but only to demonstrate the coherence of internalist intentionality. But nonetheless, it seems to me that both claims (1) and (2) could be accepted by an internalist. The important point which allows this is that internalism can understand demonstrative thought not in purely descriptive terms, but in combined descriptive-indexical terms. That is, the truth-conditions of 'that F is G' could be given, not by a description of the form 'the F which is H (etc.) is

G' where 'H' is a context-independent predicate, but rather by a mixed index-ical description, of the form 'the F which is related to me in such-and-such ways is G'.[33]

So suppose Alice is looking at a pineapple in front of her and Bob is having a perfect hallucination of one (those with doubts about the relevant idea of hallucination may look at §41). Each of them utters the words, 'that pineapple is rotting'. The externalist about demonstrative thoughts will say that while Alice is having a genuine demonstrative thought, into whose truth-conditions the pineapple itself enters, Bob is having no determinate thought at all, since there is no object to figure in the truth-conditions as the reference of 'that pineapple'. The internalist, by contrast, will say that Alice and Bob are having the same kind of thought, whose truth-conditions are given by the prop-osition *the pineapple in front of me is rotting*. It is true that, if we are not hallucinating ourselves, we would not describe Bob's thought in the following terms: 'Bob thinks that *that* pineapple is rotting', although we would say something similar about Alice's. But given what we have said above (§35) about the distinction between thoughts and the conditions for their ascrip-tions, this does not entail that Bob's thought differs from Alice's. It's just that no one would ascribe thoughts in the above way unless they themselves would refer to something by using an expression of the form 'that F'.

The kind of internalist approach sketched here, therefore, has something important in common with the internalist response to the Twin Earth argu-ment. It is this idea: thoughts do not determine their references independently of context, but rather, they get to have the references they do when the thinker is in a context.[34] But the content of the thought can nonetheless be conceived of as what is common between thinkers in different contexts—whether the context is Earth as opposed to Twin Earth, or a veridical perception as opposed to a hallucination. And the reason that content can be thought of as common across these differences in context derives from the fact that the subject's points of view, how things seem to the subject, are relevantly the same. The heart of the internalist's position is the idea that psychological similarity ultimately follows or consists in similarity in how things seem from the subject's point of view. Of course, this idea has been subjected to harsh criticism from externalists. But since my aim has only been to state a coherent internalist position, I will leave these criticisms to be explored and examined at the reader's leisure.

39. The prospects for explaining thought

I have been discussing the various kinds of thought, distinguishing thoughts from beliefs, and distinguishing the propositional attitudes from other intentional states. I have not said anything about the project, mentioned in §7 and in the Preface, of giving an account of the intentionality of thought (or mental representation generally) in physicalist or 'naturalist' terms. To simplify wildly: this normally involves giving sufficient (and necessary, in most cases) conditions for one thing to represent another in terms of the causal relations between the two things. There is much to be said about this project, but I will not say anything about it here.[35] One reason for not going into any details is that the project presupposes physicalism, but I rejected physicalism in Chapter 2. However, rejecting physicalism does not by itself remove the appeal of reductive explanations; in §15 I claimed that a genuine explanatory reduction is an advance in knowledge, so we should not set our faces against the very idea of reduction. But in this case there are some specific reasons for scepticism: for one thing, causation is (on most views) a relation between cause and effect, and yet there is in general no relation between thoughts and their objects (§7). There may be a way of answering this kind of objection, and making the reductive project work within the understanding of the concept of intentionality as I have outlined it here. But as things stand at this stage, for these reasons and others, the prospects are not good.

5

Perception

40. The problem of perception

Philosophers have been interested in sense perception for many reasons. One kind of interest is inseparable from a psychological investigation into the mechanisms of perception: how the different senses convey information to our brains about the perceived environment. Another kind of interest is epistemological: how does perception give us knowledge about the world? The psychological study is concerned with the mechanisms of perception, while the epistemological study is concerned with the ways in which perception can be knowledge, for examples by providing us with reasons for our beliefs.[1]

This chapter is about neither the psychology of perception (as understood above) nor its epistemology. It is rather about the intentionality of perception, and the problems which arise when trying to understand it. An intentionalist account of mind must be able to say something about the ways in which different states of mind differ from each other. Part of our investigation into perception will concern how perception resembles and differs from other mental states, notably belief and sensation (§45). And another part of the investigation will concern the phenomenal character of perception itself, and how to gain a clear understanding of it (§§43–4). It is important to emphasize that this approach is not in conflict with any scientific or psychological investigation of perception; rather than asking about how the mechanisms of perception work, it asks what are the most general features of anything we could reasonably call 'perception' or 'perceptual experience', and tries to give a consistent and systematic description of them. It turns out that this is a harder task than it might initially seem: quandaries, conundrums, and tensions within our conception of perception arise. I claim that these problems are independent of the psychological/scientific questions about perception, and also of the epistemological questions. The problems are phenomenological: they arise from reflection upon perception as we experience it.

What are these phenomenological problems of perception? I shall argue that, in essence, they arise from the conflict between two ideas about visual experience or visual perception which both seem intuitively plausible.[2] (I will have less to say about perception by the other senses.) The first intuitively plausible idea is what we can call the *immediacy* of visual experience: the idea that in visual perception we are normally 'immediately' aware of the material world around us. What 'immediately' (or, alternatively, 'directly') means is not entirely clear yet, but it surely means at least this: when we are aware of a material object in the world, we are not normally aware of it by first being aware of something which is *not* a material object.[3] Here visual perception seems to differ from perception through some of the other senses: arguably, when our sense of smell makes us aware of the burning toast, this is because we first come to be aware of the *smell* of the toast. While the toast is a physical object, the smell of the toast is not obviously one—not because smells are not physical, but because they are not obviously objects. (They are, as we shall see, 'intentional objects', but a physical thing which is an intentional object is not necessarily a physical object: see §5.) Sounds are a similar case.[4]

The comparison with smell and hearing brings out what is special about visual perception: while it makes good sense to say that we smell the toast by smelling its smell, or hear the bell by hearing the sound of the bell—even if ultimately we think this way of talking is misleading—it makes no sense at all to say that we see the garden by seeing a 'look' of the garden. To catch a glimpse of something is not to see it by seeing a glimpse. Vision seems to make its objects immediately available to us, without us being aware of those objects by being aware of something else. (Of course, one can be aware of a physical or material object by being aware of some other physical object—as when one sees someone or something on the television. But this is not relevant, for here one is immediately aware of a physical object too, the television.)

The second intuitively plausible idea is what Howard Robinson calls 'the phenomenal principle'.[5] I shall have more to say about this principle in the next section, but the basic idea is this: when one experiences that something is F, there is something F which one is experiencing. (A more precise version will be given below.) If one has an experience of something coloured, then it is very natural to conclude that there is something which has the colour in question. I see a goldfinch in the garden, and see its striking red and yellow plumage; there is something there, in the garden, namely the goldfinch, which has those perceptible properties. What could be more obvious?

Now one might wonder why the immediacy of visual perception and the phenomenal principle are in conflict. The first says that when one visually perceives a material thing, one does not normally perceive it by perceiving something else; and the second says that when one perceives that something has a property, there is something which has this property. So far, there is no conflict between these two ideas. The conflict comes when we come to consider a possibility which is implicit in our ideas about perception: the possibility of a certain kind of hallucination. This possibility gives rise to what has traditionally been called the argument from illusion; this argument will be discussed in §41. In §42 I shall argue that a correct understanding of the intentionality of perception provides the solution to the problem of perception. Intentionalist theories of perception of the sort I defend here have been criticized for not being able to give an adequate account of the phenomenology of perception; I discuss these criticisms in §§43–4. An adequate intentionalist theory of perception must give a proper account of the difference between perception and belief; this is discussed in §45.

41. The argument from illusion

The philosophy of perception in the first half of the twentieth century was concerned with the question of whether or not we perceive material objects— for example, people, plants, animals, artefacts—'directly'. The opposing theories were Direct Realism and versions of the Sense-Data theory. The first holds that we do perceive material objects directly or immediately. One version of the Sense-Data theory—Indirect Realism—says that we perceive material objects indirectly, by perceiving *sense-data*. The other version of the theory— Phenomenalism or Idealism—says that only sense-data are perceived, directly or indirectly, and material objects are some kind of 'construction' out of sense-data.

What are sense-data supposed to be? Literally, they are what is *given* (hence, 'data') to the senses. And in fact, when the term 'sense-data' was first introduced into philosophy by G. E. Moore, it was meant to stand for whatever it is that is 'given or presented to the senses' in acts of perception.[6] Now if they are understood in this way, as whatever is given to the senses, sense-data could be material objects themselves, or their surfaces—if these are, in fact, the things which are given to the senses in acts of perception. But Moore, and some of those who followed him, ultimately denied that material objects were the things given to the mind because of the notorious 'argument from illusion', intended to show that what is directly given to the mind is never a material (or physical) object. This argument has appeared in many forms throughout the history of philosophy.[7]

Although it is called the argument from *illusion*, it is best expressed in terms of the idea of a hallucination, an experience of a non-existent object, rather than an illusion, where this is understood merely as an incorrect perception. In essence, the argument from hallucination attempts to show that one never *directly* or *immediately* perceives a material object, because one's experience could remain the same even if there were no such object perceived. Therefore, sense-data—the immediate objects of experience—are not material objects. Put like this, it hardly looks like an argument, but more like a dogmatic assertion of a bizarre conclusion, with some implausible assumptions. So let me try to make the argument more plausible.

Suppose I am currently visually perceiving a blue flower. The nature of this particular experience, we can suppose, is partly determined by the nature of its object—for example, if the flower were (for example) a different colour, then this experience would be of a different kind. Now it seems to be a possibility which is allowed by our concept of experience that I could be in a mental state which is phenomenally indistinguishable from a perception of a real blue flower, but there is no flower there: this is a hallucination of a flower. Phenomenally indistinguishable perceptual states are mental states of the same type. Therefore, since the hallucination of the flower is phenomenally indistinguishable from a genuine perception of the flower, the nature of this type of mental state does not depend on the existence of the flower. Nonetheless, it is wrong to say that I am not aware of *anything*: it seems to me that I see a blue flower. But this thing I am aware of cannot be a physical object. Now if my experience is of the same type when I am really seeing a blue flower as when I am merely hallucinating one, and experiences of the same type have the same immediate objects, then the immediate object of the experience in the case of the genuine perception cannot be a physical object either. Generalizing from this case, we must conclude that if sense-data are the things which are immediately given to the senses in experience, then sense-data are not physical objects.

The argument presented in this form has many steps, and almost all of them have been questioned. Some of the objections of the argument are objections to particular details in the way it is set up, others are objections to general principles which the argument employs. So, for example, some people have objected to the idea of a phenomenally indistinguishable hallucination. How do we really know such a thing is possible? There are such things as hallucinations, of course, but these are unusual experiences, normally had in some disturbed or traumatic state, or under the influence of drugs, which no one would *mistake* for a normal perception. It is as implausible as supposing that one might mistake a dream-experience for the real thing; but, as Austin once pointed out, dreaming one is being presented to the Pope is nothing like really being presented to the Pope.[8] So it is claimed that, in appealing to the idea of a hallucination which is indistinguishable from a genuinely perceptual experience, the argument is making an illegitimate empirical speculation: there is no reason to suppose that such things really happen.

This response is implausible. For the idea of an experience which seems the same as a genuine perception is only supposed to be a *metaphysical possibility*, one which is allowed by our ideas of perception and experience. The argument does not require that such hallucinations actually do happen, only that they are possible. Now the response just expressed could be saying that hallucinations are impossible, or that they are only possible, just not actual. If the latter, then the response is no objection. If the former, then more has to be done to show that hallucinations are impossible.

If someone needed persuading that such hallucinations are possible, then we only need to elaborate on the original story a bit.[9] It is uncontroversial to suppose that how a visual experience seems is, as a matter of fact, a direct upshot of causal processes: the light reflected off objects and onto the light-sensitive retina, the passing of information down the optic nerve and throughout other informational pathways in the brain, and so on. To say this is not to commit ourselves to a causal *analysis* of the concept of visual experience, it is only to appeal to the facts about experience as we know them to be. Now, with any interaction between cause C and event E, it makes sense to suppose that an E-type effect could have been brought about by something other than a C-type cause. This could be done by intercepting the causal chain, bringing about an E-type event by bringing about something downstream of the normal kind of cause, C. So in our case, the experience—the effect of causal processes in the brain and outside—could be brought about by bringing about causes which are downstream of its normal cause outside the brain. For instance, the experience could be brought about by stimulating the retina in exactly the same way that it would be if the subject were really seeing a blue flower, and keeping all the other causal influences in the brain the same.

The objector may fail to be moved by this on the grounds that the experience should not be thought of as the causal upshot of events in the brain. But this is implausible.[10] To take this line is to make a much bolder and more demanding claim than the original hypothesis that hallucinations are possible. We can safely ignore it, and the objection that it sustains.

A more promising response is to deny that phenomenally indistinguishable mental states are always mental states of the same type. For why should it not be, as Austin says, that having an experience of one type seems exactly the same as having an experience of another?[11] Even if we have to accept that, in the hallucinatory case, the subject perceives a sense-datum, why should it follow that in the genuinely perceptual case the subject perceives a sense-datum too? For why shouldn't perceiving a sense-datum in certain circumstances seem exactly like perceiving a physical object? Moreover, there are general reasons for thinking that phenomenal sameness is not always sufficient for sameness of thought—this is a principle which externalists defend. (An experience of XYZ might be phenomenally the same as an experience of H_2O.) So in this particular case, someone might say that our normal ways of talking about experience do already contain the distinctions between states of mind which are needed to resist the argument from illusion: we say that someone who is merely hallucinating is *not really seeing*, whereas the person who sees the flower is *genuinely perceiving* or *seeing*. If this principle is supposed to depend solely on a claim about ordinary usage, then it is debat-able. It is not to misuse the word 'see' to say that Macbeth saw a dagger or that someone sees flashes before their eyes after a bump on the head. We may want to qualify these claims, but usage does not decide things in any straight-forward way.[12] But the distinction can appeal to more than usage: it can appeal to a proper account of the phenomenology of our states of mind.

This leads us to a further and deeper response to the argument from illu-sion. I just said that one could resist the argument by objecting that there is no reason to think that seeing a non-physical flower sense-datum is the same type of mental state as seeing a real flower. But one could go further: why suppose that there need be *any* object of any kind which one is seeing in the hallucin-atory case? Surely the only reason for thinking there is would be if one thought that someone who has an experience must have an experience of *something real*; those who see must see something real. But what is the reason for thinking this? Why can't it be that sometimes one has a visual experience yet nothing whatever is seen? What is the motive for the principle that those that see must see something?

It seems that a principle of this kind is at the heart of the argument from illusion. This is the principle mentioned above, Robinson's *Phenomenal Principle*:

If there sensibly appears to a subject to be something which possesses a particular sensible quality then there is something of which the subject is aware which does possess that sensible quality.[13]

So, for example, if it sensibly (e.g. visually) appears to me that there is a flower which is a certain shade of blue, if I have a visual experience of a blue flower, then there is something of which I am aware which does have that shade of blue. Now clearly, this principle is essential to the argument from illusion; without it, the argument collapses. The principle is endorsed by the sense-datum theory; but it is worth pointing out that a somewhat similar principle is endorsed by the theory's opponent, the Direct Realist. Let's call this the *Genuine Perception Principle*:

If a subject is genuinely perceiving that an object has a certain sensible quality, then there is an object which the subject is perceiving which seems to possess this property.

In other words, it is a constraint on something being a *genuine* perception that an object of perception exists, and it appears to have certain properties. In this terminology, a genuine perception is not yet a veridical or correct percep-tion, since one could genuinely perceive a certain object and yet misperceive its properties. We should say that a perception is *veridical* when the object does have the sensible property it appears to have. The parallel with the Phenomenal Principle is obvious: the Phenomenal Principle says that in every case of sensory experience an object is present, while the Genuine Perception Principle says that if someone is genuinely perceiving, then an object exists.

Despite the difference in these two principles, both the Sense-Datum theory and the Direct Realist share a fundamental assumption: that perception (in one or the other sense) *relates* perceivers to objects. Perception—either the Direct Realist's genuine perception, or the Sense-Datum theory's sensory experience—is a relation between perceivers and the objects of perception. This is why it is so natural to think of something being 'given' to the mind in perception, and this is why Moore thought that 'there is no doubt at all that there are sense-data, in the sense in which I am using that term'.[14] There is no doubt because this is how perception immediately strikes us: something is given to the mind. The starting point for both of these theories of perception is the idea that perceptual experiences appear to have objects, they have a relational structure, something is presented in an experience.

So it is this idea of something being *given*, it seems to me, which is the intuitive idea behind both the Sense-Datum theory and the Direct Realist theory. It is worth emphasizing that, contrary to what many commentators have said, this basis has little or nothing to do with traditional epistemological issues—for example, finding certain foundations for knowledge, or refuting scepticism. Neither the argument as presented nor Robinson's Phenomenal Principle say anything about incorrigibility, infallibility, scepticism, or the foundations of knowledge. The considerations appealed to are phenomeno-logical, not epistemological. One could, perhaps, construct an argument from epistemological premises to the same conclusion, but this would be a different kind of thing.[15]

(Some philosophers have criticized the idea of 'the given' as involving deep philosophical confusion: Wilfrid Sellars said that the whole idea of the given is a myth, and Robert Brandom and John McDowell have recently defended Sellars's idea, in rather different ways.[16] I will not say much about these criti-cisms, except to note that, insofar as these criticisms of the given are criticisms of its epistemological role, then they do not touch the phenomenological motivation for the idea that something is given.)

To the extent that the idea that something real is given in experience is compelling, then the Sense-Datum and Direct Realist theories are plausible. But, I shall argue, neither theory is completely acceptable as it stands. My position, stated without argument, is this. The Sense-Datum theory says that perception and hallucination involve a common state of mind, and that each involves a real relation to a non-physical sense-datum. The Direct Realist theory says that genuine perception and hallucination do not involve a com-mon state of mind, but only genuine perception involves a relation to a real perceived object. The Sense-Datum theory's claim that perception and hal-lucination involve a common state of mind is plausible; but it is hard to

believe in sense-data. The Direct Realist's denial that perception and hallucination are the same state of mind is implausible; but its claim that visual
perception presents us immediately with material objects is an obvious phenomenological fact. What we need to do is to preserve what is best in each of
these theories. The next section will describe a way of doing this.

42. Perception as a form of intentionality

The solution to the problem of perception is to appreciate correctly the nature
of the intentionality of perception. Both the Sense-Data theory and the Direct
Realist theory treat perception as a relation: in the first case to real sense-data,
in the second case (for genuine perception) to ordinary material objects. The
Sense-Data theory gives a satisfactory answer to the argument from illusion,
but leaves us with sense-data, mysterious non-physical objects. Direct Realism, on the other hand, commits us to the existence of no objects except those
which we would accept anyway, but on the face of it fails to account for the
sense in which perception and hallucination share a phenomenal character.
Which way should we turn?

The way out of this impasse will have already been anticipated: we should
deny that perception is a relation to real objects. Rather, perception is an
intentional state, a relation to an intentional content. Every perceptual state
has an intentional object, of course, but this is just to say that there is an
answer to the question, 'what is the object of your experience?' An intentionalist can therefore reject the Phenomenal Principle and the Genuine Perception
principle, since it is not essential to something's being an intentional state that
it has an existing object. What is essential to something's being an intentional
state is that it has an intentional structure: subject—mode—content (§8). The
rejection of the Phenomenal Principle may be motivated by a comparison
with belief. Now a version of the Phenomenal Principle is valid for
knowledge-states, but the version for belief is plainly invalid. Compare the
following:

(1) If a subject knows that a is F, then there is something a, which the subject
    knows to be F.
(2) If a subject believes that a is F, then there is something a, which the subject
    believes is F.

Principle (1) is true, but (2) is false, as any number of examples can show.
Vladimir believes that the Fountain of Youth is in Bratislava; it does not follow
from this that there is something, the Fountain of Youth, which Vladimir
believes to be in Bratislava.

Of course, there are belief ascriptions (*de re* ascriptions: see §35) of which principle (2) is true, and some Externalists will hold that it is true of certain kinds of thoughts (for instance, thoughts expressible using demonstrative expressions: 'that F is G'; see §38). But no one will think that this is a valid principle for belief (or ascriptions of belief) *in general*, let alone for other intentional states. The intentionalist view, opposed to Direct Realism and to Sense-Data theory, is that the Phenomenal Principle is not valid for perception.

Now there is a sense in which the Direct Realist theory and the Sense-Data theory are also intentionalist theories: each of them holds that the mind is directed on real objects in acts of perception. The Direct Realist holds that this is a fact only about genuine perception, while the Sense-Data theorist holds that it is a fact about all perceptual experience, 'genuine' or not.[17] So each of these theories accepts that perceptions have a relational structure: in fact, perception in one way or another relates the mind to real objects.

This might raise the question of whether, on my view, the intentionality of perception is a trivial matter. However, despite the (admittedly very general) conception of intentionality with which I am working, there is an approach to perception which is not intentional even in this general sense. This is the Adverbial theory, which holds that visually experiencing a blue object is to be understood as *visually experiencing bluely*: the predicates which other theories take as picking out properties of perceived objects are here interpreted as adverbs of the perceptual verb.[18] In other words, the qualities of the objects of perception are really qualities of the perceptual state itself. Experiencing something *F* is a matter of having one's experience modified in certain ways. The view arose as a response to what were seen to be the metaphysical excesses of the Sense-Datum theory: rather than committing ourselves to strange objects, we commit ourselves only to properties of experiences. But this fact in turn brings into relief the deepest weakness of the theory: that it is unable to account for the fact that the phenomenal character of visual perceptual states is, at the very least, the experience of a spatially arrayed arrangement of objects and properties, which cannot be captured in the adverbial reconstructions of the normal ways of describing perception.[19] As Martin puts it, perceptions have a *subject-matter*: this is the basis of the intentionalist conception I am recommending here, and this feature is shared by Sense-Data theories and Direct Realism, whatever their other deficiencies. However, to avoid any confusion with the intentionalist elements of Direct Realism or Sense-Data theories, I shall call the version of intentionalism I recommend here *standard intentionalism*.

What, then, is the nature of perceptual intentionality, according to standard intentionalism? As with any intentional state, the intentional structure of perception is given by two things: the mode and the content. The intentional modes in the case of perception are picked out by our everyday ways of picking out the senses: seeing, hearing, smelling, tasting, touching. These could be seen as determinates of the determinable concept 'perceiving through the senses'; there may be others. Since I regard bodily sensation as a form of perception, I would also include proprioception and kinesthesia as intentional modes, in the way described in §§24–5.

What about the content of perception? This is not a question that can have a simple answer, since in a sense it is the concern of the rest of this chapter. But some preliminary remarks can be made, to clarify the areas that need to be pursued here.

We can make a general distinction in our ways of thinking about perceptions, between the perception of objects or events and the perception of facts or states of affairs. In our way of talking about these experiences, this distinction corresponds roughly to the distinction between the context where a perceptual verb takes a noun phrase as complement ('God saw the light') and that where it takes a propositional or sentential complement ('God saw that it was good'). The noun phrases may refer to events ('I saw the fall of Icarus') as well as to objects in the ordinary sense. These distinctions apply to the other senses too: one can smell that the toast is burning or smell the toast burning; one can hear that the guests have arrived or hear the arrival of the guests. (Notice that this isn't the same thing being heard, though!) One can taste that the wine is sour, and one can taste the sourness of the wine. Touch is slightly different here: one can touch the carpet, but not touch *that* the carpet is a certain way. So we might express the propositional form of the sense of touch by using the verb 'feel' instead. The distinction between these two kinds of complement does not exhaust the ways we have of talking about perception, though: there are also other cases where we talk about the perception of events but the complement is neither a noun-phrase nor a sentence ('I saw my lady weep').

I mention these points to give a feel for the different kinds of perceptual content there can be, for the different kinds of entities which can be objects of perception. The objects of perception can be things and they can be events, or they can be states of affairs. The fact that there are ways of ascribing perceptual states which give them propositional objects means that perceptions are propositional attitudes. But perceptions need not all be propositional attitudes: there is such a thing as noticing an object, without necessarily noticing *that* it is a certain way. The generally liberal approach to the nature of intentional content put forward in §8 means that there is no requirement that there has to be a translation or reduction of one kind of way of talking into another.

As noted above, there seems to be a difference between the sorts of entities which can be the objects of perceptual experience in the case of vision and the other senses.[20] One can smell the rose, but also the *smell* of the rose can be an object of one's experience. One can hear the violin, but one can also hear the sound of the violin. One can taste road tar in the wine, and one can also experience the taste of road tar in the wine. In some cases, these objects seem to be the curious event/object-like things which we encountered (and dismissed) in the case of bodily sensation (§24). For example, sounds seem like events in one way (they take time, they have temporal parts) but like objects in others (they can move across a space).²¹ There are differences between these cases—while one can smell the smell of something, one does not touch the touch of something—but all of them differ from the case of vision, where there is no everyday, non-theoretical way of saying that you see the 'look' of something. When we talk about the look of something, this is never naturally understood as an event-object, as a sound is—rather, the look of something describes a property of something, the *way* something looks. The fact that one might smell smells or hear noises does not tell against standard intentionalism, as we shall see in §43. For remember: all intentionalism needs is the idea of an intentional structure (subject—mode—content). The interest in any particular intentionalist theory must be in the detailed accounts it gives of the intentional content and intentional modes.

43. **The phenomenal character of perceptual experience**

Standard intentionalism about perception holds that objects and properties in the mind-independent world are presented to the mind in experience. The strong form of this intentionalism (§25) is committed to the view that all phenomenal aspects of mental states are an aspect of its intentionality. Strong standard intentionalism therefore denies that visual experience involves awareness of qualia (as defined in §23).

In recent philosophy, those who deny that there are qualia in visual experience describe themselves as believing in the 'transparency' of experience.²² This is meant to capture the idea that when one has an experience of something blue, say, one is not aware of one's experience having certain intrinsic properties; rather one 'sees through' (hence *transparent*) to the blueness itself. The term is liable to mislead, since 'transparent' has also been used to describe those mental states whose existence entails that we know that we are in them.²³ Given these other distinct uses, perhaps another term would have removed the possibility of confusion; but having noted this, I will continue to use the term 'transparency' for this putative perceptual phenomenon.

According to Gilbert Harman and Michael Tye, support for this view comes from introspecting on experience. Tye describes his 'argument from introspection' as follows:

Standing on the beach in Santa Barbara a couple of summers ago on a bright sunny day, I found myself transfixed by the intense blue of the Pacific Ocean. Was I not here delighting in the phenomenal aspects of my visual experience? And if I was, doesn't this show that there are visual qualia?

I am not convinced. It seems to me that what I found so pleasing in the above instance, what I was focusing on, as it were, were a certain shade and intensity of the colour blue. I experienced blue as a property of the ocean not as a property of my experience. My experience itself certainly wasn't blue. Rather, it was an experience which represented the ocean as blue. What I was really delighting in, then, were specific aspects of the content of the experience.

Tye goes on to suggest that this might have been the sort of thing Moore meant when he said that the sensation of blue is 'diaphanous', and glosses this as follows: 'When one tries to focus on it in introspection one cannot help but see right through it so that what one actually ends up attending to is the real colour blue.'[24] Tye's claim about seeing the blue of the ocean is that introspection reveals only represented facts about the ocean; that it is blue. The thesis of the transparency of experience is a generalization from this kind of example: all introspection can reveal are facts about the content of the experience (how things are represented to be) or represented facts about the object of experience (what is represented or presented in the experience).

But can we give an account of the phenomenal character of experience using purely the resources of intentionality? Some philosophers say no. They say that, although perceptual experiences have intentionality, this cannot exhaust their phenomenal character. For perceptual experiences also have *qualia*, the non-intentional, non-representational, intrinsic properties of states of mind (see §23). And no adequate account of perceptual experience can be given which does not mention these intrinsic qualia.[25]

What are the qualia in visual experience supposed to be? Here the difficulty immediately arises that one cannot (as it were) 'point' to qualia as if everyone knew that it is obvious that there are qualia. For some think it is obvious that there are qualia in experience, while others think it is obvious that there are no such things. Bill Brewer, for example, asserts that 'the notion of . . . entirely non-representational mental states—or even such aspects of mental states—is a philosophers' invention of only dubious coherence, and certainly without instance in normal human life'.[26] But if this is so obvious, then how can others think otherwise? This question surely cannot be answered by appeal to the obvious. So how is the existence of qualia supposed to be established? There are two kinds of approach. The first appeals to *actual* cases of things which everyone agrees occur in experience, and attempts to persuade us that these things are qualia. The second appeals to merely *possible* cases, and attempts to elicit judgements about these cases which shows why in the actual cases there are qualia. The first kind of example are things like blurred vision, spots before the eyes, double vision, and so on. The second kind is the inverted spectrum, and Block's variation, Inverted Earth, thought-experiments. I will deal with the first kind of case in this section, and the second kind in the next section. (Note that here we focus on visual experience. Apparent counter-examples to strong intentionalism which come from bodily sensation were dealt with in §24.)

Some of the actual cases appealed to in defence of visual qualia are familiar from discussions of sense-data in the early part of the twentieth century: for example, the cases of double vision or specks before one's eyes. Here the claim that is made is that these perceptual phenomena are not exhausted by how the *world* is represented to the subject to be. When one sees specks before one's eyes, the world is not represented to the subject as containing specks before one's eyes. One would not, for example, reach out and try and touch them. If one were to lift one's finger in front of one's face in such a way that one 'sees double', the world is not represented as containing two fingers before one's eyes. One would not, for example, consider buying a six-fingered glove. These were traditional examples produced to support the Sense-Datum theory; defenders of qualia have used them to support the view that one is aware of intrinsic (non-representational, non-intentional) features of one's experience.

But I said above that the sense-data theory *is* a kind of intentionalist theory: something is given to the mind, the experience has a relational structure. So if these are supposed to be examples of sense-data, how can they also be examples of qualia? To use these examples as examples of qualia one would have to be taking an adverbial approach to them: rather than seeing two apparent fingers, one is seeing two-finger-ly, or something like that. But as noted above, the adverbial approach is phenomenologically implausible, and the translation of all claims about experience into the adverbial format is impossible. So these are better examples for the Sense-Data theory than for the qualia theory.

But we have rejected the Sense-Data theory; so how should our preferred form of intentionalism deal with this kind of example? Surely we don't want to say that the experience is representing the world as containing specks before the eyes or as containing two fingers when one is held up? Paul Boghossian and J. David Velleman take this kind of point as decisive against an intentionalist theory. They consider an example of an after-image (without illusion) of a red spot obscuring the face of someone who has just taken your photo:

Since you suffer no illusion about the nature of this spot, you do not see it as something actually existing in front of the photographer's face. In what sense, then, do you see it as occupying that location at all? The answer is that you see it as merely appearing in that location: you see it as a spot that appears in front of the photographer's face without actually being there. Now, in order for you to see the spot as appearing somewhere, it must certainly appear there. Yet it must appear there without appearing actually to be there, since you are not under the illusion that the spot actually occupies the space in question. The after-image must therefore be described as *appearing in* a location without *appearing to be in* that location; and this description is not within the capacity of any intentionalist theory. An intentionalist theory will analyse the visual appearance of location as the attribution of location to something, in the intentional content of your visual experience. But the intentional content of your visual experience is that there is nothing at all between you and the photographer.[27]

But why isn't it open to the intentionalist to say that there is a sense in which it visually appears to the subject that there is a spot before their eyes? They don't seem to the subject to be features of their experience (whatever that would precisely be) but something seems to be *there*. We should not say that the subject *believes* or *judges* that there is something there, of course; subjects can have these kinds of experience in complete knowledge of what is really before their eyes or how many fingers they have. But all this shows is that perception is not a kind of judgement or belief (more on this below: §45). What it takes for the perception to be intentional is just the subject—mode—content structure. And these examples have it. The issue of whether the content of the experience is taken as being about the external world by the subject apprised of the facts is another question. So these examples do not show that there are qualia. At most, they are evidence for sense-data. But that is evidence for a form of intentionalism.

So these cases are not relevant. The cases which present a clearer case for qualia are those where it is the *way* in which one is aware of something which seems to go beyond the intentional character of the experience, rather than the thing of which one is aware (an *object* of awareness). For example, consider the phenomenal difference between the experiences a short- (near-) sighted person has while wearing glasses and while not wearing them. The experiences seem different. But the subject does not take the world to be different in these cases. Normal subjects are not disposed to judge that the world is different. What has changed, according to the defenders of qualia, is properties of your experience. This is clearly right: your experience has changed, in the sense that it has changed its properties. The question is whether the relevant change is in the intentional properties or the non-intentional properties, the qualia.

The defenders of qualia say that the experience does not change in its intentional phenomenal properties in the two cases; so therefore it must change in its non-intentional phenomenal properties. Is this plausible? It is certainly true, once again, that subjects need not take the world to have changed, in the sense that they would judge it to have changed, or they believe that it has changed. But all this shows, again, is the difference between perception and judgement/belief. So removing your glasses does not change the way you would judge the world to be, in normal cases. But there is still a change in the content of the experience, in what you would put into words. You might say 'things look blurry now, even though I know they are not'. And it makes sense to suppose that someone might come to believe, because of some strange background belief, that things *were* actually this way. (Consider someone standing on an underground train platform, wondering why the designers of the advertisement on the wall opposite had printed the text in such small writing that those on the platform could not read it; after a while, they may realize that they need glasses.) There is, then, a change in the intentional properties of the experience, despite the fact that normal subjects would not judge the world to have changed.

So much for visual qualia. The phenomena described certainly exist, but there is no reason to suppose that they are qualia in the sense described. Does this mean that as far as reflection on actual experience goes, the transparency of experience is correct? This depends on what the transparency thesis actually says. If it says that the phenomenal character of experience is determined by the intentionality of an experience, then I endorse it. But it is more normal for the transparency thesis to be stated as follows: all differences in phenomenal character are differences in the representational content of an experience. I deny this thesis. As in the case of bodily sensation (§24), differences in the phenomenal character of perception derive from two things: intentional mode and intentional content. I claim that one needs to fix each of these things in order to fix the phenomenal character: the fact that a perceptual experience is a visual experience rather than an auditory one is clearly a phenomenal difference; and the fact that the experience is of a cat rather than a dog is (of course) a phenomenal difference too. In emphasizing that phenomenal character is determined by mode and content, I differ from many intentionalists who defend the transparency thesis.

In other ways too, my intentionalist account of the apparent counter-examples to intentionalism rests on my own particular understanding of the intentionalist doctrine: first, that intentional states must have intentional content; second, not all intentional states are beliefs, some intentional modes have psychological and logical properties which are very different from the properties of beliefs. I therefore disagree with Howard Robinson when he says that the appeal to intentionality in the theory of perception 'tends to play down or ignore the difference between perceptual experience and other kinds of mental state'.[28] On the contrary: my appeal to intentionality is only sustainable if I emphasize the differences between perceptual experience and other kinds of mental state. (For more on these differences, see §45 on non-conceptual content below.)

44. **Inverted spectrum, Inverted Earth**

So much for actual examples, and what they show about qualia. More difficult for the intentionalist is the appeal to certain possible cases: the famous inverted spectrum hypothesis and Block's ingenious variant on the story, Inverted Earth.[29] In the inverted spectrum thought-experiment, we are asked to imagine someone—let's call him 'Invert'—whose colour spectrum is inverted relative to the normal population: whenever a normal person—call her 'Norma'—sees something red, Invert sees something green, and similarly with the other colours. Yet Invert calls grass 'green' and fire engines 'red' and so on; the difference in colour perception between Norma and Invert is undetectable.

There are many versions of this old speculation, and it has been used for many purposes. For instance, one can use it as a sceptical hypothesis: since the difference between these two characters is undetectable from the outside, how can we ever know what the phenomenal character of another person's experience is like? But the purpose I am interested in here is its use in establishing that perception involves the awareness of qualia. Those who use the thought-experiment in this way argue as follows: there is a similarity between Invert and Norma, and a difference between them. The similarity is in the intentional content of their states of mind concerning colours. They both truly believe, the interpretation says, that fire engines are red, and that grass is green; and insofar as their experience has intentional content, it must be the content of the beliefs produced by experience. So the content of a visual experience of a red fire engine may be that the fire engine is red. The difference between Invert and Norma, on the other hand, is not an intentional difference, on this view: it is a difference in the qualia of the experience. Indeed, this could be used as a way of saying what is meant by visual qualia.[30]

It could be argued that the inverted spectrum hypothesis is incoherent for deep metaphysical and empirical reasons.[31] While I am sympathetic to some of the ideas behind this kind of criticism, I think that the use of the argument to show the existence of qualia can be rebutted without taking this line. I will proceed as follows. First we need to distinguish the inverted spectrum hypothesis used as an objection to intentionalism, and the way the hypothesis is used as an objection to functionalism.[32] Functionalism is the theory that mental states are distinguished from one another by their functional or causal roles. It is easy to see how the inverted spectrum has been used as an argument against this view: for Invert and Norma could be, by hypothesis, functionally identical: they have all the same dispositions to behave, to utter the same sounds, and so on. And yet they have inverted spectra, so they are psychologically different. Sometimes intentionalism and functionalism are associated, on the grounds that intentional states are the only mental states of which one could give a functionalist account, so a functionalist should be an intentionalist. But this association is not essential, and the doctrines are really quite independent. Here I am only defending intentionalism, not functionalism.

This is just as well, since it is hard to insist that there must be a functional difference between Invert and Norma. But the claim that there is no *intentional* difference between them is implausible. For after all, the way we have told the story, we have said that *red things look different* to Invert than they do to Norma (and to all the rest of us). Isn't this a difference in how things (i.e. the world) seem to them, and therefore a difference in intentional content? Why should we suppose that this is a difference in qualia?

The difficulty emerges when we try and express the way in which their states of mind differ in content. We cannot do it by using the content of the public language words which they use to express the beliefs which they acquire on the basis of the experience. For these are the same: Norma says 'that fire engine is red' and Invert says the same, thus both expressing their beliefs that *that fire engine is red*. And they are both right in these beliefs, we may suppose. This is true regardless of which view you take of the semantics of colour words: if 'red' refers to a (complex) primary quality of surfaces, then Norma and Invert are both right in saying that the fire engine has this property; and if 'red' refers to the disposition of objects to cause experiences with a certain kind of phenomenal character in *normal* perceivers (i.e. the kind had by Norma's experience), then they are both right too.

Yet the world is presented in a different way to them, I claim. Assuming that Invert does not mean something different by 'red' than the others do who speak his language, we have to locate the difference between the two somewhere else. The right thing to say, it seems to me, is that Invert's *experience* represents the fire engine as green, even though his *belief* represents the fire engine as red. There is a mismatch between his experience and his belief about the colour of the fire engine. Invert has a true belief about the fire engine's colour. But he has a false belief about how the fire engine's colour *looks* to him: he thinks that the fire engine looks red.[33] He is wrong: it doesn't look red, it looks green—that is the content of his experience. Norma, on the other hand, believes truly both that the fire engine is red, and that it looks red.

One way to express this reading of the inverted spectrum is as follows. Either Invert believes that fire engines are red, or he doesn't. If he doesn't, then he must have a different concept of red, so he is naturally taken as meaning *green* by his word 'red'. But this is implausible: it has the consequence that when he says 'that fire engine is red' he says something that sounds exactly the same as Norma's utterance, in the same circumstances, but is false. In fact, all his statements about colour would come out false; this can't be right. So we should conclude that Invert *does* believe that fire engines are red. But if he does, in what does the psychological difference from Norma consist? The non-intentionalist says that it is a difference in *qualia*. The intentionalist says it is a difference in *how things seem to be*; that is, a difference in the intentional content. Invert's experience represents the fire engine as green; his belief that it looks red is false.

This might seem satisfactory, so long as we stick with the case of Invert, who is a lone individual in a population of normal perceivers. So we can say that he means red by 'red' because he means what everyone else means by 'red'. And we can say this regardless of which theory of colour words is true, as noted above. But once we move beyond the simple case of Invert, things become harder to adjudicate. Suppose one half of the population's (group A's) spectra were inverted relative to the other half (group B's). Consider someone from each half saying 'that fire engine is red'. Which, if any, is saying something true? If 'red' means whatever gives rise to such-and-such experiences in normal perceivers in normal circumstances, then this only raises the question, what is a normal perceiver? Is it someone from A or is it someone from B? Or is it both? Or is this whole analysis of the meaning of 'red' wrong? (Would this be like the following real case, famously introduced by Jonathan Bennett: phenol-thio-urea tastes bitter to three-quarters of people, but to the rest it's tasteless.[34] Is it really bitter or really tasteless? Or is there a relevant difference between tastes and colours here, as Shoemaker claims?[35])

The most likely answer is that this account of the meaning of colour words is seriously flawed; but so is the primary quality analysis, which would say that one of A and B is right and the other is wrong.[36] But none of this need concern us here. For the difficulty we have encountered is independent of the issue we are debating here: intentionalism. When the population is split like this, then the main question which arises is whose (intentional) colour *judgements* are correct. This is a problem for the theory of *colour*; it is not a problem which only arises for the intentionalist account I have defended. So I will leave the matter here for the time being.

But a further challenge to intentionalism comes from Ned Block's variant on the inverted spectrum, the Inverted Earth thought-experiment. Inverted Earth is intended to illustrate the converse of what the inverted spectrum showed: while the inverted spectrum is supposed to be a case where intentional content is constant and qualia vary, Inverted Earth is a case where intentional content changes but qualia stay the same. So even if the inverted spectrum fails, Inverted Earth would, if successful, be enough to establish qualia in visual experience.

The Inverted Earth thought-experiment involves a version of a Twin Earth story (see §37). Imagine Inverted Earth to be a planet where everything is the same as it is on Earth, *except for two things*. First, the objective colours of things are inverted systematically to the way they are on Earth. On Inverted

Earth the sky is really yellow, fire engines are really green, and so on. Second, the way people talk about the colours of things is 'inverted' relative to how it is on Earth. So people who speak the version of English which they have on Inverted Earth say 'the sky is blue' and they call fire engines 'red' and so on. On Inverted Earth, 'red' means what 'green' does on Earth, and so on—you get the picture. So, to people on Inverted Earth fire engines look green.

Now suppose I am transported to Inverted Earth by evil scientists, but colour-inverting lenses are inserted into my eyes without my knowledge, so that the real colours of things on Inverted Earth look the way they do on Earth. So things look the same, and I call their colours by the same names. I go around talking of fire engines as red, and grass as green, and the sky as blue, and so on. Nonetheless, Block argues, there is a sense in which my words for colours come to mean something different from what they used to, and the intentional contents of my thoughts come to change. Block claims, and I agree, that when I first move to Inverted Earth my word 'red' still refers to Earthly red. So on my first day on Inverted Earth, when I say 'fire engines are red around here' I am speaking Earthly English, and saying something false. But as I start to causally interact more and more with coloured things on Inverted Earth, then my words start to acquire the meanings of words in Inverted English.[37] So after fifty years on Inverted Earth, my words and the intentional contents of my thoughts *and experiences* refer to the inverted colours; but the way the colours seem to me has remained the same, because of the inverting lenses. According to Block, what has remained the same is the qualia of my experience; what has changed is the intentional content. Hence the qualia of experience are distinct from its intentional content.

Like the inverted spectrum, Inverted Earth was partly intended as an argument against functionalism. I am functionally different from inverted-me, because (*inter alia*) the typical causes of my experience of colours and my colour judgements are different: red things cause me to say 'green' and so on. And yet, the argument goes, my qualia are the same as the qualia of inverted-me: so qualia cannot be captured by the functionalist account. But I am concerned here to defend intentionalism, not functionalism. And however good an argument this is against functionalism, it does not have much force as an argument against intentionalism, unless certain strong assumptions are made.

Note first that the way in which we most naturally talk about the similarity between me and inverted-me is in intentional terms: 'things look the same to us; fire engines look red, it's just that they are really green', and so on. Talk of how *things* look, or of how the *colours* of things look, seems to be talk about how the world is presented to perceivers. Also, we can make a distinction here between how things look or seem and how they really are; so this looks like an area of the mind where the idea of representation clearly and unproblematically applies. So why does Block say that this sameness between me and inverted-me is not an intentional one?

The reason is that he is assuming a broad functional role conception of intentional content. The intentional content of my beliefs about and experiences of colours is the actual property in the world that typically causes these beliefs and experiences. This is why the content of my inverted mature belief about the colour of fire engines is *green*, not red. This causal theory is an externalist theory of intentional content, which I am inclined to reject for the reasons given in §§37–8. But I do not want to let my rejection of Block's conclusion rest on the rejection of this theory. For Block's conclusion does not just need the externalist causal theory of the content of colour words; it also needs the assumption that this is the *only* kind of intentional content which the experiences have. For, faced with the Inverted Earth story as I have told it, it is natural to react thus: my mental states are both similar and different to those of inverted-me. They are different in that they have different broad contents: the normal causes of the experiences and beliefs about colours are different. But they are the same in that they have the same narrow contents: the colours of things seem the same to me and inverted-me. These seemings have narrow contents because they supervene on local properties of me and inverted-me. The common phenomenal properties of which we are aware are apparent properties of objects. They do not seem to be properties of me or inverted-me. And our states of mind therefore have conditions of correctness, since my inverted experience would correctly represent the colours of things if I were returned to Earth. So what is in common between me and inverted-me is the narrow content of our visual experiences.

Unless Block has a way of ruling out narrow content of this form, his conclusion will not follow. (And this is true regardless of the success of the externalist causal theory of intentional content.) He does consider such a 'two-factor' (i.e. broad plus narrow content) response, but his response is marred by the fact that he is assuming that his opponent is giving a functionalist account of narrow content; and narrow functionalist theories of content are implausible.[38] But the opponent does not have to be a functionalist; the opponent could just be an intentionalist.

Here I do not need to defend internalism. All I need is the claim, defended in §§36–8, that the notion of a narrow content (or a narrow intentional state) is a coherent notion. The narrow content in this case is how the world visually seems to be, and the world visually seems the same to me and to inverted-me. But it may still be asked how it can be that two experiences with the same intentional content (say, *looking green*) can be brought about by such different properties in the two worlds (red and green). This is not like the case of H_2O and XYZ (§37), it might be said, since the difference between these two things is (by definition) not phenomenally available. It might be plausible that water and Twin Earth's 'water' can cause the same kind of narrow intentional state, but how can red and green systematically cause the same kind of narrow intentional state?

This objection ignores the fact that what makes it the case that an object looks to be a certain colour is not just facts about the object, but facts about the object, the light it reflects, and the visual system. Since inverted-me has an altered visual system, this is enough to explain the difference in experience. Indeed, if this objection were any good, it could also be raised against very different properties causing the same qualia.

I conclude that, properly understood, neither the inverted spectrum nor the Inverted Earth arguments refute intentionalism about visual experience. There are many difficult questions about the metaphysics of colour (e.g. the question of primary and secondary qualities) and the metaphysics of the mind (e.g. functionalism) which the arguments raise; but these are questions which are largely independent of the truth or falsehood of intentionalism.

45. **Perception as non-conceptual**

In treating the objections to intentionalism, we found the need to distinguish between the intentional mode involved in perceptual states and that involved in belief or judgement. So, for example, I said that someone who saw an after-image before their eyes is not normally inclined to believe that something is there in front of their eyes. But this just underlines the point that perception or visual experience is a different mode from belief. So what is the nature of the intentional mode involved in perception?

It has been said that perceptions are judgements about the perceived environment.[39] If what is meant by this is that perceptions are a kind of propositional attitude, then the point is uncontroversial (as long as we allow that perceptions can have other kinds of intentional content too). But if it is meant that perceptions have the psychological and epistemological attributes of judgement, then the point is only half right (and therefore, not right at all). I say half right because perceptions have this in common with judgement, or the formation of belief: they 'aim' at truth. Part of the functional role of perception, unlike desire (say), is to provide true beliefs about the environment. Perception, unlike desire, informs us about the world. But the way in which perceptions aim at truth is different from the way beliefs do. For part of what it means for belief to aim at truth is illustrated by the phenomenon known as 'Moore's paradox': the oddity of an assertion of the form 'I believe that p but not-p' (see §31). My interest here is not in resolving the Moorean paradox, but in pointing out that it is specific to the attitude or intentional mode, *belief.* There is no such oddity in saying something of the form 'I desire that p but not-p'. Nor, to move to the topic of this chapter, is the same thing wrong with 'I perceive that p but not-p', or 'I see that p but not-p'. One might perceive, or see, that things are certain way but know on independent grounds that one is subject to an illusion, and that things are not that way. This fact— the persistence of illusion—is one of the features of perception which shows its independence from belief.[40]

Another feature of perception which distinguishes it from belief is the kind of content it has. One can believe that someone is smoking outside, without thereby being committed to the smoker being a man, a woman, tall, or short. One might simply come to believe it because one was told, or through having smelled the smoke. But if one sees someone smoking outside, one inevitably gets more information: normally, one cannot see someone smoking outside without seeing someone of a particular height, sex, and so on. The content of perception is *replete* in a way the content of belief is not. This is sometimes put by saying that perceptual content has a 'fineness of grain' which belief content does not have; it is also said that the content of perception rules out more possibilities, so in that sense contains more information. Your belief that someone is smoking outside is neutral on whether this is a man or a woman, and therefore does not rule either possibility out; your perception might well rule out one of these possibilities.

Here we have, then, two features of perceptual states which help us indi- viduate them. The first feature is that perception aims at truth, though in a way that is compatible with us being able to disbelieve our perceptions. Per- ception presents the world as being a certain way, it 'aims' (as it were) to tell us how the perceptible world is; but this presentation can be overridden by conflicting knowledge. And a distinctive feature of the perception here is that the perceptual state can remain even though the belief has corrected it. The second feature is that the content of perception is more detailed, more spe- cific, containing more information than the contents of beliefs and other propositional attitudes. Indeed, sometimes it is said that the 'richness' of perceptual experience defies the kind of classification which we can give of our beliefs: the content of perception outruns our modes of description of it.

This last feature has led some philosophers to claim that the content of perceptual experience is *non-conceptual*.[41] Although the terminology is in some ways confusing, I agree with them; in the rest of this section I will explain what this idea means and give reasons to believe it.

First, the terminology. The term 'non-conceptual content' suggests a con- trast with conceptual content; and in fact those who believe that perceptions have non-conceptual content often also claim that the content of belief is conceptual. But this way of talking can be misleading. For it makes it sound as if there are two kinds of intentional content, conceptual and non-conceptual, and while conceptual content is made up out of concepts, non-conceptual content isn't. But on some theories of the contents of propositional attitudes, this distinction makes no sense. For example: consider the view (introduced in §33) that the content of a belief should be given by a set of possible worlds, the set of all those worlds in which the belief is true. In the only sense in which this content has constituents, its constituents are the possible worlds and their inhabitants which are the members of this set. (Assume for the sake of argument that there are such things.) There is no sense in which the content of the belief, in the sense of the proposition believed, is composed of concepts—yet this could hardly be an objection to the thesis that the content of a belief is given by a set of possible worlds.[42] The fault seems to be rather with the idea that conceptual content is 'composed of concepts'.

The problem, however, is superficial. When we talk about the distinction between conceptual and non-conceptual contents, we are really talking about a distinction between kinds of intentional states or acts. To say that a belief has a conceptual content is to say something about the conditions for having that belief. If someone believes that *a is F*, then they must have the concept *F*, and the concept *a*. We could, then, consider concepts as the constituents of certain intentional states themselves, in the sense that being in these intentional states—conceptual states—requires having certain concepts. (Example: if one believes that fish swim, one must have the concept of a fish.) So, likewise, we can say that being in non-conceptual states does not require having certain concepts. But which concepts? The natural answer that to be in a non-conceptual state with content p, one does not have to possess the concepts which one *would* have to possess if one *were* in a conceptual state with content p.

We may call these concepts the concepts which are *canonical for being in a state with conceptual content p* (or for short: those concepts which are 'canonical for p'). Then we can say that a state with nonconceptual content is one of which the following is true:

(NCC): In order for subjects to be in a state with a content p, they do not have to possess the concepts which are canonical for p.

The idea of concepts which are canonical for a certain content is just the idea that there are certain concepts which *essentially* characterize a given content.[43] The content expressed by the sentence 'Pigs fly' is essentially characterized in terms of the concepts *pigs* and *fly*. These are the concepts which you have to possess if you are to be a conceptual state with *pigs fly* as its content. So the basic idea of a non-conceptual state, S, is the idea of a state with content, and the content has its canonical concepts, and yet these concepts do not have to be possessed by the subject in order to be in S. For example: it might be said that to believe that a certain pig is flying you have to have the concept of a pig, but that to *see* that this pig is flying you don't need to. In what follows, I may occasionally call non-conceptual states 'states with non-conceptual content'; this should be understood as a variant on 'non-conceptual state'.

That's just an illustration. Before defending in more detail how this idea applies to perceptual states, we need to clarify how I am using the idea of a concept. Someone who believed in Jerry Fodor's representational theory of mind might not be interested in the distinction I have just drawn between conceptual and non-conceptual states.[44] They might say: all intentional states have representations as constituents; this is as much the case for the perception of a flying pig as it is for a belief about a flying pig. What is the point of distinguishing, among these representations, between those which are concepts and those which are not? What is so significant about concepts?

There is one straightforward kind of answer to this question, which I reject. This is that having concepts is a matter of having a language; someone has the concept A when they have a word for A in their language. So creatures with no language have no concepts.[45] One could combine this view either with the acceptance of non-conceptual states or with the rejection of these states. If one rejects non-conceptual states, then one is committed to the view that only language-users can be in intentional states. This is John McDowell's view. But if one accepts non-conceptual states, then the conceptual/non-conceptual distinction is just the distinction between those intentional states which one can only be in by virtue of being a language-user, and those which one can be in without needing a language. And this distinction is one which many philosophers will accept; so if that is all that the conceptual/non-conceptual distinction comes to, then it is not particularly controversial.

So there are two ways of pursuing the thesis that having a concept is a matter of having a language; the first (McDowell's) is implausible, since it does not allow anything amounting to reasoning to non-linguistic creatures, while the second does not give us an interesting conceptual/non-conceptual distinction. The interesting conceptual/non-conceptual distinction comes from rejecting the association between concepts and language. To have a concept, on this view, depends on the kinds of recognitional, inferential, and other capacities one can exercise in one's thinking. Not all these capacities depend on one's mastery of a language. The suggestion is that one could have, for example, a capacity for recognizing a certain kind of animal X, and this capacity is something one also employs in reasoning about animals about this kind. One need not have a word for the kind of animal in question, but one has enough of an idea of what the thing is to qualify as having a concept of X. An analogy: we are all familiar with the phenomenon of knowing exactly the person we are thinking about without knowing (or while temporarily forgetting) their name. The sense in which we know whom we are thinking of is analogous to having the concept; forgetting the name is analogous to not having a single word to express that concept.

Employing this rough idea of a concept, then, and our definition NCC above, we can say that a non-conceptual state, then, is one where the world is presented or represented in a certain way, but the subject does not have the kinds of inferential or recognitional capacities (which are what concepts are) for each way in which the world is presented. To apply this to the case of perception, consider colour experience: is it plausible to say that each of us has a distinct concept (in the above sense) for each precise shade of colour we are able to perceive? If it isn't, then this can be a reason for holding that perceptual experiences have non-conceptual content: perception has a 'phenomenological richness' which is not constrained by the concepts the perceiver has.[46] There are various ways the claim could be filled out. One is Christopher Peacocke's theory that part of the content of visual experience is what he calls a 'scenario': a set of all those ways of filling out, with properties and relations, the space around the perceiver which are consistent with the correctness of the experience. The experience is correct when the actual filling out of space around the perceiver is a member of that set.[47] Opinions differ on whether perceptual states are wholly conceptual, wholly non-conceptual, or some mixture. McDowell holds that they are wholly conceptual, Evans that they are wholly non-conceptual, while Peacocke holds that experiences have many layers of content, some of which are conceptual and some non-conceptual.

McDowell has argued that to treat perceptions as non-conceptual is to be committed to a version of what Wilfrid Sellars called 'the Myth of the Given': the idea that experience involves being presented with an unconceptualized 'given' which the mind then goes on to conceptualize.[48] McDowell argues instead that the content of experience is wholly conceptual. So how does he account for the phenomenological richness of (say) colour experience? He claims that, where we have discrimination (between colours, say) we may not have a distinct word for each colour, but we do have 'a recognitional capacity, possibly quite short-lived, that sets in with the experience'.[49] This capacity we can express by using a complex demonstrative expression 'that shade' to refer to the shade in question. And such recognitional capacities are conceptual, given the equation between 'conceptual' and 'linguistically expressible'.

I am not able to discuss here the many things which fall under the heading of the Myth of the Given. Instead, I shall end this discussion by raising the following question: what entitles McDowell to say that what is expressed, in the envisaged case, by saying 'that shade' is a concept in any interesting sense of the word? There does not seem to be any necessary link to any of the capacities which I have claimed are associated with having a concept: I need not be able to recognize the shade again (the capacity may 'short-lived'), I need not be able to imagine it or remember it; there is nothing in what

McDowell says that makes me capable of reasoning about that shade, once the experience has passed. I cannot manipulate my idea of that shade in thought, except when I am confronting it. The main thing which seems to lie behind the idea that 'that shade' expresses a concept is McDowell's association of having a concept with speaking a language. I have rejected this view, but I cannot pretend to have refuted it. The relation between language and concepts (or thought generally) is a large and complex area which needs further investigation. But, to borrow a Czech saying from another context, we are not for the last time in this forest.

Endnotes

Chapter 1: **Mind**

1. In Steve Pyke, *Philosophers*.
2. See e.g. Richard Rorty, *Philosophy and the Mirror of Nature*, ch. 1.
3. D. C. Dennett, *Brainstorms*, Introduction, p. xviii. For a simple explanation of Church's thesis and the idea of a Turing machine, see my *The Mechanical Mind*, ch. 3.
4. See Timothy Williamson, *Vagueness*.
5. See Anita Avramides, *Other Minds*.
6. See Thomas Nagel, *The View from Nowhere*, ch. 1.
7. A. W. Moore, *Points of View*, 282.
8. F. Brentano, *Psychology from an Empirical Standpoint*, 125.
9. John Searle, *The Rediscovery of the Mind*, 155.
10. See E. Husserl, 'Phenomenology'.
11. See G. E. M. Anscombe, 'The intentionality of sensation: a grammatical feature'. Anscombe gives no further reference for this (in itself plausible) etymological claim. For further reading on the origins of the idea of intentionality, see the bibliography of my 'Intentionality'.
12. See Anthony Kenny, 'Intentionality: Aquinas and Wittgenstein'.
13. Thomas Hobbes, *Leviathan*, Part 1, ch. 4, 'Of Speech', p. 100.
14. G. W. Leibniz, *New Essays on Human Understanding*, Bk. IV, ch 17, p. 8. See Mary Spencer, 'Why the "S" in intension?', 114–5; this note corrects the attribution of the invention of the term 'intension' to Sir William Hamilton, by P. T. Geach, *Reference and Generality*, Anscombe, 'The intentionality of sensation', 159, and W. Kneale and M. Kneale, *The Development of Logic*.
15. Brentano, *Psychology from an Empirical Standpoint*, 88.
16. See Chisholm, *Perceiving: A Philosophical Study*, ch. 11.
17. W. V. Quine, *Word and Object*.
18. For further defence of this claim, see my 'Intentionality'.
19. See Hartry Field, 'Mental representation'.
20. Here I take issue with J. Searle, *Intentionality*, 24.
21. J. Searle, *Intentionality*, 117. The phrase 'ordinary object' occurs on p.18.
22. See M. G. F. Martin, 'An eye directed outward', 101.
23. See Bob Hale, *Abstract Objects*, and David Lewis, *On the Plurality of Worlds* for discussion of the idea of abstractness of objects.
24. Anscombe, 'The intentionality of sensation' 161.

25. Russell, 'On denoting'.

26. See Valberg, 'The puzzle of experience', 22.

27. Anscombe, 'The intentionality of sensation'.

28. See Quine, 'On what there is'.

29. See Quine, 'Quantifiers and propositional attitudes' and David Kaplan, 'Quantifying in'.

30. Gareth Evans, *The Varieties of Reference*, 16. I have used the more standard term 'reference' instead of Evans's 'Meaning'. Here I am following the terminological conventions introduced by A. W. Moore in *Meaning and Reference*, Introduction.

31. Evans, *The Varieties of Reference*, 62.

32. G. Frege, 'On sense and reference' 27.

33. Frege, 'Letter to Jourdain', 45.

34. Here I correct something that I said on p. 36 of *The Mechanical Mind*.

35. For a valuable discussion of this question, see Alberto Voltolini, 'Objects as intentional and as real'.

36. This, of course, bypasses many interesting questions about fiction. See David Lewis, 'Truth in fiction'.

37. Good discussions of this traditional problem can be found in Michael Dummett, *Origins of Analytical Philosophy*; A. N. Prior, *Objects of Thought*; and J. L. Mackie, 'Problems of intentionality'. For a discussion of the problem in Aristotle, see Victor Caston, 'Aristotle and the problem of intentionality'.

38. See Quine, 'On what there is', and Anscombe 'The intentionality of sensation', 161.

39. Russell, 'Descriptions', 47

40. See Evans, *The Varieties of Reference*, ch. 10.

41. See the attempt by David Lewis to clarify what is at stake in 'Allism and noneism'.

42. See Timothy Williamson, 'Is knowing a state of mind?' for the latter view.

43. See e.g. Hartry Field, 'Mental representation'; William Lyons, *Aspects of Intentionality*.

44. Brentano, *Psychology from an Empirical Standpoint*, 88.

45. For the relation between the famous passage and the idea of the non-existence of the object of thought, see my 'Intentionality as the mark of the mental', 244, n. 31.

46. Kazimir Twardowski, *On the Content and Object of Presentations*.

47. Dummett, *Frege*, 227.

48. Here I am inspired by Dummett's discussion of the distinction between sense and reference in ibid. 227ff.. See also John McDowell's 'On the sense and reference of a proper name', 114–5, for another way of treating the distinction.

49. P. T. Geach, 'Intentional identity', 147.

50. Anscombe, 'The intentionality of sensation', 161.

Chapter 2: **Body**

1. René Descartes, *Meditations on First Philosophy*, Meditation 6, p. 159.

2. Ibid. 159.

3. See the essay by Jonathan Cole and Jacques Paillard, in Bermúdez, Eilan, and Marcel (eds.), *The Body and the Self.*

4. For Descartes's views on substance, see Descartes, *Principles of Philosophy*, §§51–3.

5. For an excellent brief account of substance in one traditional sense see David Wiggins, 'Substance', in A. C. Grayling (ed.), *Philosophy: A Guide through the Subject.* I take the terminology of a substance being 'wholly present' from D. H. Mellor, *Real Time*, ch. 8.

6. Among those who would deny that persons are substances in this sense are Derek Parfit, 'Personal identity', and David Lewis, 'Survival and identity'; Lewis is generally sceptical about the traditional idea of something's identity through time consisting of its persistence over time; see *On the Plurality of Worlds*, section on persistence.

7. These matters are well reviewed by Roger Woolhouse, *The Concept of Substance in Seventeenth Century Metaphysics.*

8. See also Susan James, 'The emergence of the Cartesian mind'.

9. See Howard Robinson, 'The anti-materialist strategy and the "knowledge argument"'.

10. See e.g. Paul Churchland, *Matter and Consciousness*, 8.

11. The first view is that of P. F. Strawson in *Individuals*, ch. 3; the second view is very common; it is well represented by Nagel, *The View from Nowhere*, 51.

12. I therefore disagree with those theorists who call these entities 'events' (see Kim, 'Events as property-exemplifications'). I follow Davidson's clarification of these issues (see the various papers on events in *Essays on Actions and Events*). See also the useful ch. 8 of Mellor, *Real Time.*

13. Peter T. Geach, *Mental Acts*, 9.

14. Here I follow Mellor, *Real Time*, ch. 8.

15. See *The Philosophical Works of Rene Descartes*, vol. III.

16. See David Fair, 'Causation and the flow of energy'.

17. Jerry Fodor, 'The mind–body problem', 25.

18. A dualist view which holds that minds are extended in space is W. D. Hart's view in *The Engines of the Soul.*

19. For the idea of two things in the same place at the same time, see David Wiggins, 'On being in the same place at the same time'.

20. See David Papineau, 'The rise of physicalism'.

21. David Lewis, 'An argument for the identity theory', 105.

22. See David Owens, 'Levels of explanation'. In my paper 'All God has to do', I suggest a way in which a non-physicalist might employ the image.

23. See Papineau, 'Why supervenience?'

24. See 'There is no question of physicalism', where much (too much, perhaps) is made of this open-ended character. See also Pettit, 'A definition of physicalism', and Papineau, 'The reason why: response to Crane'.

25. Contrary to what is claimed by Jeffrey Poland, *Physicalism: The Philosophical Foundations.*

26. See Frank Jackson, 'Epiphenomenal qualia', for this combination of dualism and the completeness of physics.

27. This is a very crude version of the counterfactual analysis, but that doesn't matter for our purposes. See David Lewis, 'Causation' (and the Postscripts to this paper) and Laurie Paul and Ned Hall (eds.), *The Counterfactual Analysis of Causation.*

28. See Fred Dretske, *Explaining Behavior*, Preface.

29. I have in mind here Lewis, 'An argument for the identity theory', and D. M. Armstrong, *A Materialist Theory of the Mind*; an epiphenomenalist approach is defended by Chalmers, *The Conscious Mind.*

30. And this is the way he argues for it: see Davidson, 'Mental events'. In 'The mental causation debate' I spell out why Davidson's argument is an instance of the kind of argument described in §13 above.

31. Hume, *Treatise of Human Nature*, on 'rules by which to judge causes and effects'.

32. See e.g. Paul Churchland, 'Eliminative materialism and the propositional attitudes'. For a discussion of the view, see my *The Mechanical Mind*, ch. 2.

33. See Peter Smith, 'Modest reductions and the unity of science'.

34. Davidson, 'Mental events', is an example.

35. 'The nature of mental states', 228. I have replaced Putnam's 'brain state theory' with 'identity theory'.

36. Ibid. 228

37. For the first response, see David Lewis, 'Review of Putnam'; Berent Enç, 'In defense of the identity theory'; Jaegwon Kim, 'Physicalism and the multiple realizability of mental states'; and Christopher Hill, *Sensations.* For the second, see Kim, 'Physicalism and the multiple realizability of mental states', esp. 235–6. For discussion of this objection, I am grateful to Lorien Vecellio.

38. For other reasons for being suspicious about the idea of token identity, see my 'Dualism, monism, physicalism', and Kim *The Philosophy of Mind*, 60.

39. See Kim, *Mind in a Physical World*, ch. 1, for an excellent statement of this kind of point.

40. Here I skip over many difficult metaphysical questions: see e.g. Allan Gibbard, 'Contingent identity', who argues that this is a case of identity; the idea of

constitution is defended by David Wiggins, *Sameness and Substance*, ch. 1, and E. J. Lowe, *Kinds of Being*.

41. Horgan, 'From supervenience to superdupervenience: meeting the demands of a material world'.

42. For a different route to the same conclusion, see A. D. Smith, 'Non-reductive physicalism'.

43. This is the approach taken by Tyler Burge, 'Mind–body causation and explanatory practice', and by Lynne Rudder Baker, 'Metaphysics and mental causation'. Both are effectively criticized by Kim, *Mind in a Physical World*, ch. 3.

44. See e.g. Frank Jackson and Philip Pettit, 'Functionalism and broad content', Fred Dretske, *Explaining Behavior*, and my 'The mental causation debate', for discussion of these views.

45. Jackson, *From Metaphysics to Ethics*, ch. 1. What 'minimal' means need not worry us here. See also David Lewis, 'Reduction of mind'.

46. I am indebted in my discussion of this view to Barry Loewer's paper, 'From physics to physicalism' and to discussions with Loewer.

47. See Chalmers, *The Conscious Mind*.

48. 'Mental events' and 'Thinking causes'.

49. Davidson's response to the charge that he has a problem in explaining mental causation is in 'Thinking causes'; but the response is really implicit in his 'Causal relations' (see esp. p. 150). I defend the coherence of Davidson's position in 'The mental causation debate', §8.

50. McLaughlin argues in addition that downward causation and configurational forces are not incompatible with quantum mechanics, nor with special and general relativity. See 'The rise and fall of British emergentism', 53–4, and 74–5. But the essential point can be made in relation to classical mechanics. I should emphasize that McLaughlin himself does not accept the existence of such configurational forces. For more on this issue, see my 'The significance of emergence'.

51. C. D. Broad, *Scientific Thought*, 177.

52. For further defence of this point, see 'The significance of emergence'.

53. Lewis, *Counterfactuals*.

54. This is a lesson I take from Stephen Yablo's fine paper, 'Mental causation'.

55. This is Papineau's view in 'The rise of physicalism'.

56. For further defence of the completeness of physics, see Barry Loewer, 'From physics to physicalism'; for the first way of rejecting the completeness of physics, see Nancy Cartwright, 'Fundamentalism vs. the patchwork of laws'. The second way of rejecting the completeness thesis is implicit in Tim Crane and D. H. Mellor, 'There is no question of physicalism'.

57. Sydney Shoemaker, 'The mind–body problem', 55. Representative statements of the kind of point Shoemaker is making here can be found in Colin McGinn, 'Can we

solve the mind–body problem?', and most famously, Thomas Nagel, 'What is it like to be a bat?'

58. The story is reported in O. R. Jones, 'The way things look and the way things are'.

59. David Lewis, 'Mad pain and martian pain', *Philosophical Papers*, vol. I.

60. Frank Jackson, 'Epiphenomenal qualia'; Howard Robinson, *Matter and Sense*.

61. See Crane and Mellor, 'There is no question of physicalism'.

Chapter 3: **Consciousness**

1. See Neil Campbell Manson, ' "A tumbling-ground for whimsies?" The history and contemporary relevance of the conscious/unconscious contrast'.

2. Jean-Paul Sartre, *Being and Nothingness*, p. xxvii.

3. See David Rosenthal, 'Two concepts of consciousness', and Ned Block, 'On a confusion about a function of consciousness', 384.

4. Block, 'On a confusion about a function of consciousness', 377.

5. Nagel, 'What is it like to be a bat?', 519.

6. Block, 'On a confusion about a function of consciousness', 380.

7. See McCulloch, 'The very idea of the phenomenological'.

8. Block, 'On a confusion about a function of consciousness', 382.

9. Ibid. 384.

10. David Rosenthal, 'Identity theories', 349.

11. Kim, *Philosophy of Mind*, 13.

12. See John McDowell, *Mind and World*; Armstrong, *A Materialist Theory of the Mind*.

13. See McCulloch, 'The very idea of the phenomenological'. To note this difference is not to go as far as McCulloch and deny that phrases like 'visual sensation' make sense. Of course they make sense: see Geach, *Mental Acts*, 122–3.

14. Block, 'Inverted earth', 677; see also Dennett's use of the word in *Consciousness Explained*, 372.

15. For 'higher-order thought' or HOT theories of consciousness, see David Rosenthal, 'Two concepts of consciousness'; D. H. Mellor, 'Conscious belief'; Peter Carruthers, 'Brute experience'. Sometimes HOT theories are put forward as theories of all conscious states, not just conscious thoughts. This has the consequence that a sensation is not conscious unless it is the object of a higher-order thought. Also, sometimes consciousness is explained in terms of the *availability* to higher-order thought, in other cases it is explained in terms of an actual episode or act of thinking. I find all these views implausible, but I will not discuss them here.

16. Searle, *The Rediscovery of the Mind*, 84.

17. See Michael Tye, *Ten Problems of Consciousness*, ch. 4; Armstrong, *A Materialist Theory of the Mind*, ch. 14.

18. I am indebted here to M. G. F. Martin, 'Bodily awareness: a sense of ownership'. See also D. M. Armstrong, *Bodily Sensations.*

19. Tye, *Ten Problems of Consciousness.*

20. The example comes from Roberto Casati, 'Space, objects and intuition'; he does not draw the analogy with Block's argument.

21. Frank Jackson, 'The existence of mental objects', 115. Jackson is criticizing Bruce Aune, *Knowledge, Mind and Nature,* 130.

22. For weak intentionalist theories of visual perception, see Ned Block, 'Inverted earth'; Brian Loar, 'Transparent experience'; Christopher Peacocke, *Sense and Content,* ch. 1; Sydney Shoemaker, 'Qualities and qualia: what's in the mind?'

23. This is a point well made by Tye, 'A representational theory of pains and their phenomenal nature', 333.

24. See J. J. Valberg, *The Puzzle of Experience,* ch. 2. For related conceptions of the 'transparency' of experience, see Gilbert Harman, 'The intrinsic quality of experience'; Michael Tye, 'Visual qualia and visual content'. Brian Loar ('Transparent experience') argues for the unusual position that the existence of qualia is compatible with the facts about transparency. For an illuminating general discussion of transparency, see M. G. F. Martin, 'The transparency of experience' (forthcoming).

25. Tye, *Ten Problems of Consciousness,* chs. 3–7.

26. Tye is, of course, well aware of this sort of objection, and responds to it in *Ten Problems of Consciousness;* I reject this response for the reasons given in my paper, 'The intentional structure of consciousness'.

27. The view derives from D. M. Armstrong. See his *Bodily Sensations* and *A Materialist Theory of the Mind,* ch. 14.

28. See also Fred Dretske, *Naturalizing the Mind,* 102–3.

29. Christopher Peacocke, 'Consciousness and other minds', 115. I am indebted in this paragraph to Peacocke's discussion of the concepts of pain and hurting, though I do not mean to imply that Peacocke holds a perceptual theory of sensation in my sense of that term.

30. For an elementary exposition of the fundamental problems, see my *The Mechanical Mind;* ch. 5.

31. For a good general discussion of the three arguments, see Robert van Gulick, 'Understanding the phenomenal mind'.

32. See David Chalmers, *The Conscious Mind.*

33. The term 'explanatory gap' was introduced by Joseph Levine; see 'Materialism and qualia: the explanatory gap'. In *The Conscious Mind,* Chalmers helpfully distinguishes five separate arguments for the inexplicability of consciousness (ch. 3) and distinguishes questions about inexplicability from ontological questions (ch. 4). The present discussion simplifies somewhat on the question on explicability, but in a way which I hope captures the central lines of thought in this debate.

34. See Terence Horgan, 'From supervenience to superdupervenience', 560; Levine, 'On leaving out what it's like', 548.

35. Levine, 'On leaving out what it's like', 548.

36. McGinn, 'Can we solve the mind–body problem?'

37. See David Papineau, 'Mind the gap', for this point.

38. Levine, 'On leaving out what it's like', 550.

39. Ibid. 549.

40. Van Gulick ('Understanding the phenomenal mind', 564) construes the explanatory gap argument in a rather different (but not incompatible) way.

41. See David Lewis, 'What experience teaches', 281; see also D. H. Mellor, 'Nothing like experience'.

42. For these views, see G. Frege, 'The thought'; D. H. Mellor, *The Facts of Causation*; J. L. Austin, 'Unfair to facts'; and Donald Davidson, 'True to the facts'.

43. For a useful catalogue of responses to the knowledge argument, see Robert Van Gulick, 'Understanding the phenomenal mind', 559–63.

44. See Lewis, 'What experience teaches'; Lawrence Nemirow, 'Physicalism and the cognitive role of acquaintance'; Mellor, 'Nothing like experience'.

45. A. W. Moore, *Points of View*, 171. For present purposes, 'non-representational' can be read as 'non-propositional'. I am indebted here to Moore's book (especially ch. 8, §1) and to Paul Snowdon, 'Knowing how and knowing that: a distinction and its uses reconsidered'.

46. Brian Loar, 'Phenomenal states', 607. I must ignore here the bearing this point has on the famous 'Frege–Geach' problem.

47. But see Churchland, 'Reduction, qualia and the direct introspection of brain states'. In *Consciousness Explained*, Dennett questions the methodology of thought-experiments as a way of learning about consciousness.

48. For the use of the parallel with indexicals as a response to the knowledge argument, see Georges Rey, 'Sensational sentences'.

49. See John Perry, 'The problem of the essential indexical'.

50. So I disagree with Van Gulick ('Understanding the phenomenal mind', 562–3) that this is the most fruitful line to pursue.

51. Here I agree with Tye, *Ten Problems of Consciousness*.

52. See Frank Jackson, 'Postscript' to 'What Mary did not know'; and Lewis, 'What experience teaches'.

53. See e.g. Frank Jackson, *From Metaphysics to Ethics*, ch. 1 and 2.

54. See Kripke, *Naming and Necessity*; and Chalmers, *The Conscious Mind*, 148–9.

55. See Shoemaker, 'Functionalism and qualia'; Chalmers, *The Conscious Mind*, ch. 4.

56. This point is clearly made by Janet Levin in her article 'Qualia' in the *Routledge Encyclopedia of Philosophy*. It is worth mentioning that all three arguments are implicit in Nagel's seminal 1974 discussion, 'What is it like to be a bat?'.

57. Daniel Dennett makes a bold attempt to do this to the thought-experiments in *Consciousness Explained* (though not with the aim of defending the idea of a conceptual connection).

Chapter 4: **Thought**

1. Frege, 'The thought'.
2. The terminology derives from W. E. Johnson, *Logic*.
3. I have been persuaded of this thesis by M. G. F. Martin (see his unpublished paper 'Events and states') though he may not agree with much of what I say about it in this chapter.
4. For a useful discussion, see Christopher Peacocke, 'Conscious attitudes, attention and self-knowledge', 88ff.
5. See Jane Heal, 'Moore's paradox: a Wittgensteinian approach'.
6. For a discussion of the idea of belief aiming at truth, see J. David Velleman, 'Truth as the aim of belief'.
7. See Geach, *Mental Acts*, 8–9.
8. For a clear account of the functionalist theory of the mind, see Daniel Braddon-Mitchell and Frank Jackson, *Philosophy of Mind and Cognition*.
9. Ibid. 123.
10. Gareth Evans, *The Varieties of Reference*, 225.
11. Bertrand Russell, *The Analysis of Mind*.
12. See Christopher Peacocke, *A Study of Concepts*, ch. 1.
13. A systematic metaphysics which is based on the idea of a state of affairs is D. M. Armstrong's *A World of States of Affairs*.
14. Some of the standard approaches are collected in Salmon and Soames (eds.), *Propositions and Attitudes*.
15. See Nathan Salmon, *Frege's Puzzle*, for a defence of this view.
16. See Searle, *Intentionality*, ch. 1, for this kind of proposal.
17. This is one of the lessons of Quine's 'Quantifiers and propositional attitudes'.
18. By Quine, in ibid.
19. Notably, Burge, 'Belief *de re*'.
20. See ch. 2 of Gabriel Segal's *A Slim Book about Narrow Content* for a persuasive internalist case based on the phenomenon of empty concepts.
21. For a contemporary account of Russell's theory and its significance for philosophy of language, see Stephen Neale, *Descriptions*. For an account of the historical

background and an account of Russell's original motivations, see Peter Hylton, 'The theory of descriptions'.

22. W. V. Quine, *Mathematical Logic*, 147

23. John McDowell, 'Having the world in view: Sellars, Kant and intentionality', 482.

24. Ibid. 483.

25. See Segal, *A Slim Book*, ch. 2.

26. See e.g. Lewis, 'Psychophysical and theoretical identifications', § II.

27. Hilary Putnam, 'The meaning of "meaning"'. For a useful anthology on this kind of argument, see Goldberg and Pessin (eds.), *The Twin Earth Chronicles*.

28. Some of these issues are distinguished in my paper, 'All the difference in the world'.

29. For an excellent discussion of the general form of the argument, see Gregory McCulloch, *The Life of the Mind*.

30. See Gregory McCulloch, 'The spirit of Twin Earth', which effectively rebuts my 'All the difference in the world' on this point.

31. This is, of course, Fodor's solution to the Twin Earth problem in *Psychosemantics*, ch. 2, though I arrive at it from a somewhat different route. Nor do I accept Fodor's view that narrow content is 'inexpressible'.

32. P. F. Strawson, *Individuals*, ch. 1.

33. See John Searle, *Intentionality*, ch. 9.

34. See again Fodor, *Psychosemantics*, ch. 2.

35. See *The Mechanical Mind*, ch. 5 for a survey.

Chapter 5: **Perception**

1. A recent example of such an approach is Bill Brewer, *Perception and Reason*.

2. I am indebted here to the important discussions of the problem of perception by M. G. F. Martin; see esp. 'Beyond dispute: sense-data, intentionally and the mind–body problem' and 'Perceptual content'.

3. For a useful discussion of 'direct' see Paul Snowdon, 'How to interpret "direct perception"'.

4. For smells and sounds as the objects of the senses of smell and hearing, see A. D. Smith, *The Object of Perception*.

5. Howard Robinson, *Perception*, 32.

6. G. E. Moore, *Selected Writings*, 48.

7. See Martin, 'Beyond dispute'.

8. Austin, *Sense and Sensibilia*.

9. This kind of elaboration is given in J. J. Valberg, *The Puzzle of Experience*, ch. 1.

10. See Valberg, 'The puzzle of experience'.

11. *Sense and Sensibilia*, 32.

12. For more examples, see Anscombe, 'The intentionality of sensation'.

13. Robinson, *Perception*, 32.

14. 'A defence of common sense', 128. For a discussion of this central point in Sense-Datum theories, see my 'The origins of qualia'. I am especially indebted to M. G. F. Martin here and in the paragraph that follows: see his 'J. L. Austin: *Sense and Sensibilia* reconsidered'.

15. See e.g. Bertrand Russell, *The Problems of Philosophy*, ch. 1 and 2.

16. Wilfred Sellars, *Empiricism and the Philosophy of Mind*; Robert Brandom, *Making it Explicit*; John McDowell, *Mind and World*.

17. Notice that it is only this narrow notion of an intentional state which M. G. F. Martin classifies as intentional in his 'Perceptual content' and 'Setting things before the mind'. Martin takes as a defining feature of an intentional perceptual state that it represents mind-independent entities and that it does not imply the existence of these entities. I prefer to think of Martin's Naive Realism and the Sense-Datum theory as intentionalist accounts in a more general sense, since they all involve the idea that something is given to the mind. The disagreement with Martin's position is terminological, at least where perception is concerned.

18. For the adverbial theory, see Chisholm, *Perceiving*.

19. See Frank Jackson, 'The existence of mental objects', and Robinson, *Perception*, ch. 7, §§5–10.

20. This difference is noted by G. Warnock, Introduction to *The Philosophy of Perception*, pp.6–7; but he does not try to explain it.

21. I am indebted here to discussions with Matthew Nudds.

22. See Loar, 'Transparent experience'.

23. See Williamson, 'Is knowing a state of mind?', 535.

24. Michael Tye, 'Visual qualia and visual content', 160. See also Gilbert Harman, 'The intrinsic quality of experience'.

25. For a version of this view, see Peacocke, *Sense and Content*, ch. 1.

26. Bill Brewer, *Perception and Reason*, 156.

27. Paul A. Boghossian and J. David Velleman, 'Colour as a secondary quality', 91–2.

28. Robinson, *Perception* , 165.

29. For the first, see Shoemaker, 'The inverted spectrum'; for the second, see Block, 'Inverted earth'. Block credits the example to Gilbert Harman.

30. See Block, 'Inverted earth', 677.

31. For an interesting solution along these lines, see David R. Hilbert and Mark Eli Kalderon, 'Color and the inverted spectrum'.

32. These two issues are run together in Harman, 'The intrinsic quality of experience'.

33. Here I follow Tye, 'Visual qualia and visual content', 168.

34. Jonathan Bennett, 'Substance, reality and primary qualities'.

35. Shoemaker, 'Phenomenal character'.

36. For criticisms of both the primary quality view and the dispositionalist view of colour see Justin Broackes's excellent 'The autonomy of colour'.

37. For the defence of this claim, see Block's 'Inverted earth', 683.

38. Ibid. 687.

39. See E. J. Craig, 'Sensory experience and the foundations of knowledge'.

40. For the belief-independence of perception, see Evans, *The Varieties of Reference*, 123, and M. G. F. Martin, 'The rational role of experience'.

41. Evans, *The Varieties of Reference, passim*; Peacocke, *A Study of Concepts*, ch. 3; Bermúdez, *The Paradox of Self-Consciousness*.

42. This point is made by Robert Stalnaker, 'What might non-conceptual content be?'

43. See Adrian Cussins, 'The connectionist construction of concepts', 382–3.

44. See Fodor, *Psychosemantics*, Introduction and ch. 1.

45. John McDowell defends this view in *Mind and World*.

46. See Evans, *The Varieties of Reference*, 229.

47. Peacocke, *A Study of Concepts*, ch. 3.

48. McDowell, *Mind and World*, ch. 3; Sellars, *Empiricism and the Philosophy of Mind*.

49. McDowell, *Mind and World* , 57.

References

When a reprinting is listed, this is intended to imply that pages references in the text are to this reprint. When an item is listed as being in a volume, and no bibliographical details are given for that volume, then the volume has been referred to more than once, and it will be found as a separate entry in the bibliography.

ANSCOMBE, G. E. M., 'The intentionality of sensation: a grammatical feature', in R. J. Butler (ed.), *Analytical Philosophy: 2nd Series* (Oxford: Blackwell, 1965).

ARMSTRONG, D. M., *Bodily Sensations* (London: Routledge and Kegan Paul, 1962).

—— *A Materialist Theory of the Mind* (London: Routledge and Kegan Paul, 1968).

—— *A World of States of Affairs* (Cambridge: Cambridge University Press, 1997).

AUNE, BRUCE, *Knowledge, Mind and Nature* (New York: Random House, 1967).

AUSTIN, J. L., 'Unfair to facts', in *Philosophical Papers* (Oxford: Clarendon Press, 1961).

—— *Sense and Sensibilia* (Oxford: Clarendon Press, 1962).

AVRAMIDES, ANITA, *Other Minds* (London: Routledge, 2000).

BENNETT, JONATHAN, 'Substance, reality and primary qualities', *American Philosophical Quarterly*, 2 (1965).

BERMÚDEZ, JOSÉ LUIS, *The Paradox of Self-Consciousness* (Cambridge, Mass.: MIT Press, 1998).

BLOCK, NED, 'Troubles with functionalism', in Block (ed.), *Readings in the Philosophy of Psychology*, Vol. I.

—— 'On a confusion about a function of consciousness', *Behavioral and Brain Sciences*, 18 (1995), 227–247; repr. Block, Flanagan, and Güzeldere (eds.), *The Nature of Consciousness*.

—— 'Inverted earth', in Block, Flanagan, and Güzeldere (eds.), *The Nature of Consciousness*.

—— (ed.), *Readings in the Philosophy of Psychology*, 2 vols. (London: Methuen, 1980).

—— OWEN FLANAGAN, and GÜVEN GÜZELDERE (eds.), *The Nature of Consciousness* (Cambridge, Mass.: MIT Press, 1997).

BOGHOSSIAN, PAUL and J. DAVID VELLEMAN, 'Colour as a secondary quality', *Mind*, 98 (1989), 81–103; repr. in Byrne and Hilbert (eds.), *Readings on Color, Volume I.*

BRADDON-MITCHELL, DAVID, and FRANK JACKSON, *Philosophy of Mind and Cognition* (Oxford: Blackwell, 1996).

BRANDOM, ROBERT, *Making It Explicit: Reasoning, Representing and Discursive Commitment* (Cambridge, Mass.: Harvard University Press, 1994).

BRENTANO, FRANZ, *Psychology From An Empirical Standpoint*, originally published 1874; English edition ed. L. McAlister (London: Routledge and Kegan Paul, 1973).

BREWER, BILL, *Perception and Reason* (Oxford: Clarendon Press, 1999).

BROACKES, JUSTIN, 'The autonomy of colour', in David Charles and Kathleen Lennon (eds.) *Reduction, Explanation, and Realism* (Oxford: Oxford University Press, 1992); repr. Byrne and Hilbert (eds.), *Readings on Color, Volume I.*

BROAD, C. D., *Scientific Thought* (London: Routledge and Kegan Paul, 1921).

—— *The Mind and its Place in Nature* (London: Routledge and Kegan Paul, 1925).

BURGE, TYLER, 'Belief *de re*', *Journal of Philosophy*, 74 (1977), 338–62.

—— 'Mind–body causation and explanatory practice', in Heil and Mele (eds.), *Mental Causation.*

—— 'Two kinds of consciousness', in Block, Flanagan and Güzeldere (eds.), *The Nature of Consciousness.*

BURWALL, STEPHEN, PAUL GILBERT, and KATHLEEN LENNON, *Philosophy of Mind* (London: UCL Press, 1997).

BYRNE, ALEX, and DAVID HILBERT (eds.), *Readings on Color, Volume I: The Philosophy of Color* (Cambridge, Mass.: MIT Press, 1997).

CARRUTHERS, PETER, 'Brute experience', *Journal of Philosophy*, 86 (1988), 435–51.

CARTWRIGHT, NANCY, 'Fundamentalism vs. the Patchwork of Laws', *Proceedings of the Aristotelian Soc.*, 93 (1994), 279–92.

CASATI, ROBERTO, 'Space, objects and intuition', in *Space or Spaces as Paradigms of Mental Categories* (Milan: Fondazione Carlo Erba, 2000).

CASTON, VICTOR, 'Aristotle and the problem of intentionality', *Philosophy and Phenomenological Research*, 58 (1998), 249–98.

CHALMERS, DAVID, *The Conscious Mind* (Oxford and New York: Oxford University Press, 1996).

CHISHOLM, R. M. (ed.), *Realism and the Background of Phenomenology* (London: George Allen and Unwin, 1960).

CHURCHLAND, PAUL M., 'Eliminative materialism and the propositional attitudes', *Journal of Philosophy*, 78 (1981), 67–90.

—— 'Reduction, qualia and the direct introspection of brain states', *Journal of Philosophy*, 82 (1985), 8–28.

—— *Matter and Consciousness*, 2nd edn (Cambridge, Mass.: MIT Press, 1988).

CRAIG, E. J., 'Sensory experience and the foundations of knowledge', *Synthese*, 33 (1976), 1–24.

CRANE, TIM, 'All God has to do', *Analysis*, 51 (1991), 235–44

—— 'All the difference in the world', *Philosophical Quarterly*, 41 (1991), 1–26; repr. in Goldberg and Pessin (eds.), *The Twin Earth Chronicles.*

—— *The Mechanical Mind* (Harmondsworth: Penguin Books, 1995).

—— 'The mental causation debate', *Proceedings of the Aristotelian Soc.*, suppl. Vol. 69 (1995), 211–36.

—— 'Intentionality as the mark of the mental', in A. O'Hear (ed.), *Current Issues in the Philosophy of Mind* (Cambridge: Cambridge University Press, 1998).

—— 'Intentionality' in E. J. Craig (ed.), *Encyclopedia of Philosophy* (London: Routledge, 1998).

—— 'Dualism, monism, physicalism', *Mind and Society*, 2 (2000), 73–85.

—— 'The significance of emergence', in Carl Gillett and Barry Loewer (eds.), *Physicalism and its Discontents* (Cambridge: Cambridge University Press, 2001).

—— 'The intentional structure of consciousness', in A. Jokic and Q. Smith (eds.), *Aspects of Consciousness* (Oxford and New York: Oxford University Press, forthcoming).

—— (ed.), *The Contents of Experience* (Cambridge: Cambridge University Press, 1992).

—— and D. H. MELLOR, 'There is no question of physicalism', *Mind*, 99 (1990), 185–206

—— and SARAH PATTERSON (eds.), *History of the Mind–Body Problem* (London: Routledge, 2000).

CUSSINS, ADRIAN, 'The connectionist construction of concepts', in M. Boden (ed.) *The Philosophy of Artificial Intelligence* (Oxford: Oxford University Press, 1990).

DANCY, JONATHAN, (ed.), *Perceptual Knowledge* (Oxford: Oxford University Press, 1988).

DAVIDSON, DONALD, 'Causal relations', in *Essays on Actions and Events*.

—— 'True to the facts', in *Inquiries into Truth and Interpretation*.

—— 'Mental events', in *Essays on Actions and Events*.

—— *Essays on Actions and Events* (Oxford: Oxford University Press, 1980).

—— *Inquiries into Truth and Interpretation* (Oxford: Oxford University Press 1984).

—— 'Thinking causes', in Heil and Mele (eds.), *Mental Causation*.

DAVIES, MARTIN and GLYN HUMPHREYS (eds.), *Consciousness* (Oxford: Blackwell, 1993).

DENNETT, DANIEL C., *Brainstorms* (Cambridge, Mass.: Bradford Books, 1978).

—— *Consciousness Explained* (London: Allen Lane, 1991).

DESCARTES, RENÉ, *Meditations on First Philosophy*, in J. Cottingham, R. Stoothof, and D. Murdoch (eds.), *The Philosophical Writings of René Descartes*, 3 vols. (Cambridge: Cambridge University Press, 1985).

DRETSKE, FRED I., *Naturalizing the Mind* (Cambridge, Mass.: MIT Press, 1995).

—— *Seeing and Knowing* (London: Routledge and Kegan Paul, 1969).

DUMMETT, MICHAEL, *Frege: Philosophy of Language* (London: Duckworth, 1973).

—— *Origins of Analytical Philosophy* (London: Duckworth, 1993).

ENÇ, BERENT, 'In defense of the identity theory', *Journal of Philosophy*, 80 (1983), 279–98.

EVANS, GARETH, *The Varieties of Reference* (Oxford: Clarendon Press, 1982).

FAIR, DAVID, 'Causation and the flow of energy', *Erkenntnis*, 14 (1979), 219–50.

FIELD, HARTRY, 'Mental representation', in Block (ed.), *Readings in the Philosophy of Psychology*, vol.2.

FODOR, JERRY, *Psychosemantics: The Problem of Meaning in the Philosophy of Mind* (Cambridge, Mass.: MIT Press, 1987).

—— 'The mind–body problem', in Warner and Szubka (eds.), *The Mind–Body Problem.*

FREGE, GOTTLOB, 'On sense and reference', in Moore (ed.), *Meaning and Reference.*

—— 'Letter to Jourdain', in Moore (ed.), *Meaning and Reference.*

—— 'The thought: a logical inquiry', in P. F. Strawson (ed.), *Philosophical Logic* (Oxford: Oxford University Press, 1967).

GEACH, PETER T., *Mental Acts* (London: Routledge and Kegan Paul, 2nd impression, 1960).

—— *Reference and Generality* (Ithaca: Cornell University Press, 1962).

—— 'Intentional identity', in *Logic Matters* (Oxford: Blackwell, 1972).

GIBBARD, ALLAN, 'Contingent identity', *Journal of Philosophical Logic*, 4 (1975), 187–222.

GOLDBERG, S. and A. PESSIN (eds.), *The Twin Earth Chronicles* (New York and London: M. E. Sharpe, 1996).

GOLDMAN, ALVIN, *Epistemology and Cognition* (Cambridge, Mass.: Harvard University Press, 1986)

GUTTENPLAN, SAMUEL (ed.), *A Companion to the Philosophy of Mind* (Oxford: Blackwell, 1994).

HALE, BOB, *Abstract Objects* (Oxford: Blackwell, 1987).

HARMAN, GILBERT, 'The intrinsic quality of experience', in J. Tomberlin (ed.), *Philosophical Perspectives*, 4 (Atascadero: Ridgeview, 1990); repr. in Block, Flanagan, and Güzeldere (eds.), *The Nature of Consciousness.*

HART, W. D., *The Engines of the Soul* (Cambridge: Cambridge University Press, 1988).

HEAL, JANE, 'Moore's paradox: a Wittgensteinian approach', *Mind*, 103 (1994), 3–24.

HEIL JOHN, and ALFRED MELE (eds.), *Mental Causation* (Oxford: Clarendon Press, 1992).

HILBERT, DAVID R. and MARK ELI KALDERON, 'Color and the inverted spectrum', in S. Davis (ed.), *Color Perception: Philosophical, Psychological, Artistic and Computational Perspectives*, Vancouver Studies in Cognitive Science, 9 (New York and Oxford: Oxford University Press, 2000).

HILL, CHRISTOPHER, *Sensations* (Cambridge: Cambridge University Press, 1991).

HOBBES, THOMAS, *Leviathan*, originally published 1651; ed. C. B. Macpherson, (Harmondsworth: Penguin Books, 1968).

HORGAN, TERENCE, 'From supervenience to superdupervenience: meeting the demands of a material world', *Mind*, 102 (1995), 555–86.

HUME, DAVID, *A Treatise of Human Nature*, originally published 1739–40; ed. P. H. Nidditch (Oxford: Clarendon Press, 1978).

HUSSERL, EDMUND, 'Phenomenology', *Encyclopedia Britannica* (London, 1929); repr. in *Realism and the Background of Phenomenology* (London: George Allen and Unwin, 1960).

HYLTON, PETER, 'The theory of descriptions', in *The Cambridge Companion to Russell* (Cambridge: Cambridge University Press, forthcoming).

JACKSON, FRANK, 'The existence of mental objects', *American Philosophical Quarterly*, 13 (1976), 23–40; repr. in Dancy (ed.), *Perceptual Knowledge*.

—— 'Epiphenomenal qualia', *Philosophical Quarterly*, 32 (1982), 127–36.

—— 'Postscript' to 'What Mary did not know', in P. Moser and J. D. Trout (eds.), *Contemporary Materialism* (London: Routledge, 1995).

—— *From Metaphysics to Ethics* (Oxford: Oxford University Press, 1998).

—— and PHILIP PETTIT, 'Functionalism and Broad Content', *Mind*, 97 (1988), 381–400.

JAMES, SUSAN, 'The emergence of the Cartesian mind', in Crane and Patterson (eds.), *History of the Mind–Body Problem*.

JOHNSON, W. E., *Logic*, Part I (Cambridge: Cambridge University Press, 1921).

KAPLAN, DAVID, 'Quantifying in', in Linsky (ed.), *Reference and Modality*.

KENNY, ANTHONY, 'Intentionality: Aquinas and Wittgenstein', in Ted Honderich (ed.), *Philosophy Through its Past* (Harmondsworth: Penguin, 1984).

—— *The Metaphysics of Mind* (Oxford: Oxford University Press, 1989).

KIM, JAEGWON, 'Physicalism and the multiple realizability of mental states', in Block (ed.), *Readings in the Philosophy of Psychology*, vol. I.

—— *Supervenience and Mind* (Cambridge: Cambridge University Press, 1993).

—— *Mind in a Physical World* (Cambridge, Mass.: MIT Press, 1998).

—— *Philosophy of Mind* (Boulder: Westview, 1996).

KNEALE, W. and M. KNEALE, *The Development of Logic* (Oxford: Clarendon Press, 1961).

KRIPKE, SAUL, *Naming and Necessity* (Oxford: Blackwell, 1980).

LEIBNIZ, G. W. *New Essays on Human Understanding*, originally published 1765; ed. Jonathan Bennett and Peter Remnant (Cambridge: Cambridge University Press, 1981).

LEVIN, JANET, 'Qualia', in E. J. Craig (ed.), *Encyclopedia of Philosophy* (London: Routledge, 1998).

LEVINE, JOSEPH, 'Materialism and qualia: the explanatory gap', *Pacific Philosophical Quarterly*, 64 (1986), 356–61.

—— 'On leaving out what it's like', in Davies and Humphreys (eds.), *Consciousness*.

LEWIS, DAVID, 'An argument for the identity theory', in *Philosophical Papers*, vol. I.

—— *Counterfactuals* (Oxford: Blackwell, 1969).

—— 'Causation', in *Philosophical Papers*, vol. II.

—— 'Review of Putnam', in Block (ed.), *Readings in the Philosophy of Psychology*, vol. I.

—— 'Survival and identity', in *Philosophical Papers*, vol. I.

—— 'Truth in fiction', in *Philosophical Papers*, vol. I.

Lewis, David, 'Mad pain and martian pain', in *Philosophical Papers*, vol. I.

—— *Philosophical Papers*, vol. I (Oxford: Oxford University Press, 1983).

—— *On the Plurality of Worlds* (Oxford: Blackwell, 1986).

—— *Philosophical Papers*, vol. II (Oxford: Oxford University Press, 1986).

—— 'Noneism and allism', in *Papers in Epistemology and Metaphysics*.

—— 'What experience teaches', in Lycan (ed.), *Mind and Cognition*; repr. in *Papers in Metaphysics and Epistemology*.

—— *Papers in Metaphysics and Epistemology* (Cambridge: Cambridge University Press. 1999)

Linsky L. (ed.), *Reference and Modality* (Oxford: Oxford University Press, 1971).

Loar, Brian, 'Phenomenal states', in Block, Flanagan, and Güzeldere (eds.), *The Nature of Consciousness*.

—— 'Transparent experience', in A. Jokic and Q. Smith (eds.), *Aspects of Consciousness* (Oxford: Clarendon Press, forthcoming).

Loewer, Barry, 'From physics to physicalism', in Carl Gillett and Barry Loewer (eds.), *Physicalism and its Discontents* (Cambridge: Cambridge University Press, 2001).

Lowe, E. J., *Kinds of Being* (Oxford: Blackwell, 1989).

—— *An Introduction to the Philosophy of Mind* (Cambridge: Cambridge University Press, 2000).

Lycan, W. G., *Consciousness and Experience* (Cambridge, Mass.: MIT Press, 1996).

—— (ed.) *Mind and Cognition* (Oxford: Blackwell, 1990).

Lyons, William, *Approaches to Intentionality* (Oxford: Oxford University Press, 1995).

Mackie, J. L., 'Problems of intentionality', in *Logic and Knowledge: Philosophical Papers*, vol. I (Oxford: Oxford University Press. 1985).

Manson, Neil Campbell, ' "A tumbling-ground for whimsies?" The history and contemporary relevance of the conscious/unconscious contrast', in Crane and Patterson (eds.), *History of the Mind–Body Problem*.

Martin, M. G. F., 'The rational role of experience', *Proceedings of the Aristotelian Soc.*, 93 (1992), 71–88.

—— 'Perceptual content', in Guttenplan (ed.), *A Companion to the Philosophy of Mind*.

—— 'Bodily awareness: a sense of ownership', in J. Bermúdez, N. Eilan, and A. Marcel (eds.), *The Body and the Self* (Cambridge, Mass.: MIT Press, 1995).

—— 'An eye directed outward', in C. Wright, B. C. Smith and C. Macdonald (eds.), *Knowing Our Own Minds* (Oxford: Oxford University Press, 1998).

—— 'Beyond dispute: sense-data, intentionality and the mind–body problem', in Crane and Patterson (eds.), *History of the Mind–Body Problem*.

McCulloch, Gregory, 'The very idea of the phenomenological', *Proceedings of the Aristotelian Soc.*, 93 (1993), 39–57.

—— *The Life of the Mind* (London: Routledge, forthcoming).

McDOWELL, JOHN, 'On the sense and reference of a proper name', in Moore (ed.), *Meaning and Reference.*

—— *Mind and World* (Cambridge, Mass.: Harvard University Press, 1994).

—— 'Having the world in view: Sellars, Kant and intentionality', (The Woodbridge Lectures, 1997), *Journal of Philosophy*, 95 (1998), 431–90.

McGINN, COLIN, 'Can we solve the mind-body problem?', *Mind*, 98 (1989), 349–66; repr. in Block, Flanagan, and Güzeldere (eds.), *The Nature of Consciousness.*

McLAUGHLIN, BRIAN, 'The rise and fall of British emergentism', in A. Beckerman *et al.* (eds.), *Emergence or Reduction?* (Berlin: de Gruyter, 1992).

MELLOR, D. H., 'Conscious belief', *Proceedings of the Aristotelian Soc.*, 78 (1977–78), 87–101.

—— *Real Time* (Cambridge: Cambridge University Press, 1981).

—— 'Nothing like experience', *Proceedings of the Aristotelian Soc.*, 93 (1992–3), 1–16.

MOORE, A. W., *Points of View* (Oxford: Clarendon Press, 1997).

—— (ed.), *Meaning and Reference* (Oxford: Oxford University Press, 1993).

MOORE, G. E., 'A defence of common sense', in Thomas Baldwin (ed.), *G. E. Moore: Selected Writings* (London: Routledge, 1993).

MORAN, DERMOT, *Introduction to Phenomenology* (London: Routledge, 2000).

NAGEL, THOMAS, 'What is it like to be a bat?', *Philosophical Review*, 83 (1974), 435–50.

—— *The View from Nowhere* (Oxford: Oxford University Press, 1986).

NEALE, STEPHEN, *Descriptions* (Cambridge, Mass.: MIT Press, 1990).

NEMIROW, LAWRENCE, 'Physicalism and the cognitive role of acquaintance', in Lycan (ed.), *Mind and Cognition.*

OWENS, DAVID, *Causes and Coincidences* (Cambridge: Cambridge University Press, 1992).

PAPINEAU, DAVID, 'Why supervenience?', *Analysis*, 50 (1990), 66–71.

—— 'The reason why: response to Crane', *Analysis*, 51 (1991), 37–40.

—— 'The rise of physicalism', in Stone and Wolff (eds.), *The Proper Ambition of Science.*

—— 'Mind the gap', *Philosophical Perspectives* (forthcoming).

PARFIT, DEREK, 'Personal identity', *Philosophical Review*, 80 (1971), 3–27.

PAUL, LAURIE and NED HALL (eds.), *The Counterfactual Analysis of Causation* (Cambridge, Mass.: MIT Press, forthcoming).

PEACOCKE, CHRISTOPHER, *Sense and Content* (Oxford: Oxford University Press, 1983).

—— 'Consciousness and other minds', *Proceedings of the Aristotelian Soc.*, 48 (1984), 97–117.

—— *A Study of Concepts* (Cambridge, Mass.: MIT Press, 1992).

PEACOCKE, CHRISTOPHER, 'Conscious attitudes, attention and self-knowledge', in Crispin Wright, Barry C. Smith, and Cynthia Macdonald (eds.), *Knowing Our Own Minds* (Oxford: Oxford University Press, 1998).

PERRY, JOHN, 'The problem of the essential indexical', *Nous*, 13 (1979), 3–21.

PETTIT, PHILIP, 'A definition of physicalism', *Analysis*, 53 (1993), 213–233.

POLAND, JEFFREY, *Physicalism: The Philosophical Foundations* (Oxford: Oxford University Press, 1994).

PRIOR, A. N., *Objects of Thought* (Oxford: Clarendon Press, 1971).

PUTNAM, HILARY, 'The nature of mental states', in Block (ed.), *Readings in the Philosophy of Psychology*, vol. I.

—— 'The meaning of "meaning"', in *Philosophical Papers, Vol. II: Mind, Language and Reality* (Cambridge: Cambridge University Press, 1975).

—— *Renewing Philosophy* (Cambridge, Mass.: MIT Press, 1992).

PYKE, STEVE, *Philosophers* (Manchester: Cornerhouse Publications, 1993).

QUINE, W. V., *Mathematical Logic* (Cambridge, Mass.: Harvard University Press, 1940; revised 1979).

—— 'On what there is', in *From a Logical Point of View* (Cambridge, Mass.: Harvard University Press, 1953).

—— 'Quantifiers and propositional attitudes', in Linsky (ed.), *Reference and Modality*.

—— *Word and Object* (Cambridge, Mass.: Harvard University Press, 1960).

—— 'Epistemology naturalized', in *Ontological Relativity and Other Essays* (Cambridge, Mass.: Harvard University Press, 1969).

REY, GEORGES, 'Sensational sentences', in Davies, Martin, and Humphreys (eds.), *Consciousness*.

ROBINSON, HOWARD, *Matter and Sense* (Cambridge: Cambridge University Press, 1982).

—— 'The anti-materialist strategy and the "knowledge argument"', in Robinson (ed.), *Objections to Physicalism*.

—— *Perception* (London: Routledge, 1994).

—— (ed.), *Objections to Physicalism* (Oxford: Oxford University Press, 1993).

RORTY, RICHARD, *Philosophy and the Mirror of Nature* (Oxford: Blackwell, 1979).

ROSENTHAL, DAVID, 'Identity theories', in Guttenplan (ed.), *A Companion to the Philosophy of Mind*.

—— 'Two concepts of consciousness', *Philosophical Studies*, 49 (1986), 329–59.

RUDDER BAKER, LYNNE, 'Metaphysics and mental causation', in Heil and Mele (eds.), *Mental Causation*.

RUSSELL, BERTRAND, 'Descriptions', in Moore (ed.), *Meaning and Reference*.

—— *The Analysis of Mind* (London: George Allen and Unwin, 1921).

SALMON, NATHAN, *Frege's Puzzle* (Cambridge, Mass.: MIT Press, 1986).

—— and SCOTT SOAMES (eds.), *Propositions and Attitudes* (Oxford: Oxford University Press, 1988).

SARTRE, JEAN PAUL, *Being and Nothingness*, originally published 1943 (London: Methuen, 1958).

SEARLE, JOHN R., *Intentionality: An Essay in the Philosophy of Mind* (Cambridge: Cambridge University Press, 1983).

—— *The Rediscovery of the Mind* (Cambridge, Mass.: MIT Press, 1992).

SEGAL, GABRIEL, *A Slim Book about Narrow Content* (Cambridge, Mass.: MIT Press, 2000).

SELLARS, WILFRID, *Empiricism and the Philosophy of Mind* (1956), repr. with a Study Guide by Robert Brandom (Cambridge, Mass.: Harvard University Press, 1997).

SHOEMAKER, SYDNEY, 'The mind–body problem', in Warner and Szubka (eds.), *The Mind–Body Problem*.

—— 'Functionalism and qualia', in *Identity, Cause and Mind* (Cambridge: Cambridge University Press, 1984).

—— 'Qualities and qualia: what's in the mind?', *Philosophy and Phenomenological Research*, 50 (1990), 109–31.

—— 'The inverted spectrum', in Block, Flanagan and Güzeldere (eds.), *The Nature of Consciousness*.

SMITH, A. D., 'Non-reductive physicalism', in Robinson (ed.), *Objections to Physicalism*.

—— *The Object of Perception* (Cambridge, Mass.: Harvard University Press, forthcoming).

SMITH, PETER, 'Modest reductions and the unity of science', in David Charles and Kathleen Lennon (eds.), *Reduction, Explanation and Realism* (Oxford: Oxford University Press, 1992).

SNOWDON, PAUL, 'How to interpret "direct perception"', in Crane (ed.), *The Contents of Experience*.

—— 'Knowing how and knowing that: a distinction and its uses reconsidered' (unpublished).

SOSA, E. and MICHAEL TOOLEY (eds.), *Causation* (Oxford: Oxford University Press, 1993).

SPENCER, MARY, 'Why the "S" in intension?', *Mind*, 80, (1971), 114–15.

STALNAKER, ROBERT, 'What might non-conceptual content be?', in E. Villanueva (ed.), *Philosophical Issues (Concepts)*, 9 (1998).

STONE, M. W. F. and JONATHAN WOLFF (eds.), *The Proper Ambition of Science* (London: Routledge, 2000).

STRAWSON, GALEN, *Mental Reality* (Cambridge, Mass.: MIT Press, 1994).

STRAWSON, P. F., *Individuals* (London: Methuen, 1959).

TWARDOWSKI, KAZIMIR, *On the Content and Object of Presentations*, originally published 1894; trans. R. Grossman (The Hague: Nijhoff, 1977).

TYE, MICHAEL, 'Visual qualia and visual content', in Crane (ed.), *The Contents of Experience*.

—— 'A representational theory of pains and their phenomenal nature', in Block, Flanagan, and Güzeldere (eds.), *The Nature of Consciousness*.

—— *Ten Problems of Consciousness* (Cambridge, Mass.: MIT Press, 1995)

VALBERG, J. J., *The Puzzle of Experience* (Oxford: Clarendon Press, 1992).

—— 'The puzzle of experience', in Crane (ed.), *The Contents of Experience*.

VAN GULICK, ROBERT, 'Understanding the phenomenal mind: are we all just armadillos?', in Davies and Humphreys (eds.), *Consciousness*; repr. in Block, Flanagan, and Güzeldere (eds.), *The Nature of Consciousness*.

VOLTOLINI, ALBERTO, 'Objects as intentional and as real', *Grazer Philosophische Studien*, 41 (1991), 1–32.

WARNER R. and T. SZUBKA (eds.), *The Mind–Body Problem* (Oxford: Blackwell, 1994).

WARNOCK, GEOFFREY, (ed.), *The Philosophy of Perception* (Oxford: Oxford University Press, 1967).

WIGGINS, DAVID, 'On being in the same place at the same time', *Philosophical Review*, 77 (1968), 90–5.

—— *Sameness and Substance* (Oxford: Blackwell, 1980).

—— 'Substance', in A. C. Grayling (ed.), *Philosophy: A Guide Through the Subject* (Oxford: Oxford University Press, 1995).

WILLIAMSON, TIMOTHY, *Vagueness* (London: Routledge, 1994).

—— 'Is knowing a state of mind?', *Mind*, 104 (1995), 533–65.

WOOLHOUSE, ROGER, *The Concept of Substance in Seventeenth Century Metaphysics* (London: Routledge, 1993).

WRIGHT, BARRY C. SMITH and CYNTHIA MACDONALD (eds.), *Knowing Our Own Minds* (Oxford: Oxford University Press, 1998).

YABLO, STEPHEN, 'Mental Causation', *Philosophical Review*, 101 (1992), 245–80.

Index